ULTIMATE COMICS SPIDER-MAN

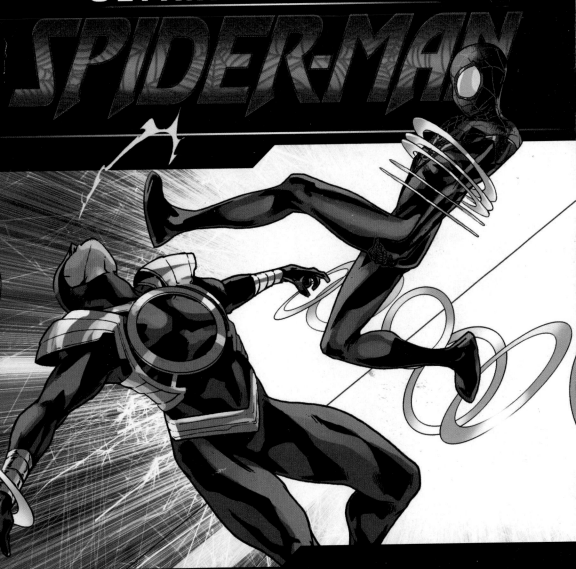

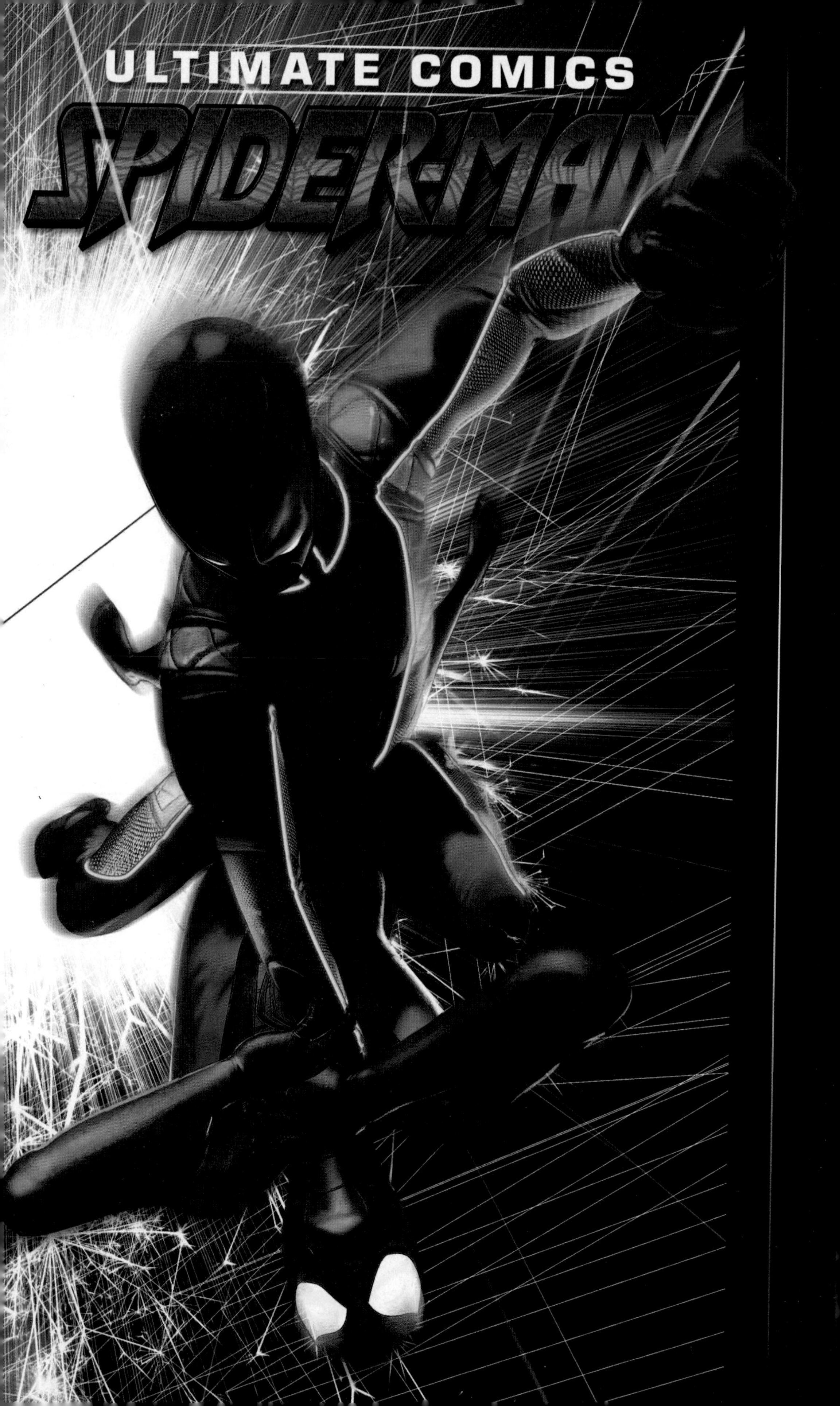
ULTIMATE COMICS
SPIDER-MAN

WRITER: **BRIAN MICHAEL BENDIS**

ARTISTS: **CHRIS SAMNEE** (#6-7), **SARA PICHELLI** (#8)
& **DAVID MARQUEZ** (#9-10)

COLOR ARTIST: **JUSTIN PONSOR**

LETTERER: **VC'S CORY PETIT**

COVER ART: **KAARE ANDREWS**

ASSISTANT EDITOR: **JON MOISAN**

ASSOCIATE EDITOR: **SANA AMANAT**

EDITOR: **MARK PANICCIA**

COLLECTION EDITOR: **JENNIFER GRÜNWALD**

ASSISTANT EDITORS: **ALEX STARBUCK & NELSON RIBEIRO**

EDITOR, SPECIAL PROJECTS: **MARK D. BEAZLEY**

SENIOR EDITOR, SPECIAL PROJECTS: **JEFF YOUNGQUIST**

SENIOR VICE PRESIDENT OF SALES: **DAVID GABRIEL**

SVP OF BRAND PLANNING & COMMUNICATIONS: **MICHAEL PASCIULLO**

BOOK DESIGNER: **RODOLFO MURAGUCHI**

EDITOR IN CHIEF: **AXEL ALONSO**

CHIEF CREATIVE OFFICER: **JOE QUESADA**

PUBLISHER: **DAN BUCKLEY**

EXECUTIVE PRODUCER: **ALAN FINE**

PREVIOUSLY:

Months before Peter Parker was shot and killed, grade-schooler Miles Morales was about to start a new chapter in his life at a new school--when he was suddenly bitten by a stolen, genetically altered spider that gave him incredible arachnid-like powers.

He has only shared this with his best friend Ganke. The Ultimates, a team of renowned superhumans, gave Miles a newly designed costume as thanks for saving them during a battle with the super villain known as Electro.

Miles just found out that his father and his Uncle Aaron used to run on the wrong side of the law. His dad took the high road but his uncle is a world-class criminal known as the Prowler.

-MAN BY BRIAN MICHAEL BENDIS VOL. 2. Contains material originally published in magazine form as ULTIMATE COMICS SPIDER-MAN #6-10. First printing 2012. Hardcover ISBN# ...ver ISBN# 978-0-7851-5715-1. Published by MARVEL WORLDWIDE, INC., a subsidiary of MARVEL ENTERTAINMENT, LLC. OFFICE OF PUBLICATION: 135 West 50th Street, New York, ...2 Marvel Characters, Inc. All rights reserved. Hardcover: $24.99 per copy in the U.S. and $27.99 in Canada (GST #R127032852). Softcover: $19.99 per copy in the U.S. and $21.99 in . Canadian Agreement #40668537. All characters featured in this issue and the distinctive names and likenesses thereof, and all related indicia are trademarks of Marvel Characters, Inc. the names, characters, persons, and/or institutions in this magazine with those of any living or dead person or institution is intended, and any such similarity which may exist is purely U.S.A. ALAN FINE, EVP - Office of the President, Marvel Worldwide, Inc. and EVP & CMO Marvel Characters B.V.; DAN BUCKLEY, Publisher & President - Print, Animation & Digital Divisions; ...e Officer; TOM BREVOORT, SVP of Publishing; DAVID BOGART, SVP of Operations & Procurement, Publishing; RUWAN JAYATILLEKE, SVP & Associate Publisher, Publishing; C.B. CEBULSKI, ...velopment; DAVID GABRIEL, SVP of Publishing Sales & Circulation; MICHAEL PASCIULLO, SVP of Brand Planning & Communications; JIM O'KEEFE, VP of Operations & Logistics; DAN CARR, ...ing Technology; SUSAN CRESPI, Editorial Operations Manager; ALEX MORALES, Publishing Operations Manager; STAN LEE, Chairman Emeritus. For information regarding advertising in ...com, please contact John Dokes, SVP Integrated Sales and Marketing, at jdokes@marvel.com. For Marvel subscription inquiries, please call 800-217-9158. **Manufactured between** ...hardcover), and 4/30/2012 and 11/19/2012 (softcover), by R.R. DONNELLEY, INC., SALEM, VA, USA.

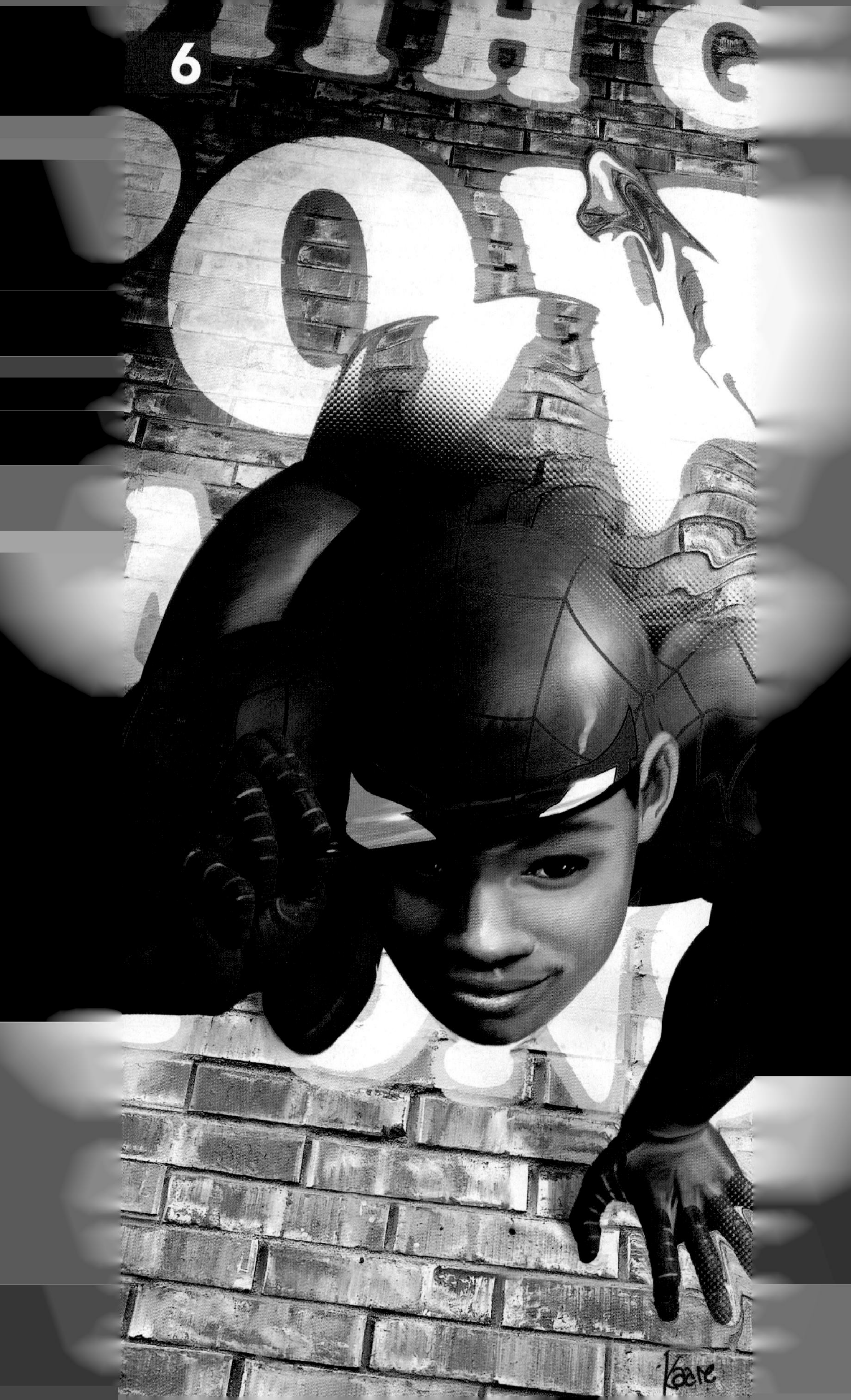
6

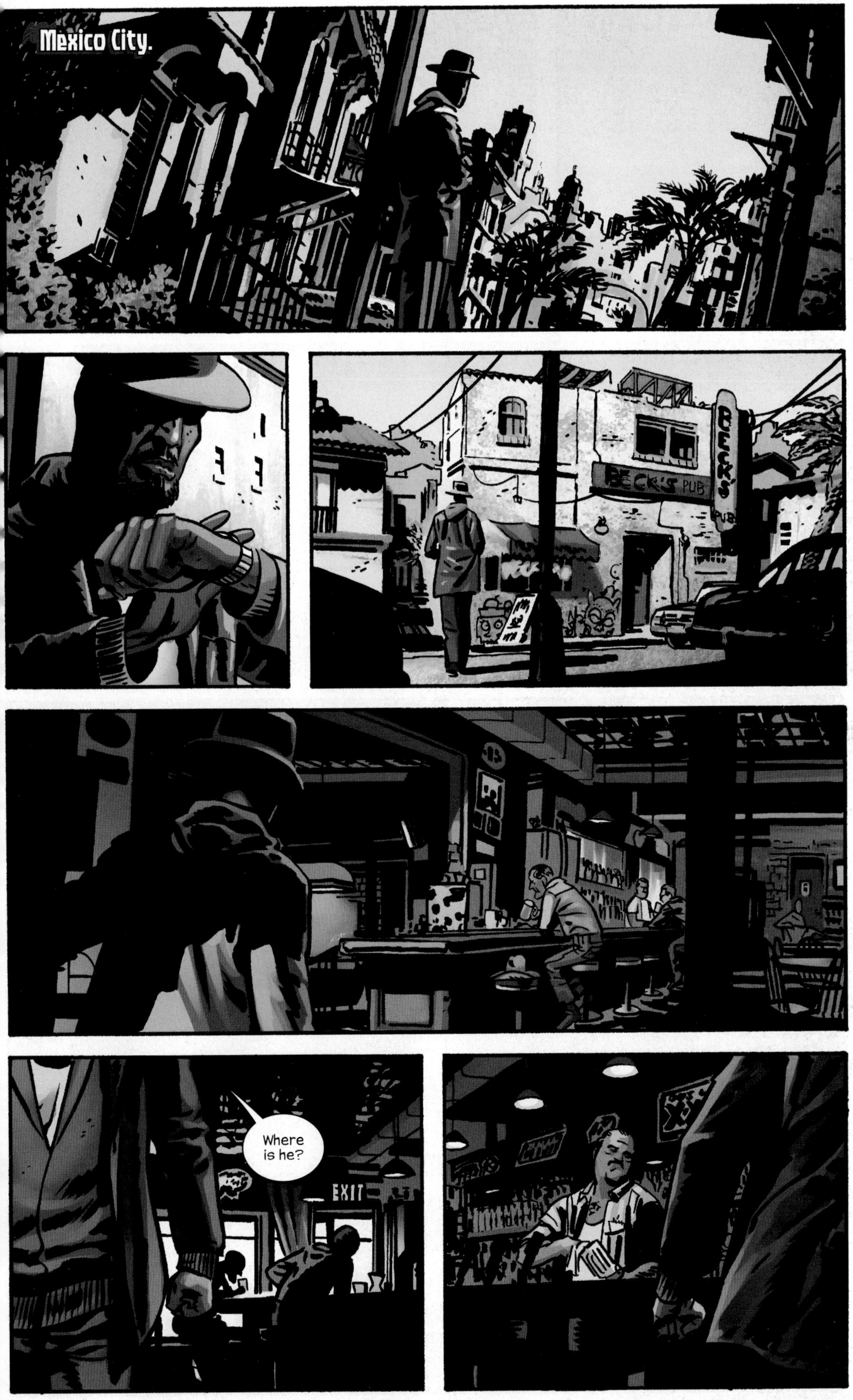
Mexico City.
BECK'S
PUB
BECK'S PUB
EXIT
Where is he?

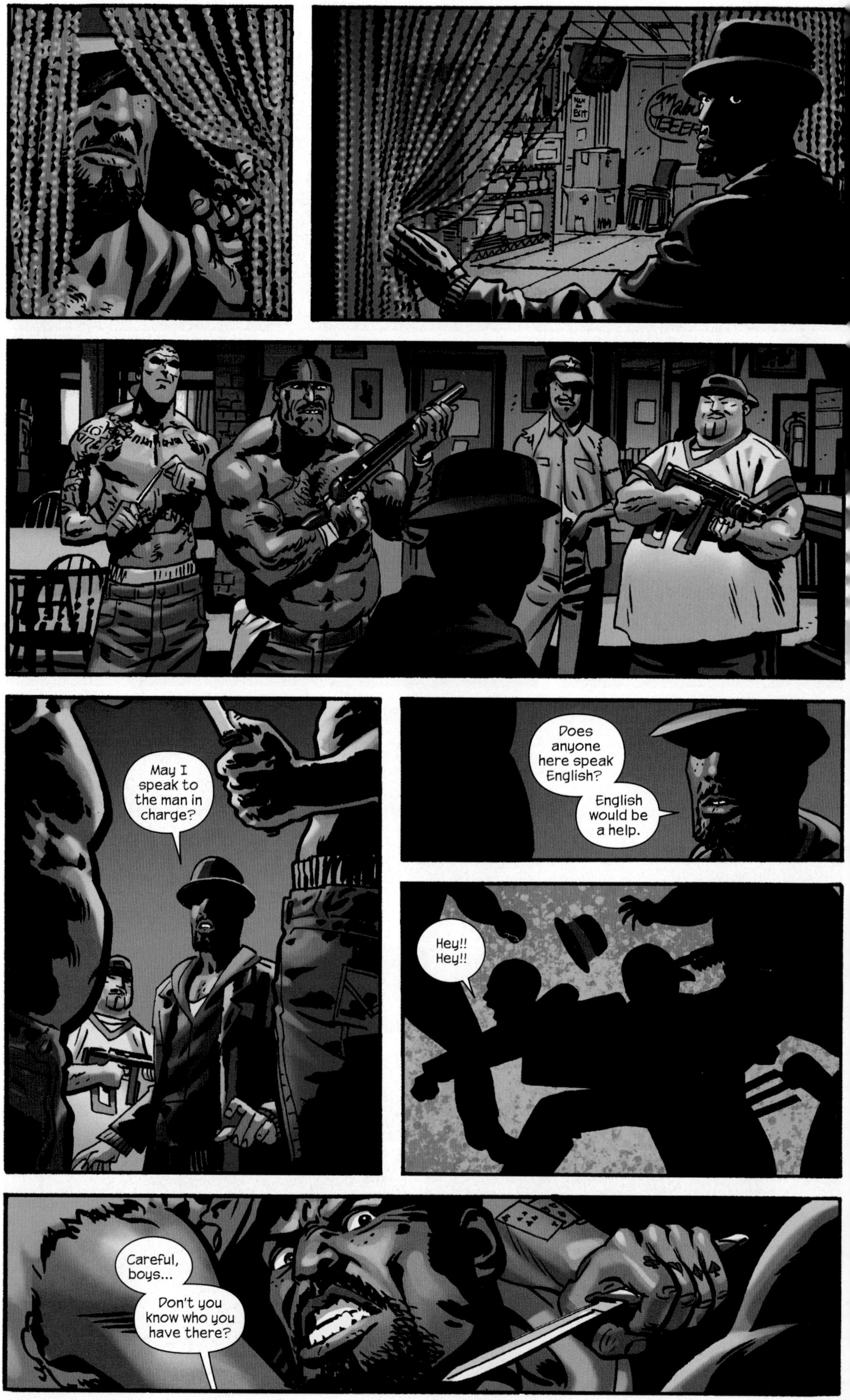
May I speak to the man in charge?
Does anyone here speak English?
English would be a help.
Hey!! Hey!!
Careful, boys...
Don't you know who you have there?

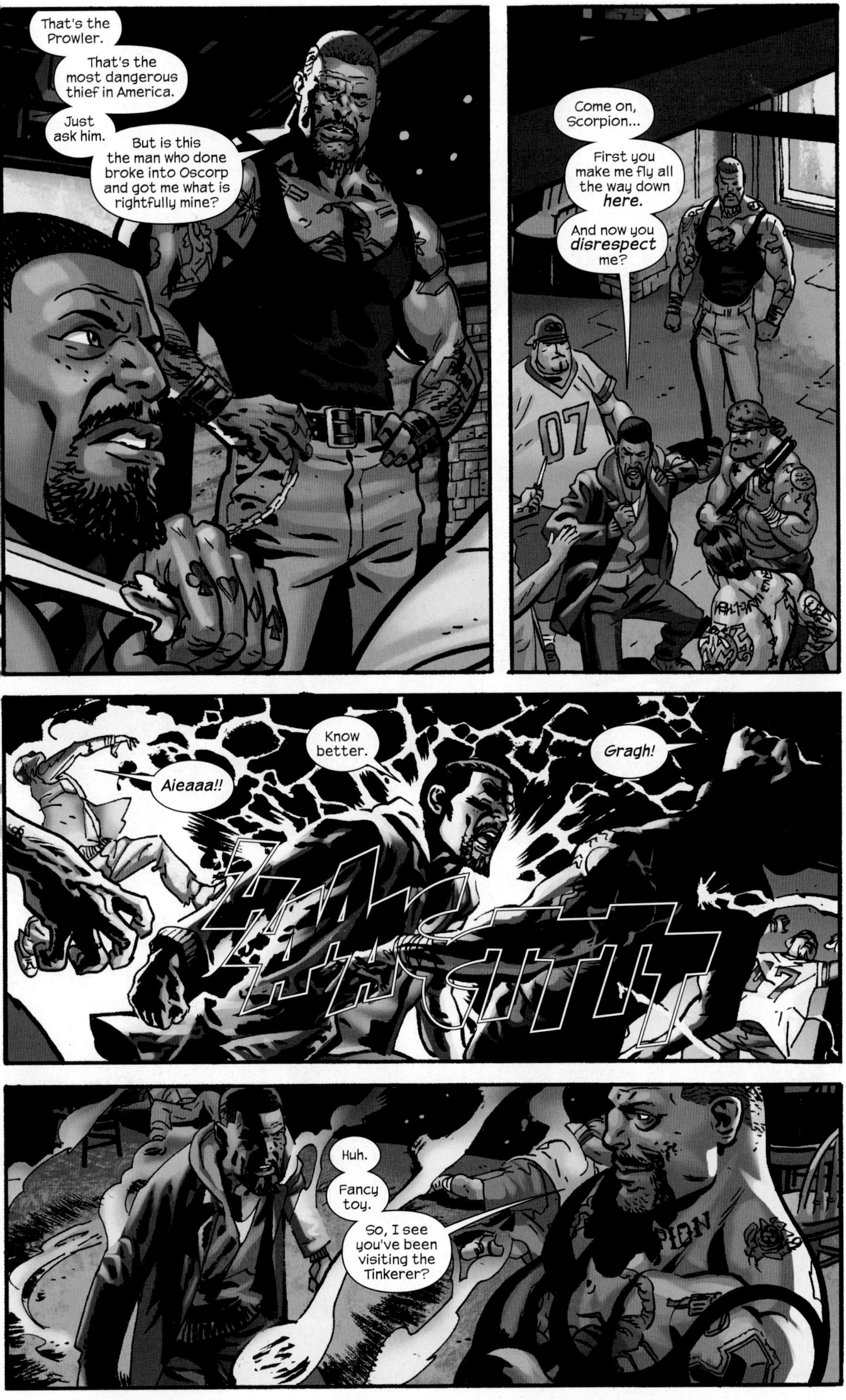
That's the Prowler.
That's the most dangerous thief in America.
Just ask him.
But is this the man who done broke into Oscorp and got me what is rightfully mine?
Come on, Scorpion...
First you make me fly all the way down *here.*
And now you *disrespect* me?
Aieaaa!!
Know better.
Gragh!
Huh.
Fancy toy.
So, I see you've been visiting the Tinkerer?

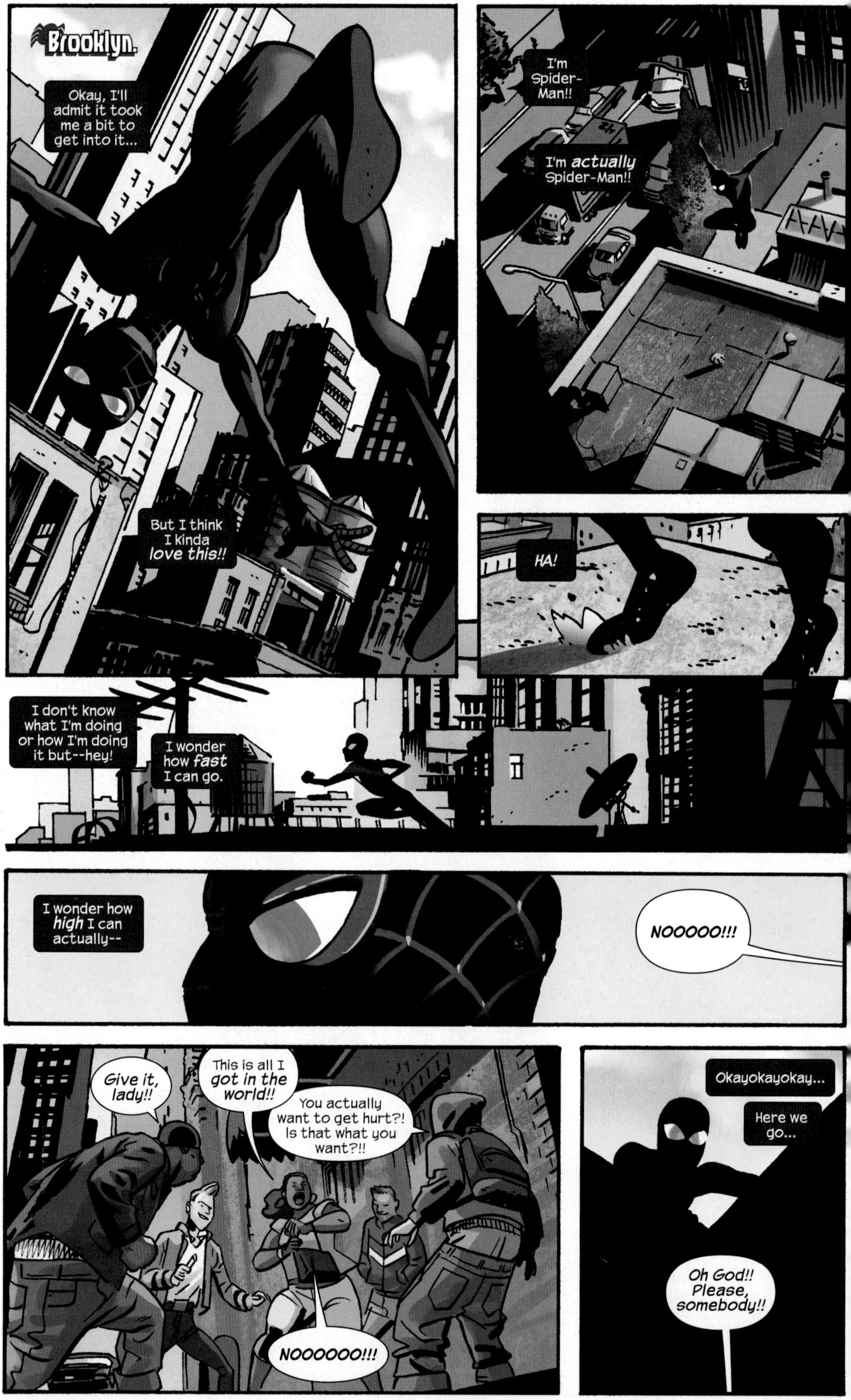
Brooklyn.
Okay, I'll admit it took me a bit to get into it...
But I think I kinda love this!!
I'm Spider-Man!!
I'm actually Spider-Man!!
HA!
I don't know what I'm doing or how I'm doing it but--hey!
I wonder how fast I can go.
I wonder how high I can actually--
NOOOOO!!!
Give it, lady!!
This is all I got in the world!!
You actually want to get hurt?! Is that what you want?!!
NOOOOOO!!!
Okayokayokay...
Here we go...
Oh God!! Please, somebody!!

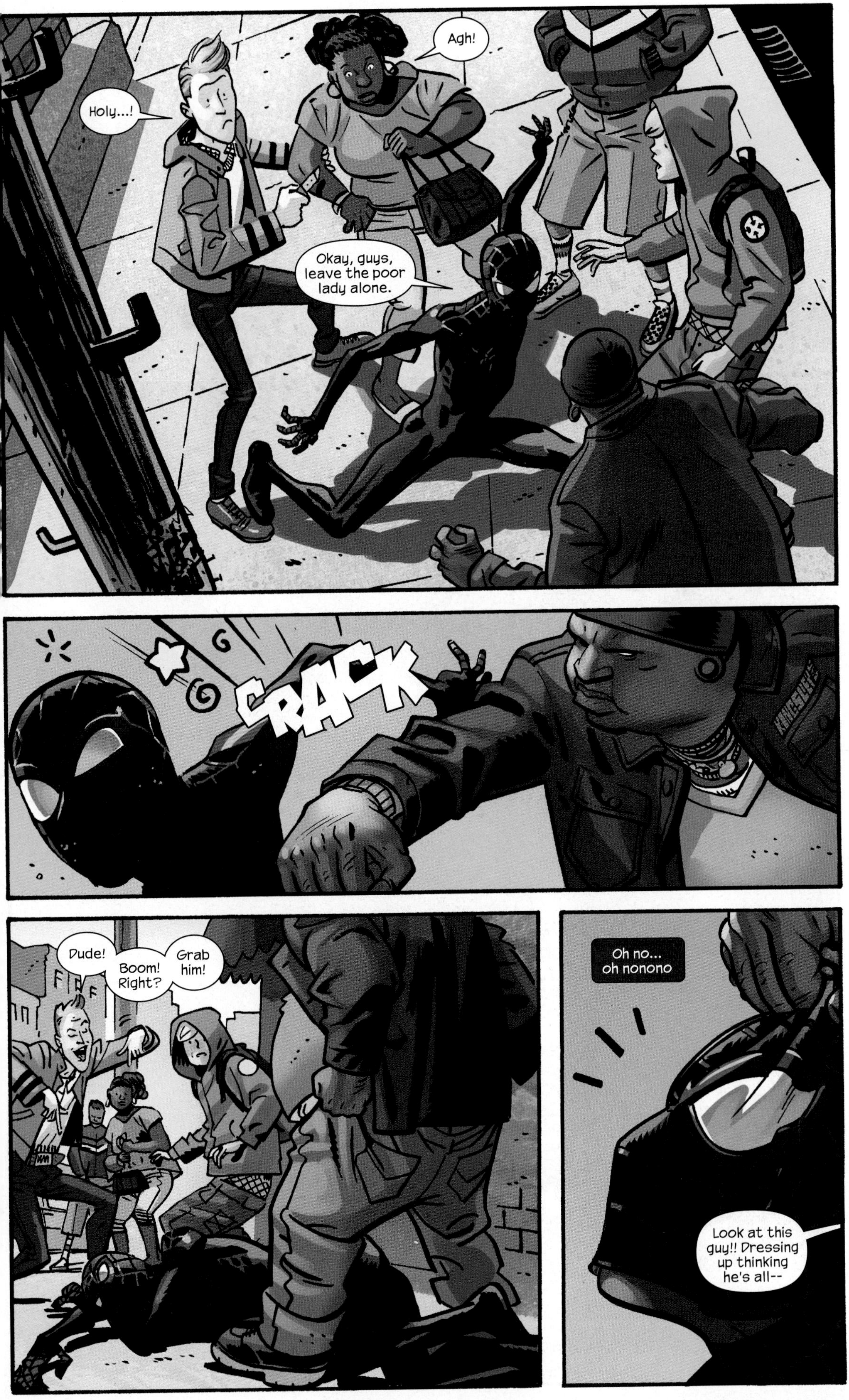
Agh!
Holy...!
Okay, guys, leave the poor lady alone.
CRACK
Dude!
Boom! Right?
Grab him!
Oh no... oh nonono
Look at this guy!! Dressing up thinking he's all--

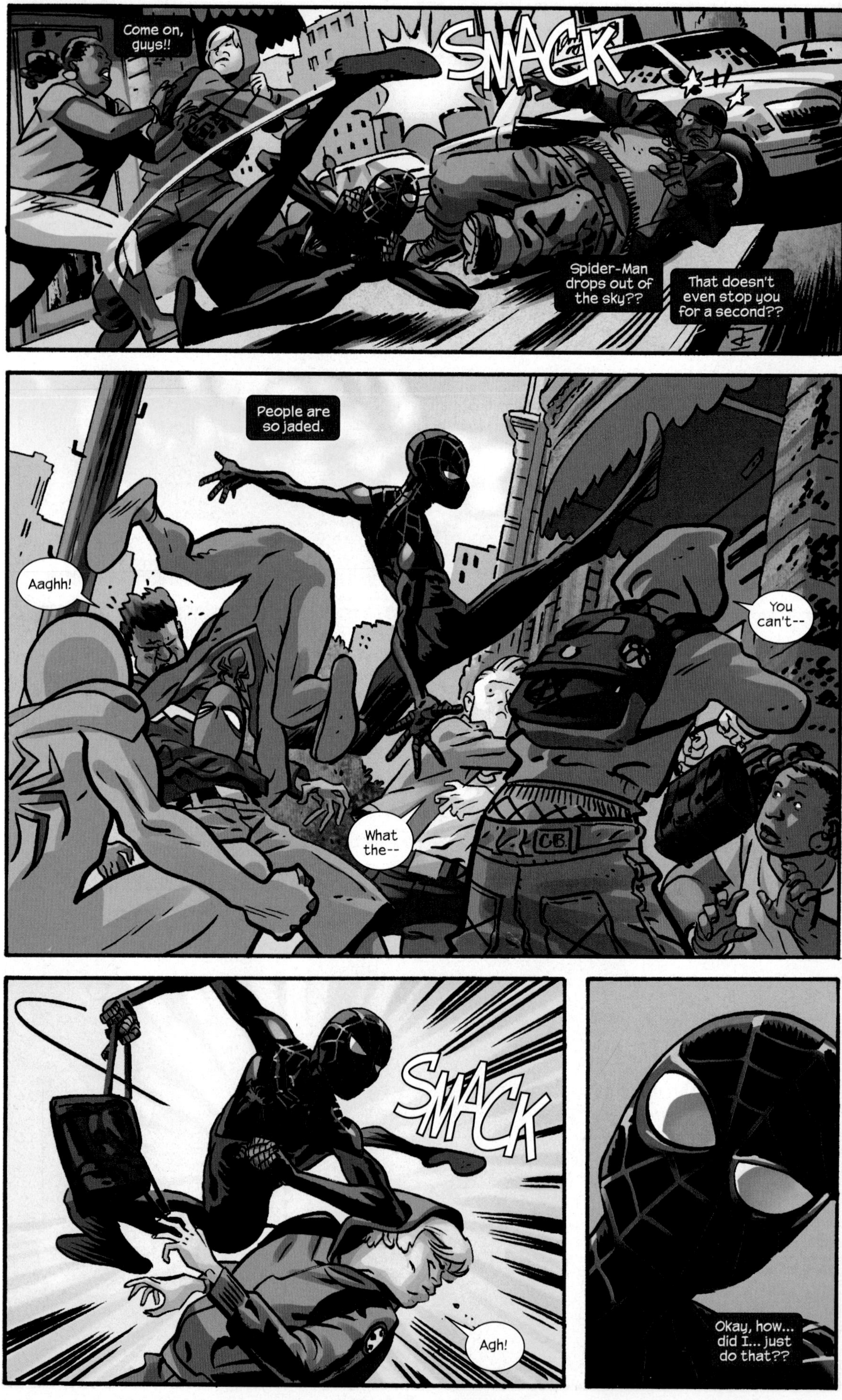
Come on, guys!!
SMACK
Spider-Man drops out of the sky??
That doesn't even stop you for a second??
People are so jaded.
Aaghh!
You can't--
What the--
SMACK
Agh!
Okay, how... did I... just do that??

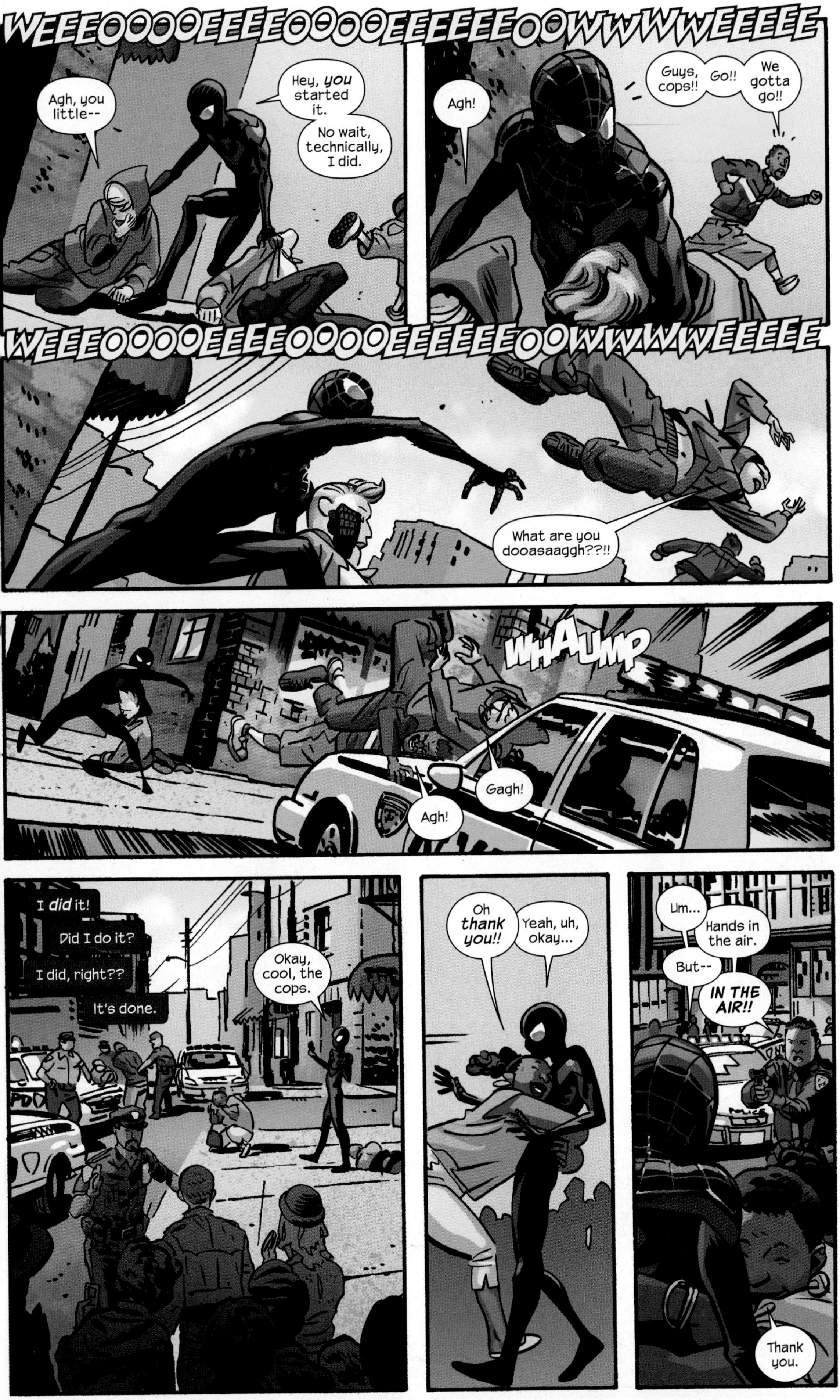
WEEEOOOOEEEEOOOOEEEEEEOOWWWWWEEEEE
Agh, you little--
Hey, you started it.
No wait, technically, I did.
Agh!
Guys, cops!!
Go!!
We gotta go!!
WEEEOOOOEEEEOOOOEEEEEEOOWWWWWEEEEE
What are you dooasaaggh??!!
WHAUMP
Gagh!
Agh!
I did it!
Did I do it?
I did, right??
It's done.
Okay, cool, the cops.
Oh thank you!!
Yeah, uh, okay...
Um...
Hands in the air.
But--
IN THE AIR!!
Thank you.

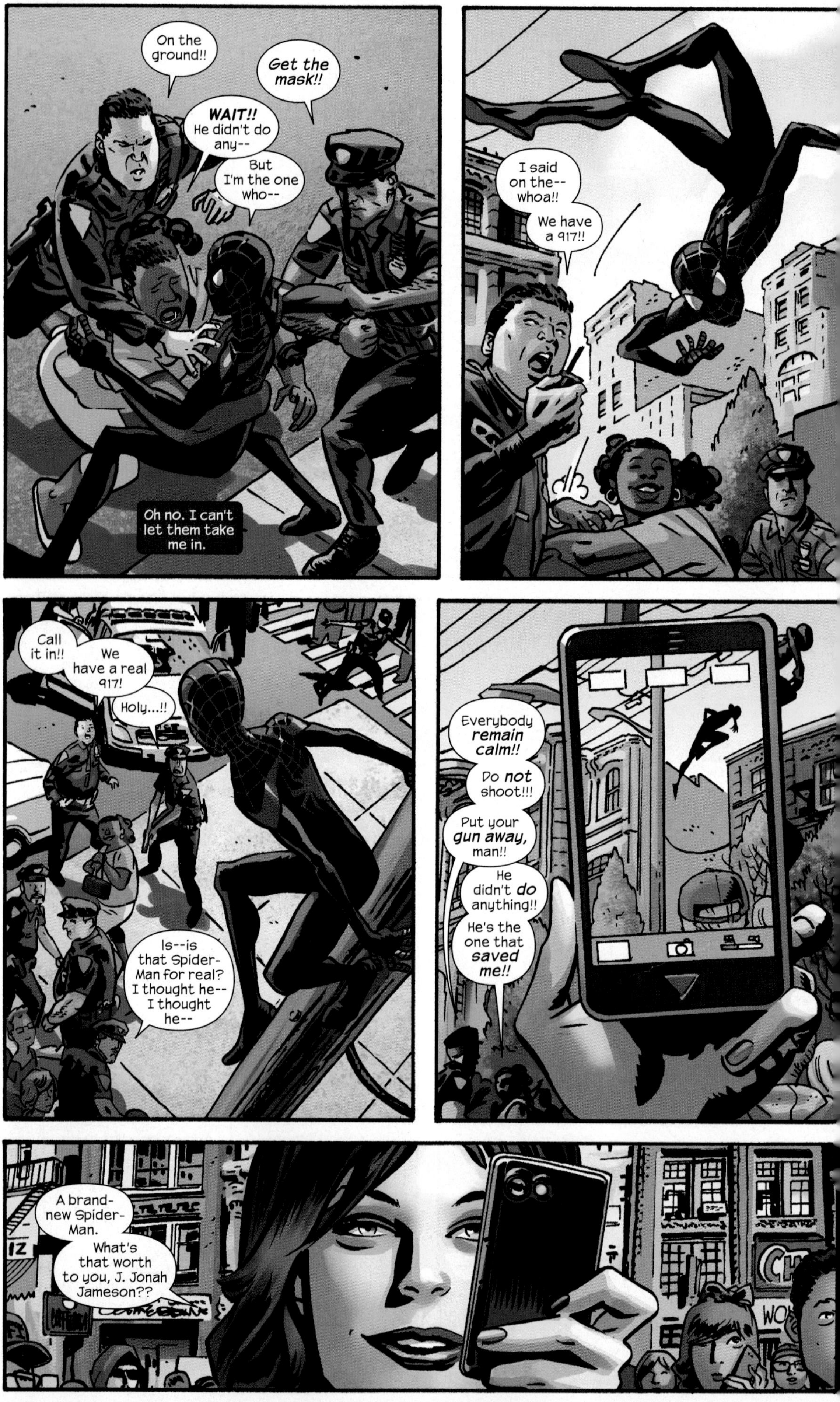
On the ground!!
Get the mask!!
WAIT!! He didn't do any--
But I'm the one who--
Oh no. I can't let them take me in.
I said on the-- whoa!!
We have a 917!!
Call it in!!
We have a real 917!
Holy...!!
Is--is that Spider-Man for real? I thought he-- I thought he--
Everybody remain calm!!
Do not shoot!!!
Put your gun away, man!!
He didn't do anything!!
He's the one that saved me!!
A brand-new Spider-Man.
What's that worth to you, J. Jonah Jameson??

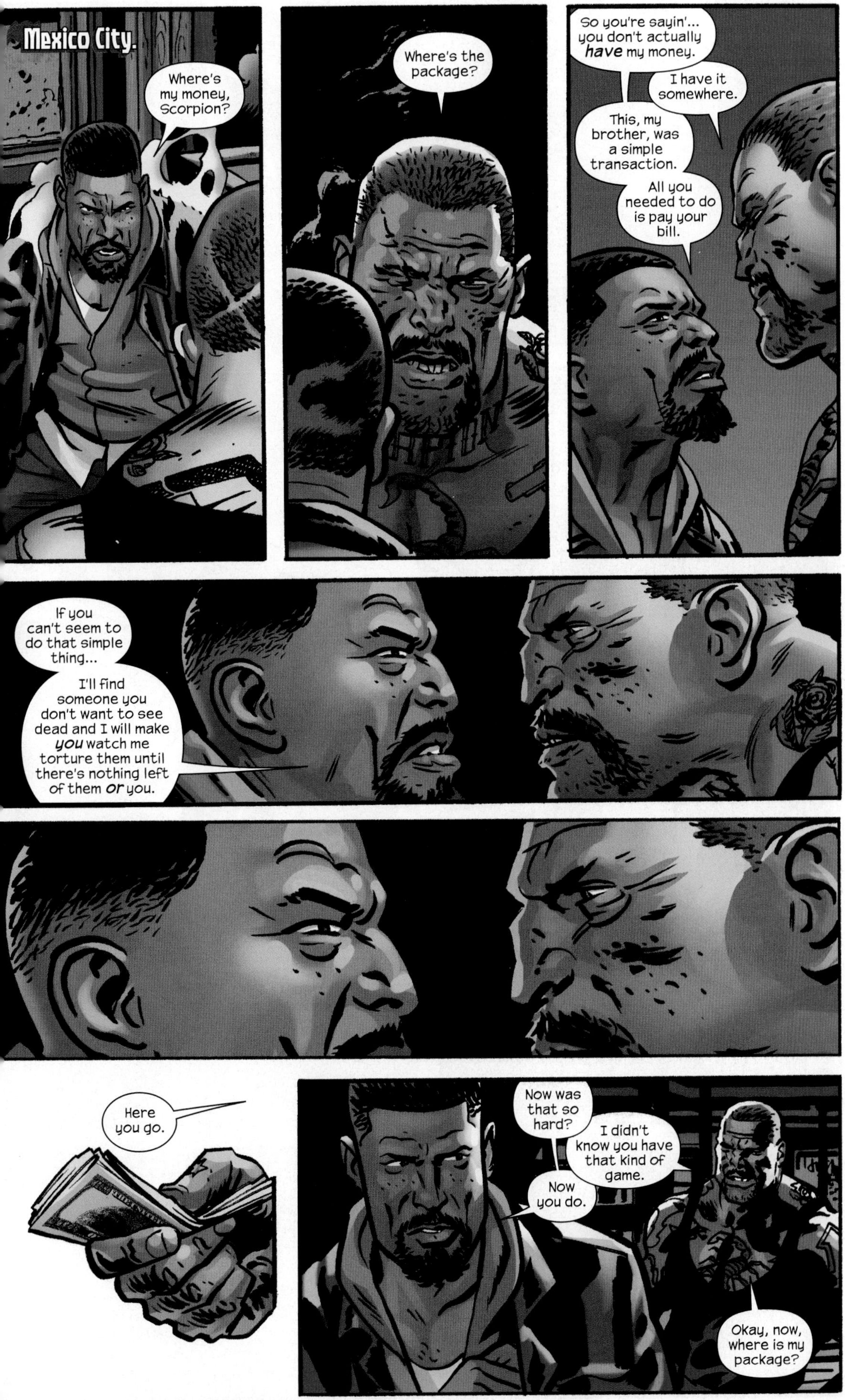
Mexico City.
Where's my money, Scorpion?
Where's the package?
So you're sayin'... you don't actually *have* my money.
I have it somewhere.
This, my brother, was a simple transaction.
All you needed to do is pay your bill.
If you can't seem to do that simple thing...
I'll find someone you don't want to see dead and I will make *you* watch me torture them until there's nothing left of them *or* you.
Here you go.
Now was that so hard?
I didn't know you have that kind of game.
Now you do.
Okay, now, where is my package?

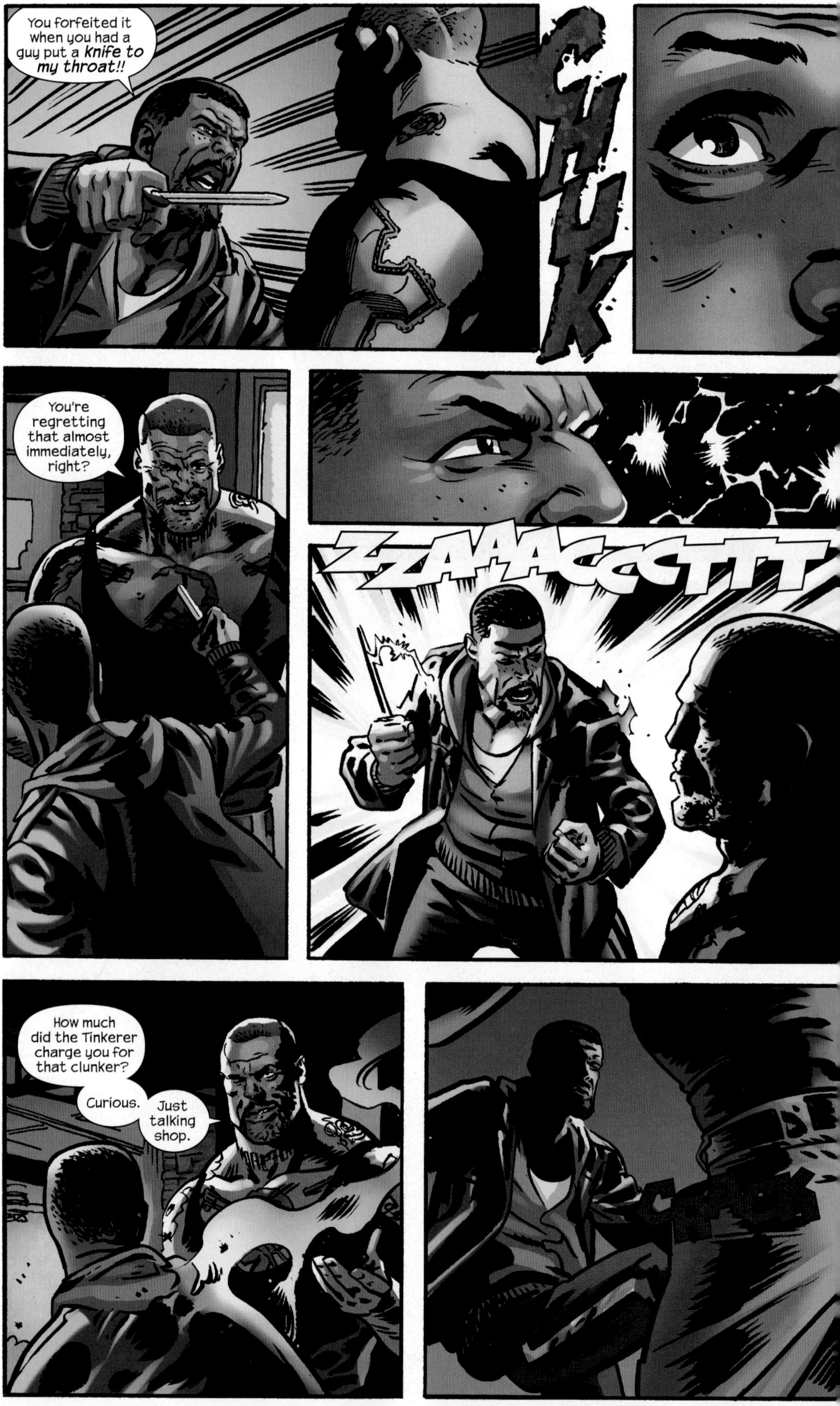
You forfeited it when you had a guy put a *knife to my throat!!*
CHUK
You're regretting that almost immediately, right?
ZZAAACCCTTT
How much did the Tinkerer charge you for that clunker?
Curious.
Just talking shop.

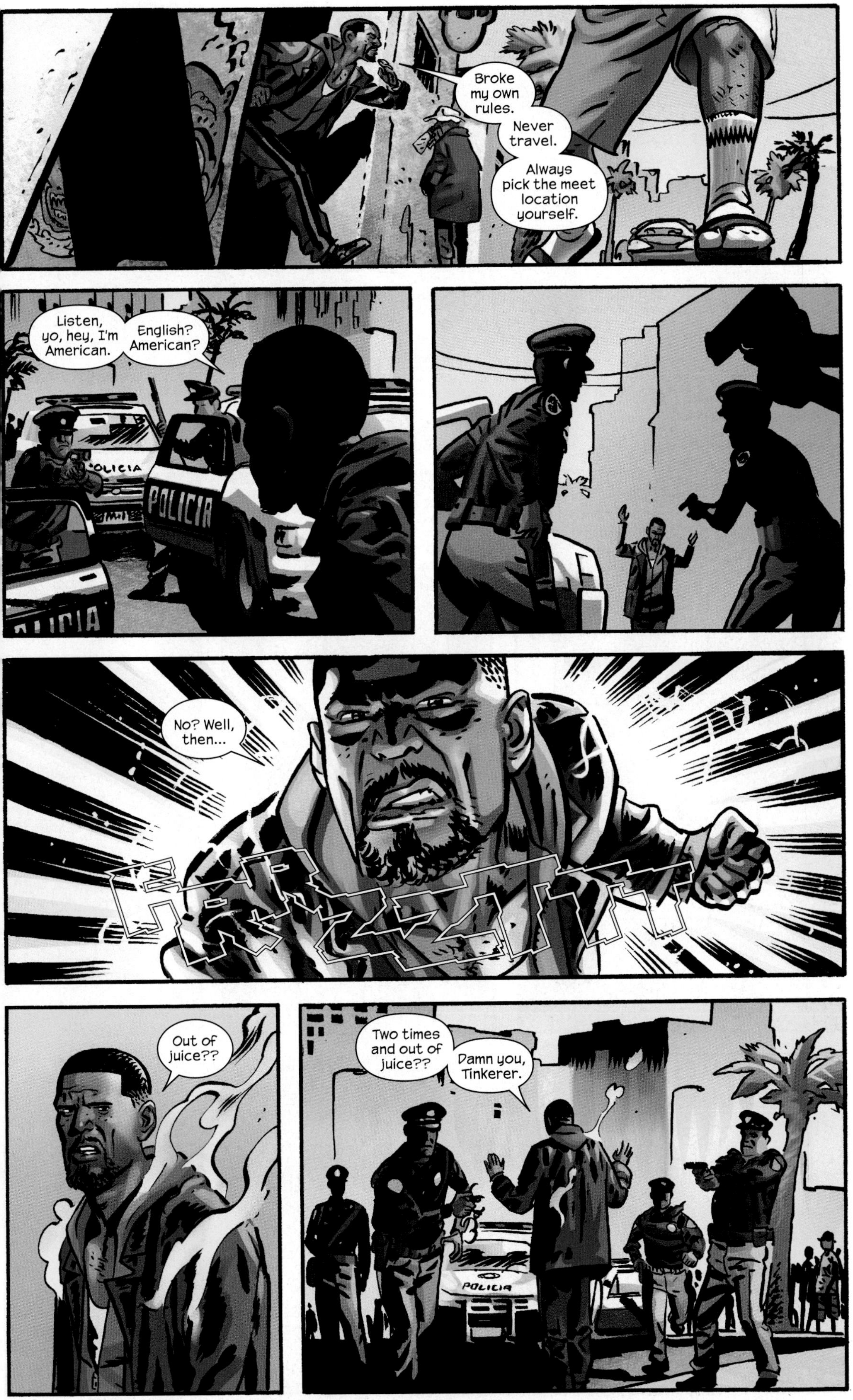
Broke my own rules.
Never travel.
Always pick the meet location yourself.
Listen, yo, hey, I'm American.
English? American?
POLICIA
POLICIA
No? Well, then...
Out of juice??
Two times and out of juice??
Damn you, Tinkerer.
POLICIA

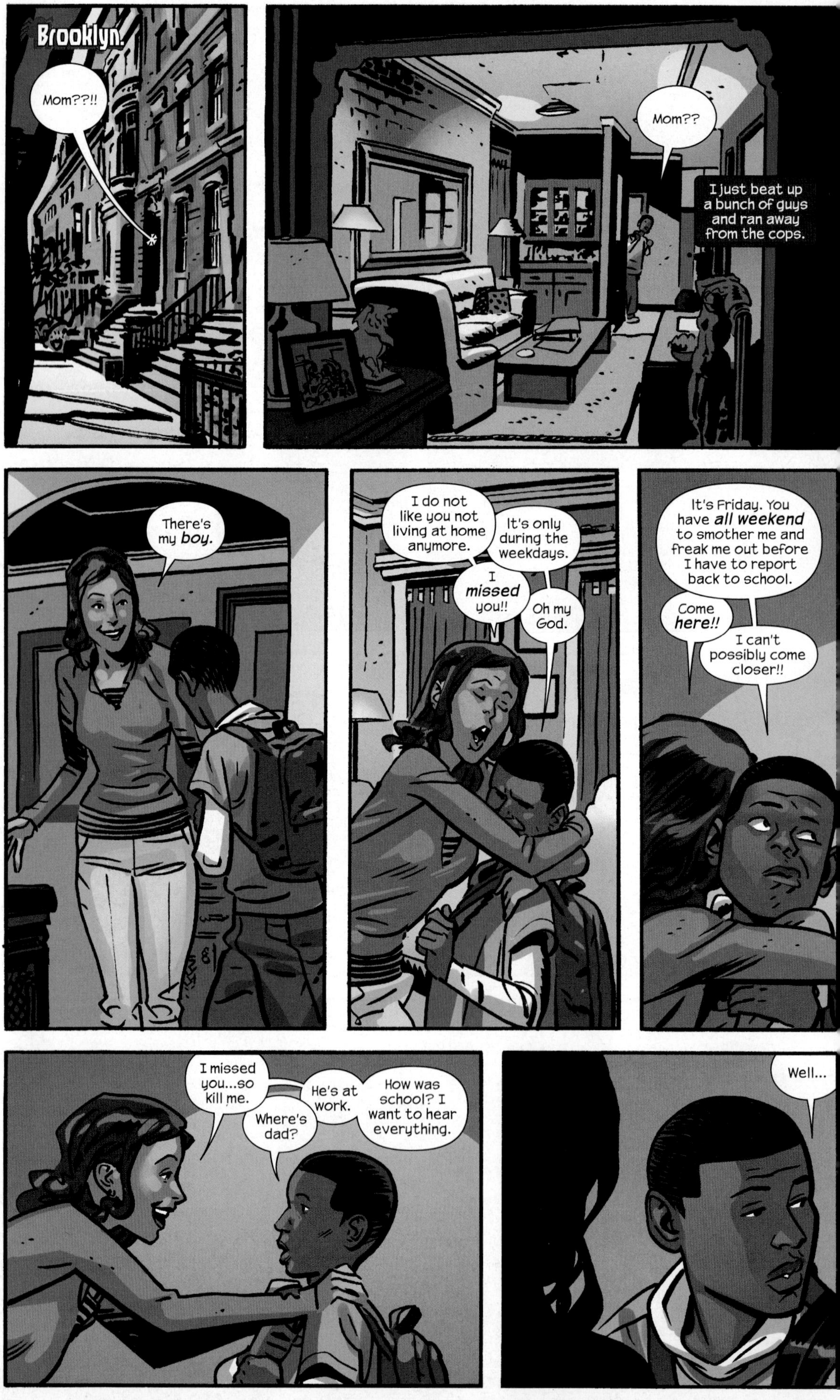
Brooklyn.
Mom??!!
Mom??
I just beat up a bunch of guys and ran away from the cops.
There's my boy.
I do not like you not living at home anymore.
It's only during the weekdays.
I missed you!!
Oh my God.
It's Friday. You have all weekend to smother me and freak me out before I have to report back to school.
Come here!!
I can't possibly come closer!!
I missed you...so kill me.
Where's dad?
He's at work.
How was school? I want to hear everything.
Well...

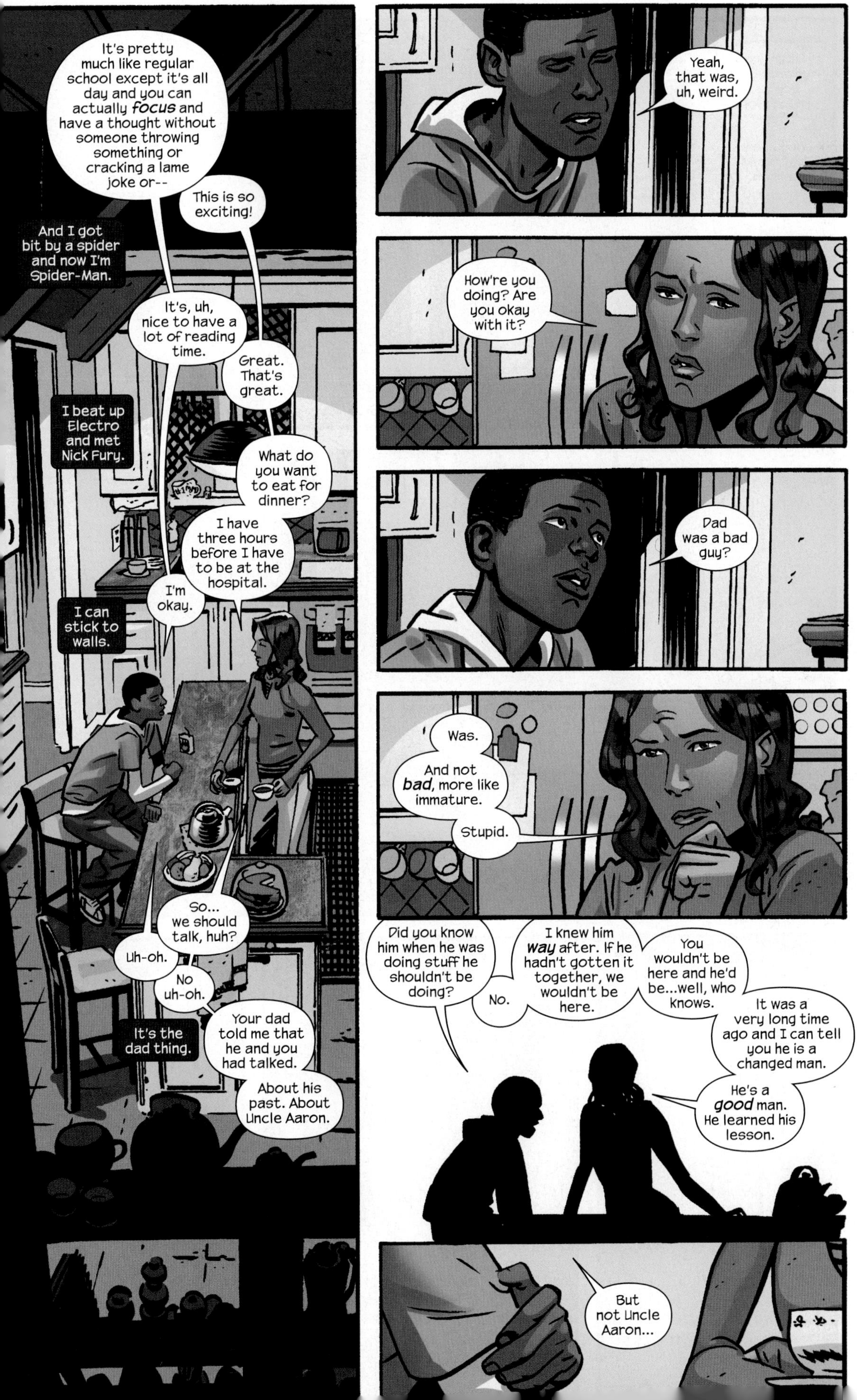
It's pretty much like regular school except it's all day and you can actually *focus* and have a thought without someone throwing something or cracking a lame joke or--
This is so exciting!
And I got bit by a spider and now I'm Spider-Man.
It's, uh, nice to have a lot of reading time.
Great. That's great.
I beat up Electro and met Nick Fury.
What do you want to eat for dinner?
I have three hours before I have to be at the hospital.
I'm okay.
I can stick to walls.
So... we should talk, huh?
Uh-oh.
No uh-oh.
It's the dad thing.
Your dad told me that he and you had talked.
About his past. About Uncle Aaron.
Yeah, that was, uh, weird.
How're you doing? Are you okay with it?
Dad was a bad guy?
Was.
And not *bad*, more like immature.
Stupid.
Did you know him when he was doing stuff he shouldn't be doing?
No.
I knew him *way* after. If he hadn't gotten it together, we wouldn't be here.
You wouldn't be here and he'd be...well, who knows.
It was a very long time ago and I can tell you he is a changed man.
He's a *good* man. He learned his lesson.
But not Uncle Aaron...

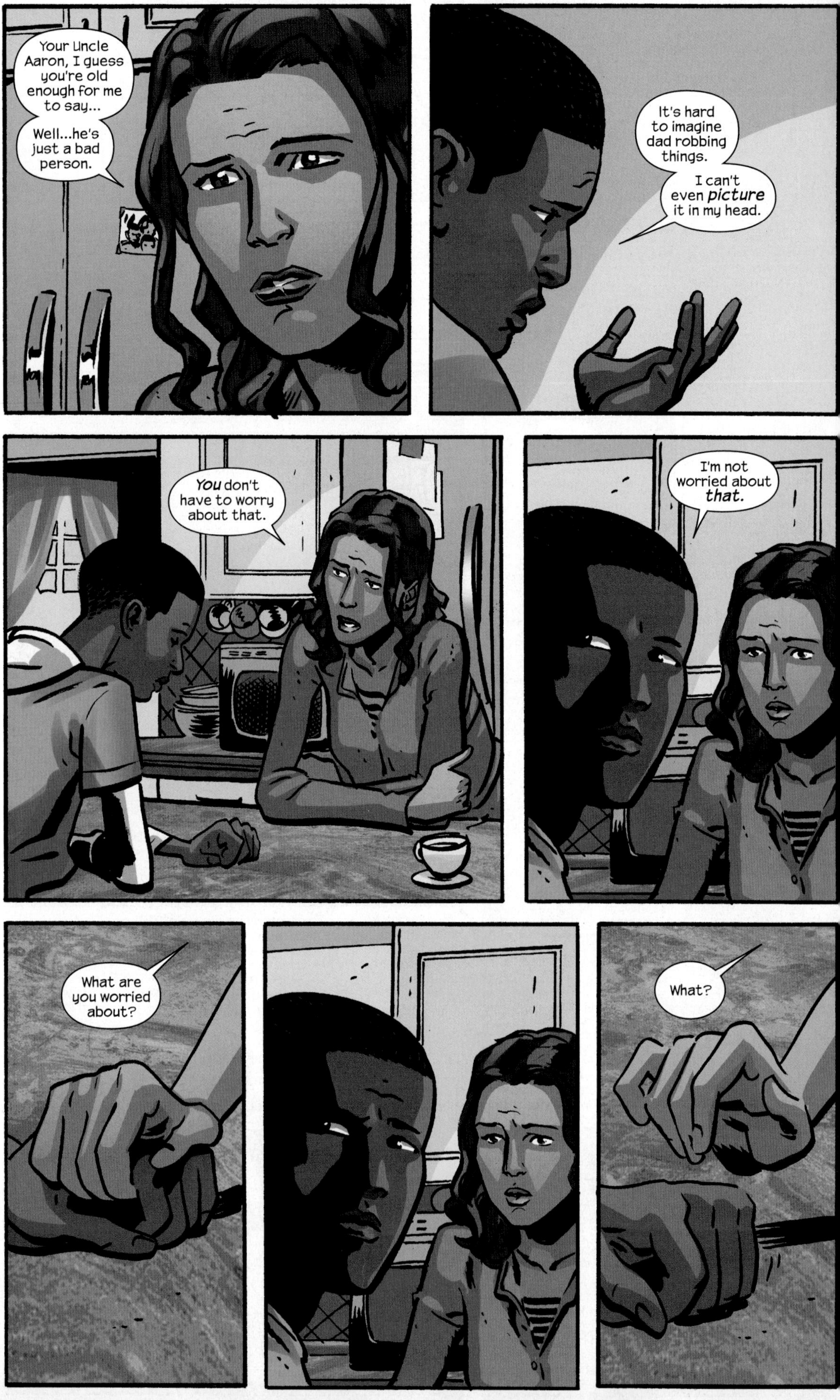
Your Uncle Aaron, I guess you're old enough for me to say...
Well...he's just a bad person.
It's hard to imagine dad robbing things.
I can't even *picture* it in my head.
You don't have to worry about that.
I'm not worried about ***that.***
What are you worried about?
What?

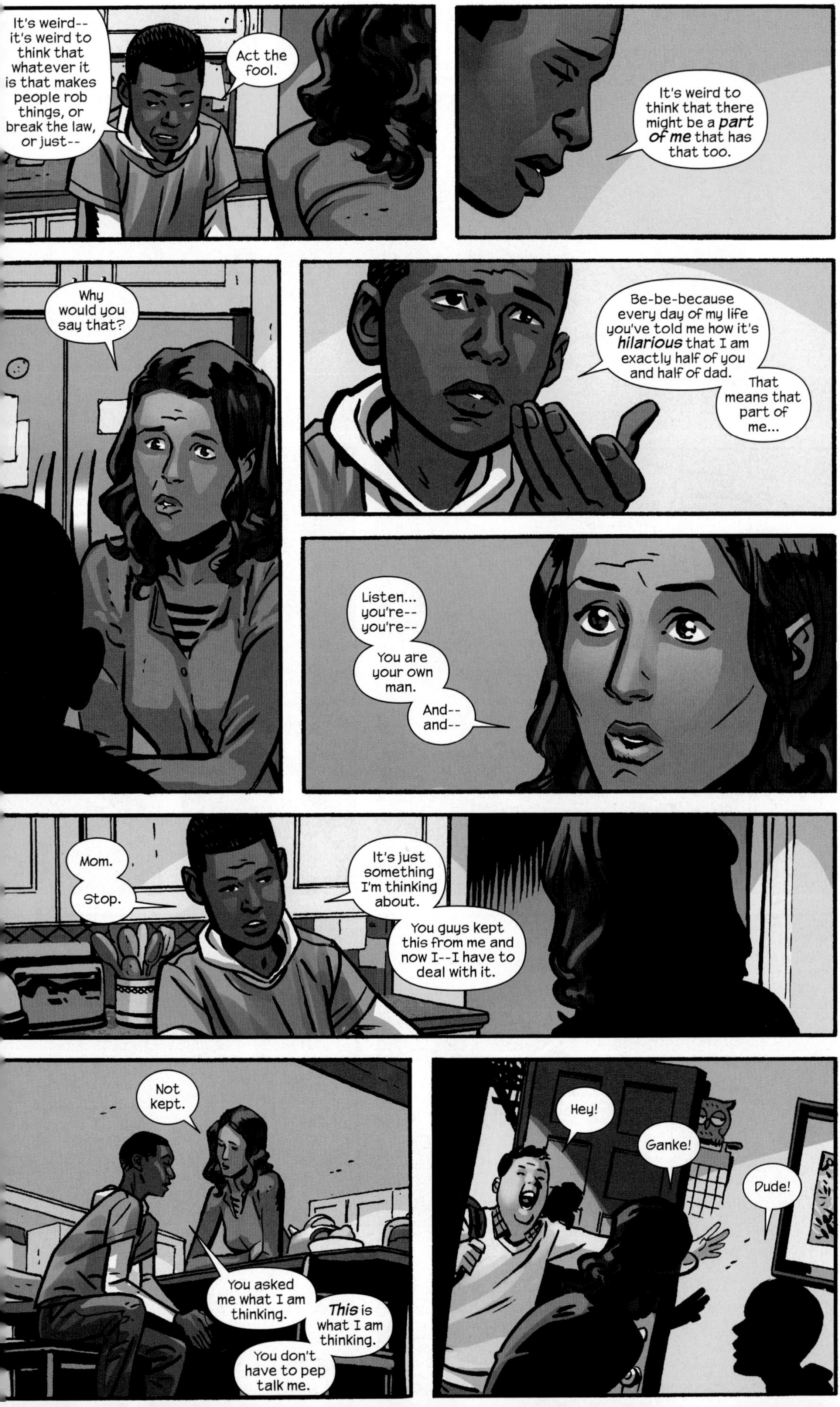
It's weird-- it's weird to think that whatever it is that makes people rob things, or break the law, or just--
Act the fool.
It's weird to think that there might be a *part of me* that has that too.
Why would you say that?
Be-be-because every day of my life you've told me how it's *hilarious* that I am exactly half of you and half of dad.
That means that part of me...
Listen... you're-- you're--
You are your own man.
And-- and--
Mom.
Stop.
It's just something I'm thinking about.
You guys kept this from me and now I--I have to deal with it.
Not kept.
You asked me what I am thinking.
This is what I am thinking.
You don't have to pep talk me.
Hey!
Ganke!
Dude!

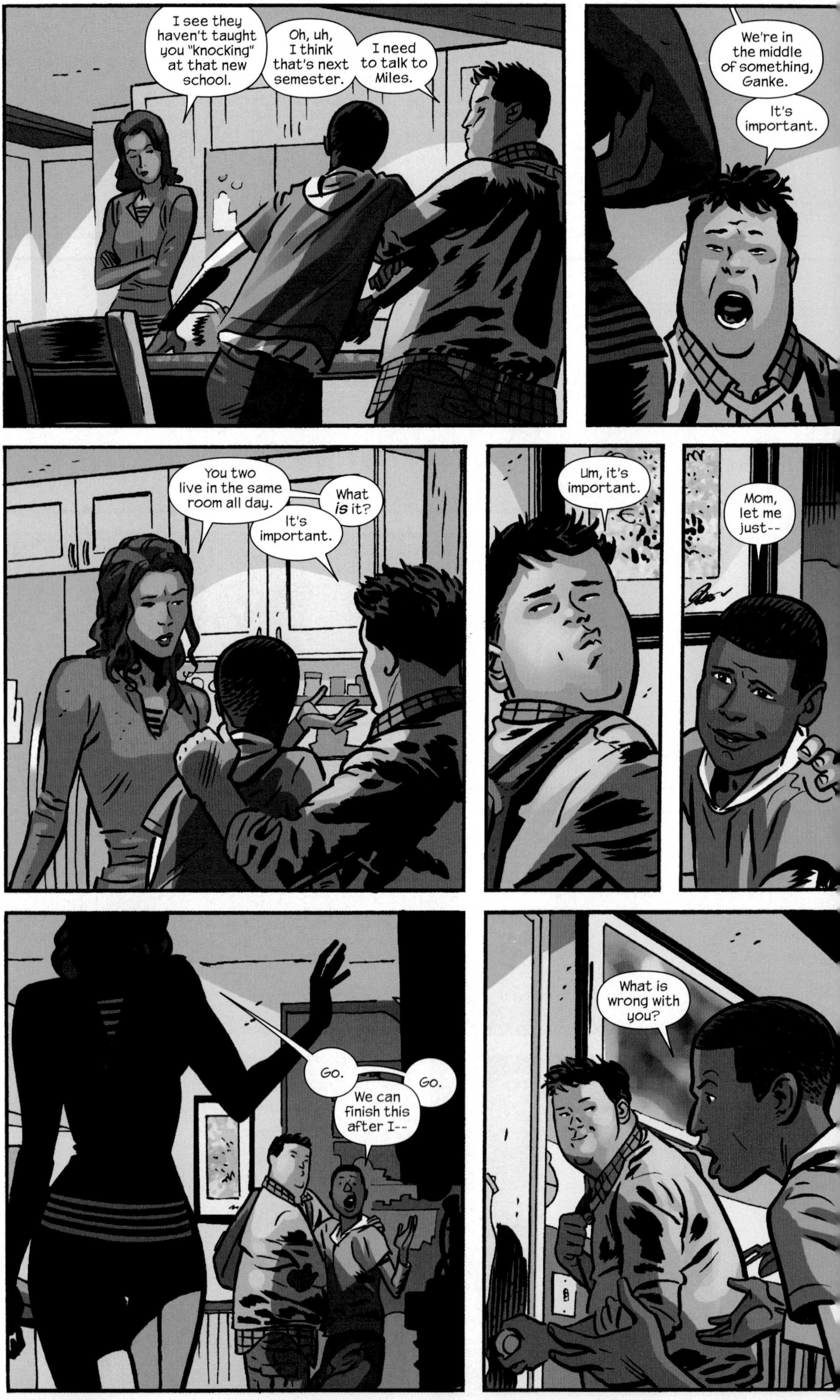
I see they haven't taught you "knocking" at that new school.
Oh, uh, I think that's next semester.
I need to talk to Miles.
We're in the middle of something, Ganke.
It's important.
You two live in the same room all day.
What *is* it?
It's important.
Um, it's important.
Mom, let me just--
Go.
Go.
We can finish this after I--
What is wrong with you?

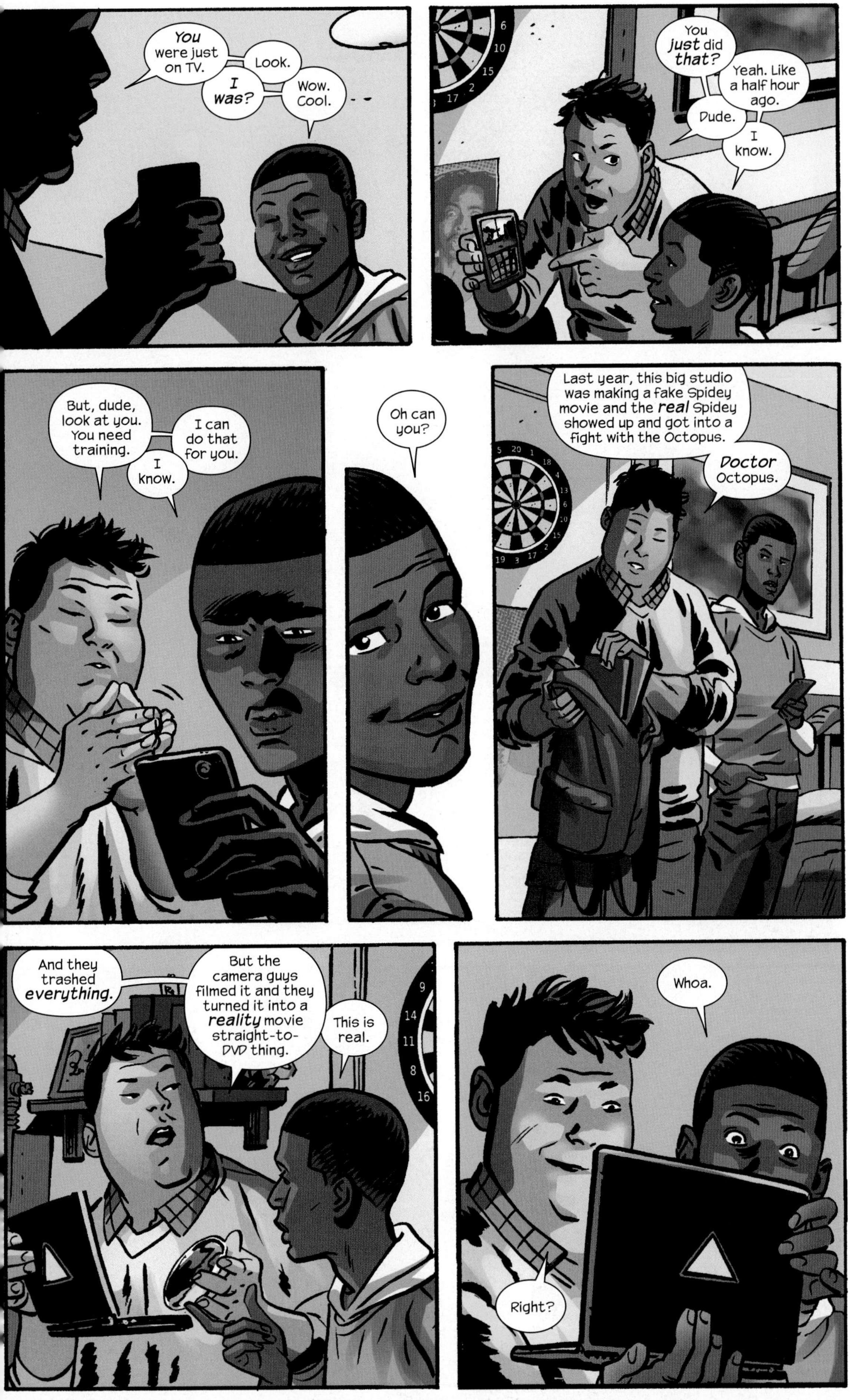
You were just on TV.
Look.
I was?
Wow. Cool.
You just did that?
Yeah. Like a half hour ago.
Dude.
I know.
But, dude, look at you. You need training.
I can do that for you.
I know.
Oh can you?
Last year, this big studio was making a fake Spidey movie and the real Spidey showed up and got into a fight with the Octopus.
Doctor Octopus.
And they trashed everything.
But the camera guys filmed it and they turned it into a reality movie straight-to-DVD thing.
This is real.
Whoa.
Right?

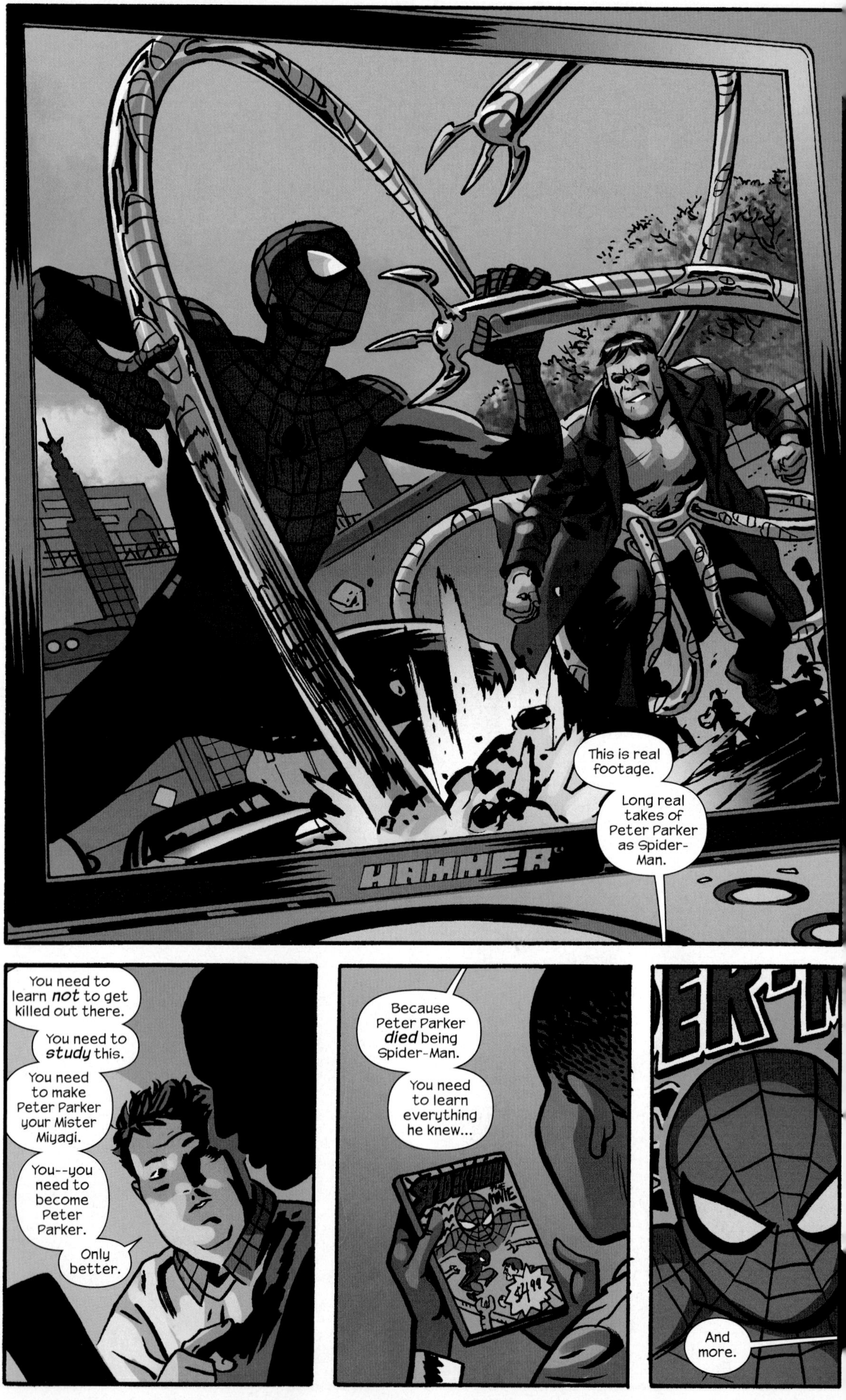
HAMMER
This is real footage.
Long real takes of Peter Parker as Spider-Man.
You need to learn *not* to get killed out there.
You need to *study* this.
You need to make Peter Parker your Mister Miyagi.
You--you need to become Peter Parker.
Only better.
Because Peter Parker *died* being Spider-Man.
You need to learn everything he knew...
And more.

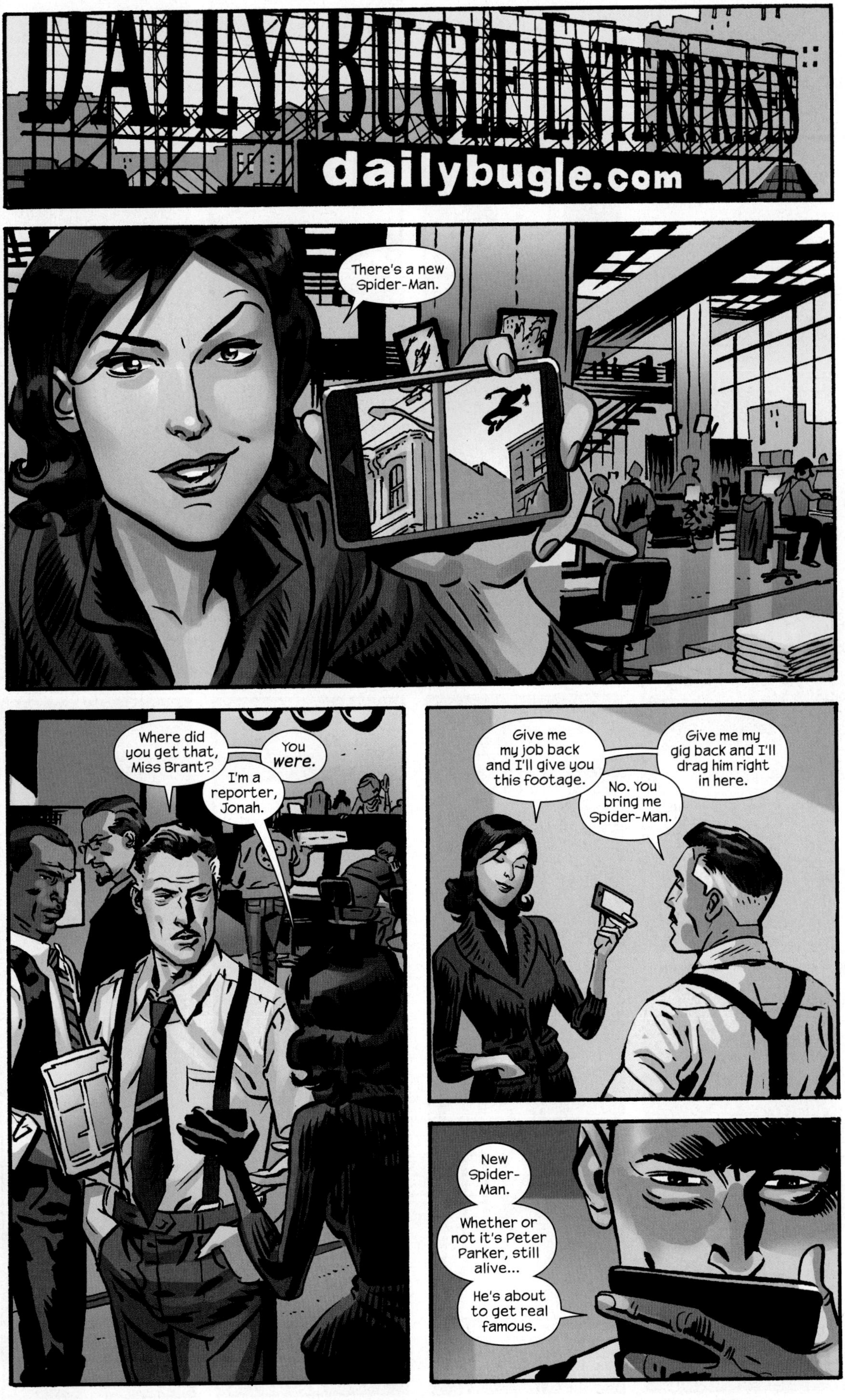
DAILY BUGLE ENTERPRISES
dailybugle.com
There's a new Spider-Man.
Where did you get that, Miss Brant?
You were.
I'm a reporter, Jonah.
Give me my job back and I'll give you this footage.
Give me my gig back and I'll drag him right in here.
No. You bring me Spider-Man.
New Spider-Man.
Whether or not it's Peter Parker, still alive...
He's about to get real famous.

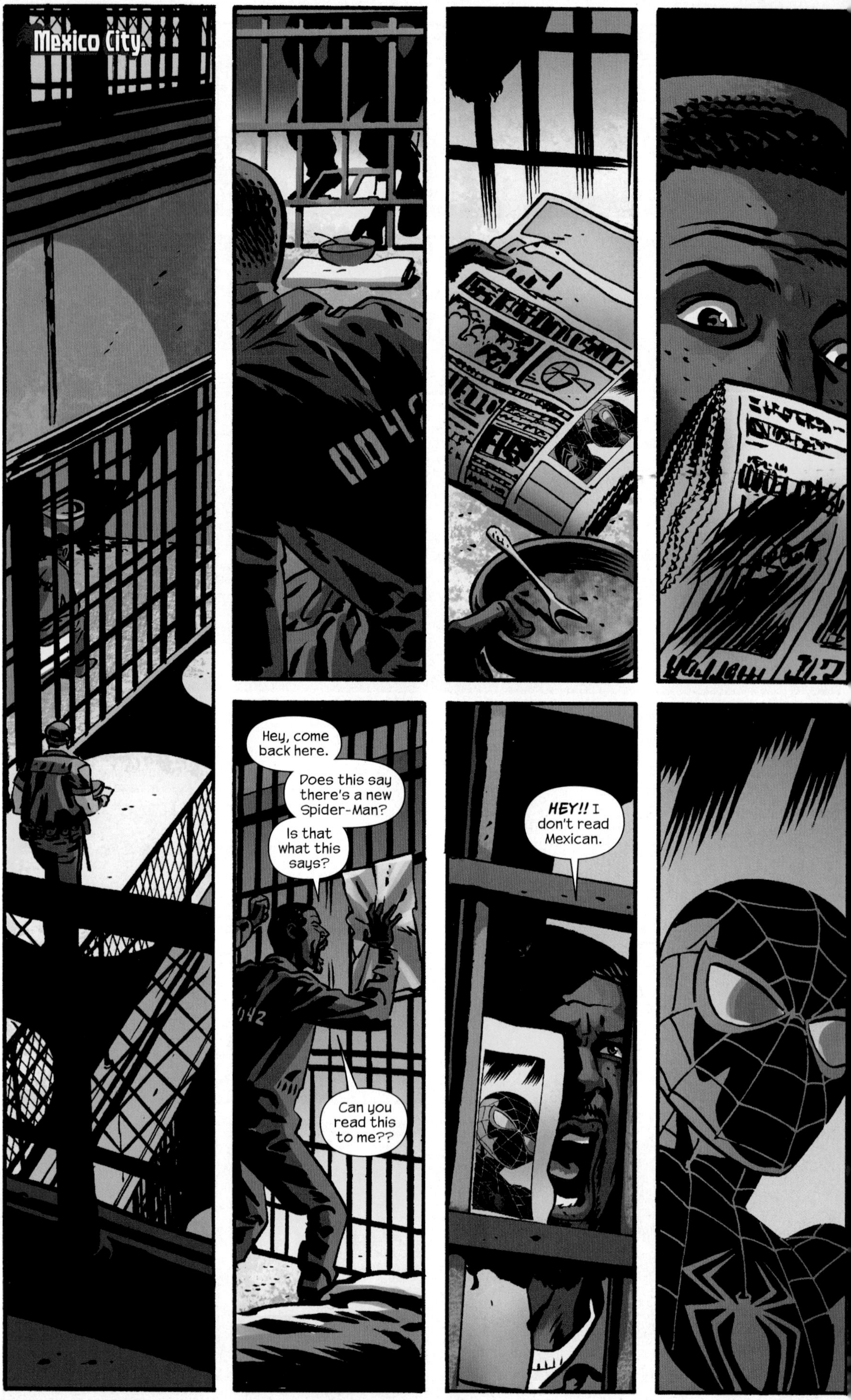
Mexico City.
Hey, come back here.
Does this say there's a new Spider-Man?
Is that what this says?
Can you read this to me??
HEY!! I don't read Mexican.

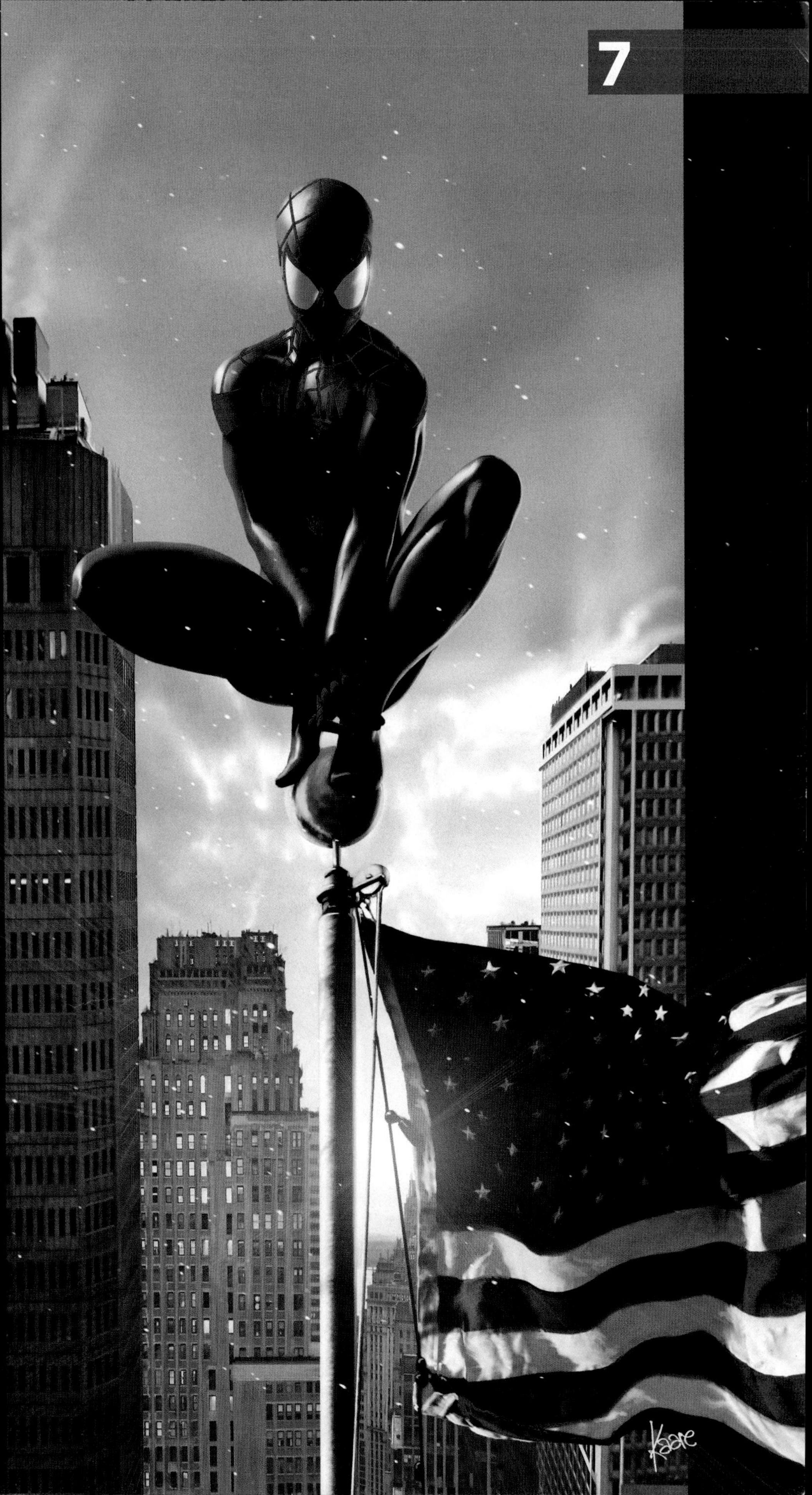
7

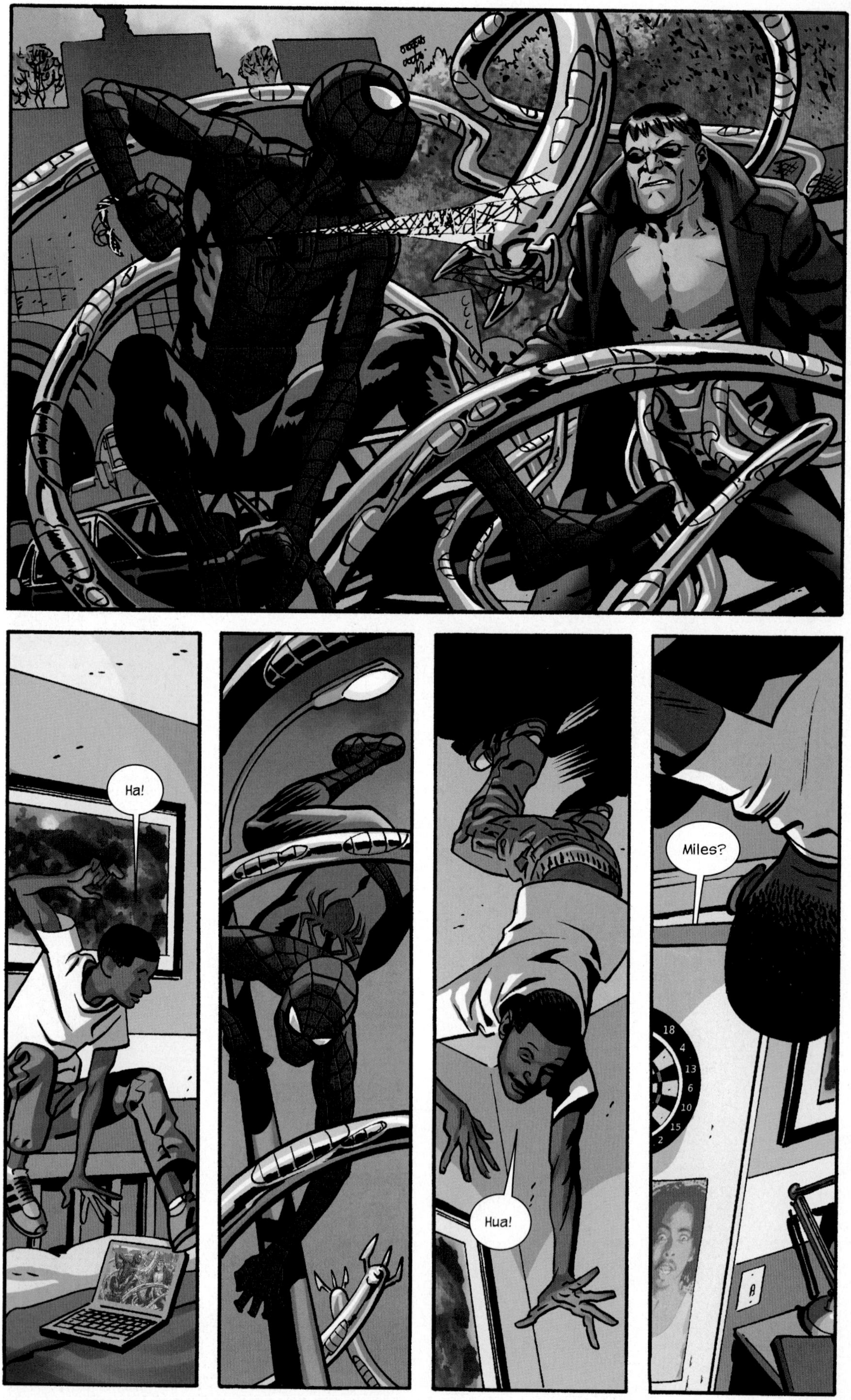
Ha!
Hua!
Miles?

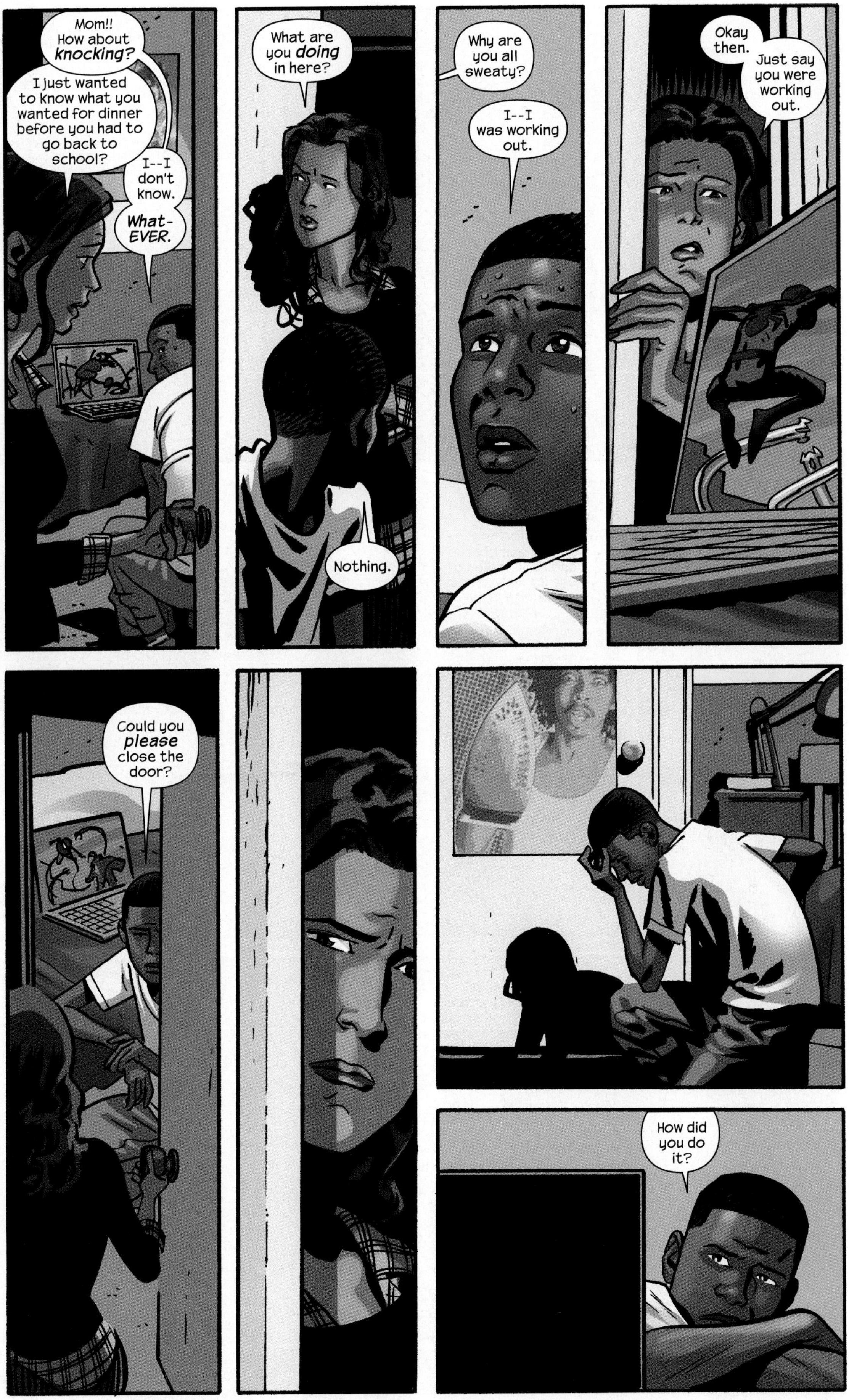

Mom!! How about knocking?
I just wanted to know what you wanted for dinner before you had to go back to school?
I--I don't know.
What-EVER.
What are you doing in here?
Nothing.
Why are you all sweaty?
I--I was working out.
Okay then.
Just say you were working out.
Could you please close the door?
How did you do it?

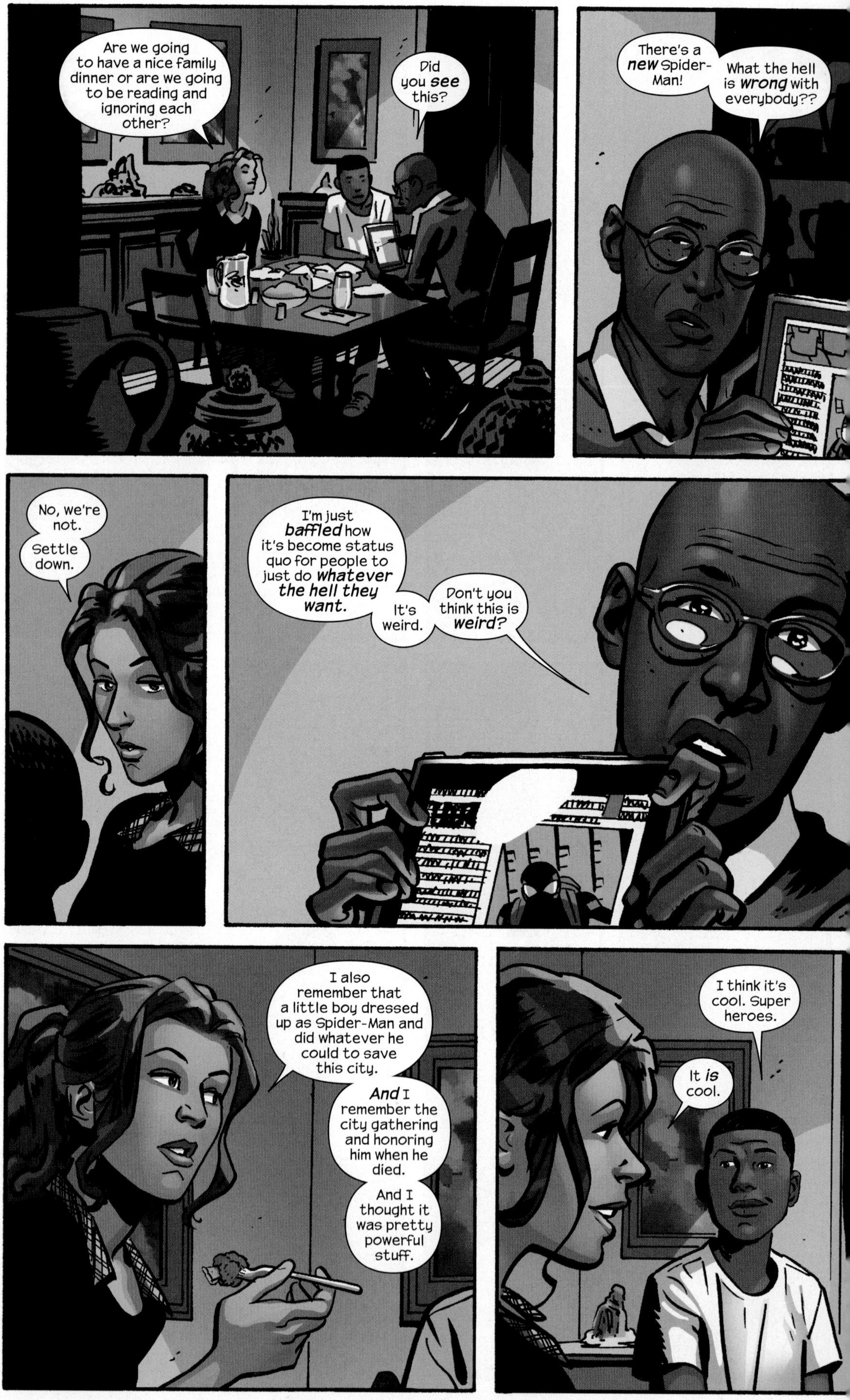
Are we going to have a nice family dinner or are we going to be reading and ignoring each other?
Did you *see* this?
There's a *new* Spider-Man!
What the hell is *wrong* with everybody??
No, we're not.
Settle down.
I'm just *baffled* how it's become status quo for people to just do *whatever the hell they want.*
It's weird.
Don't you think this is *weird?*
I also remember that a little boy dressed up as Spider-Man and did whatever he could to save this city.
And I remember the city gathering and honoring him when he died.
And I thought it was pretty powerful stuff.
I think it's cool. Super heroes.
It *is* cool.

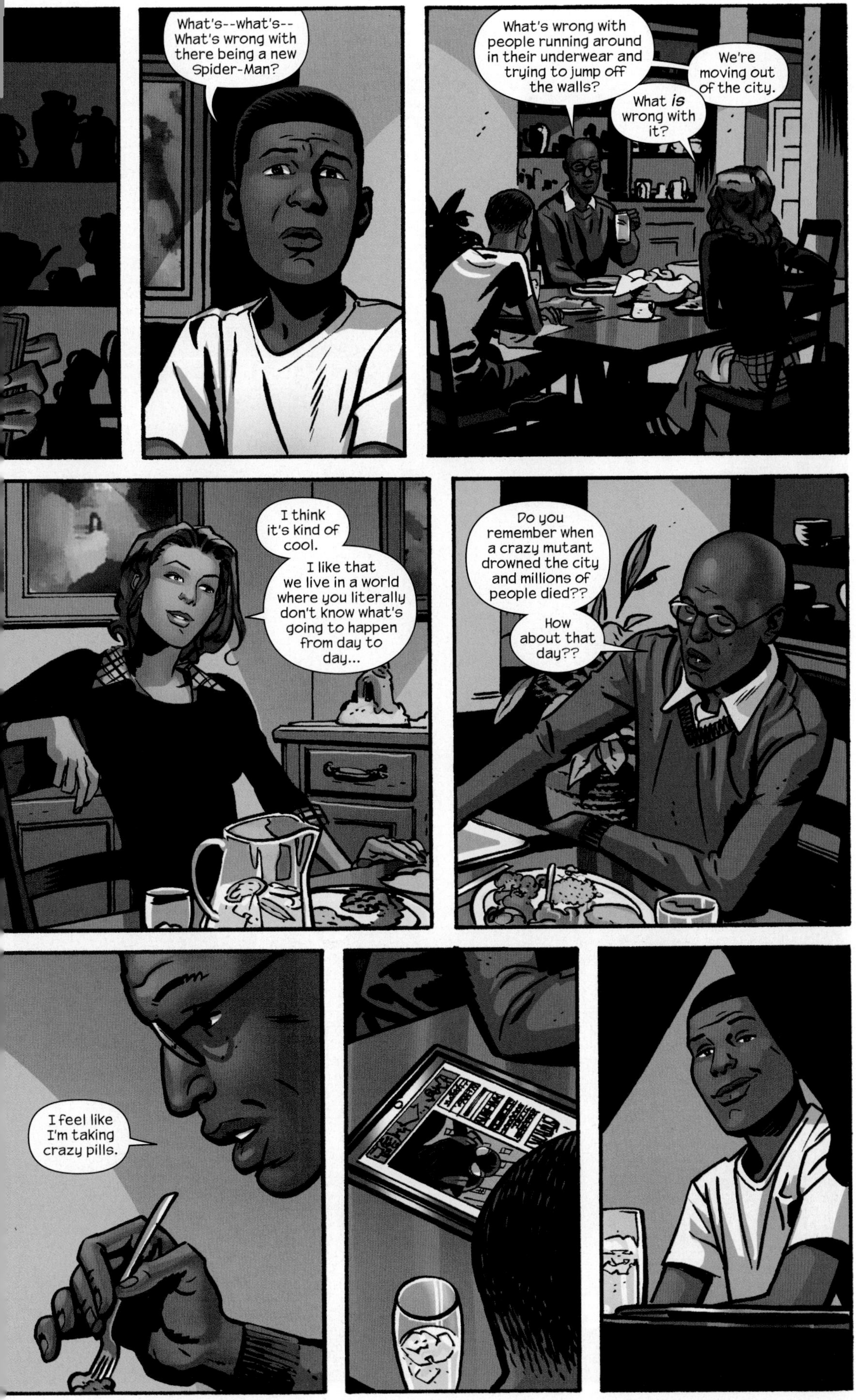
What's--what's--
What's wrong with there being a new Spider-Man?
What's wrong with people running around in their underwear and trying to jump off the walls?
What *is* wrong with it?
We're moving out of the city.
I think it's kind of cool.
I like that we live in a world where you literally don't know what's going to happen from day to day...
Do you remember when a crazy mutant drowned the city and millions of people died??
How about that day??
I feel like I'm taking crazy pills.

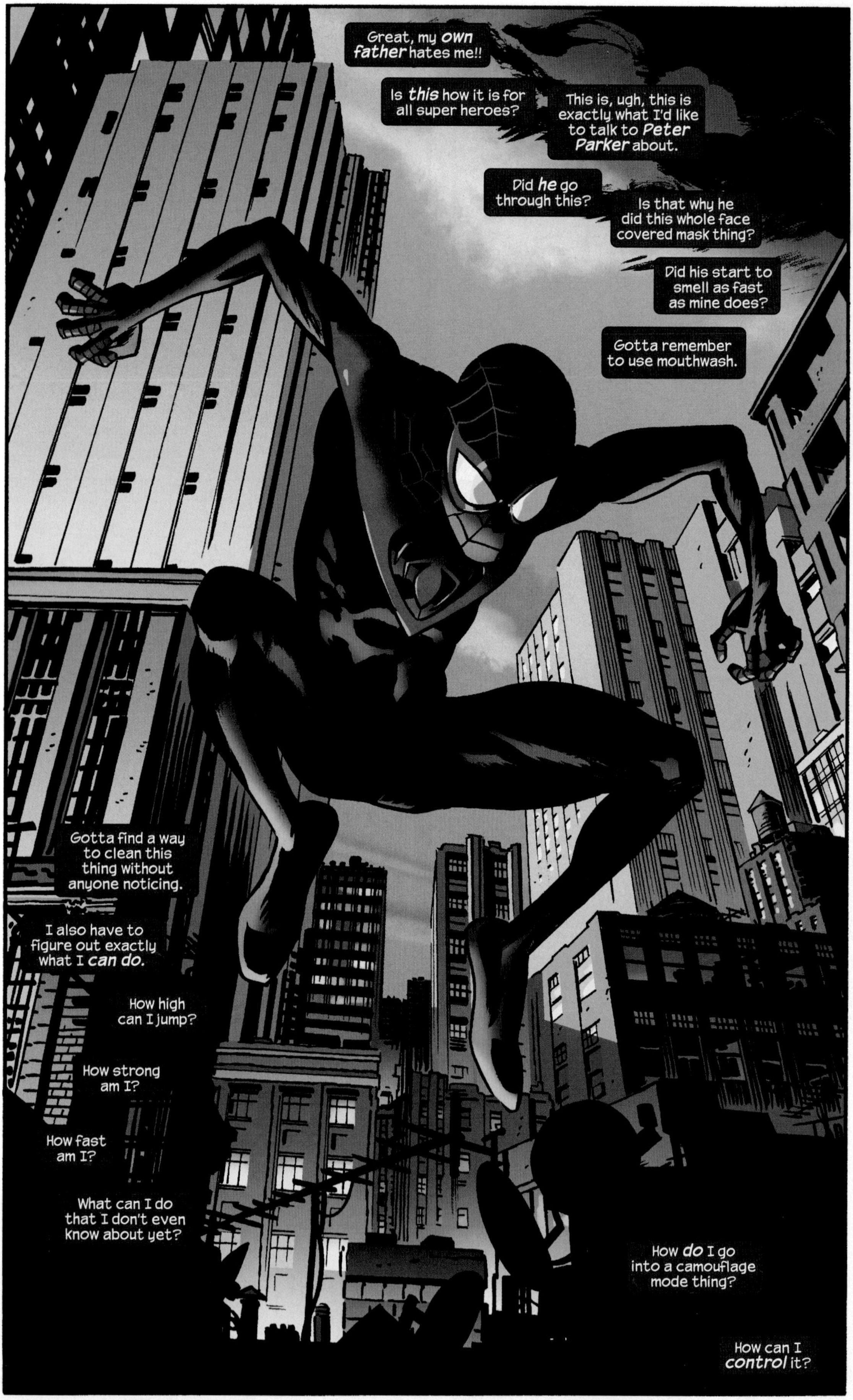
Great, my own father hates me!!
Is this how it is for all super heroes?
This is, ugh, this is exactly what I'd like to talk to Peter Parker about.
Did he go through this?
Is that why he did this whole face covered mask thing?
Did his start to smell as fast as mine does?
Gotta remember to use mouthwash.
Gotta find a way to clean this thing without anyone noticing.
I also have to figure out exactly what I can do.
How high can I jump?
How strong am I?
How fast am I?
What can I do that I don't even know about yet?
How do I go into a camouflage mode thing?
How can I control it?

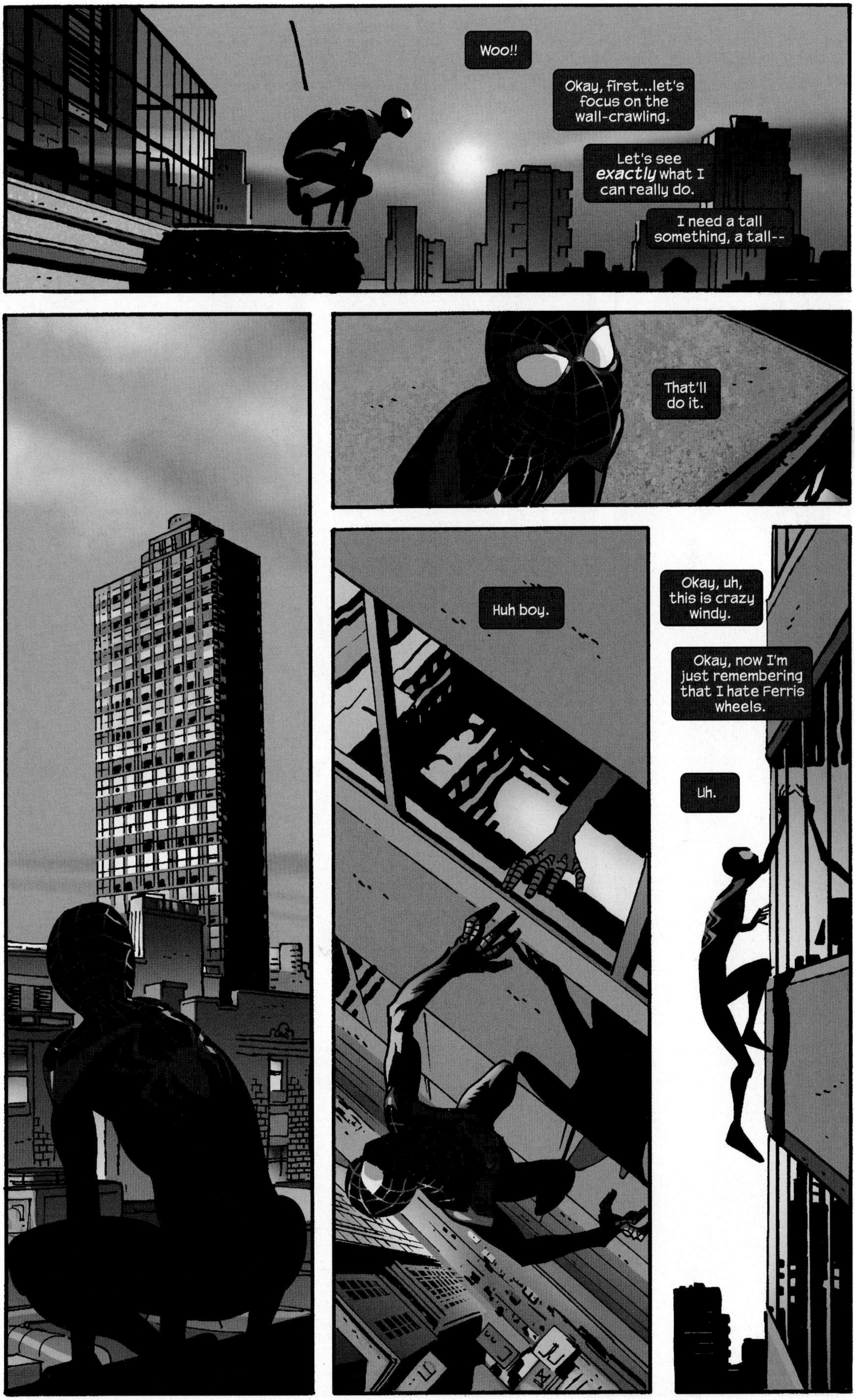
Woo!!
Okay, first...let's focus on the wall-crawling.
Let's see *exactly* what I can really do.
I need a tall something, a tall--
That'll do it.
Huh boy.
Okay, uh, this is crazy windy.
Okay, now I'm just remembering that I hate Ferris wheels.
Uh.

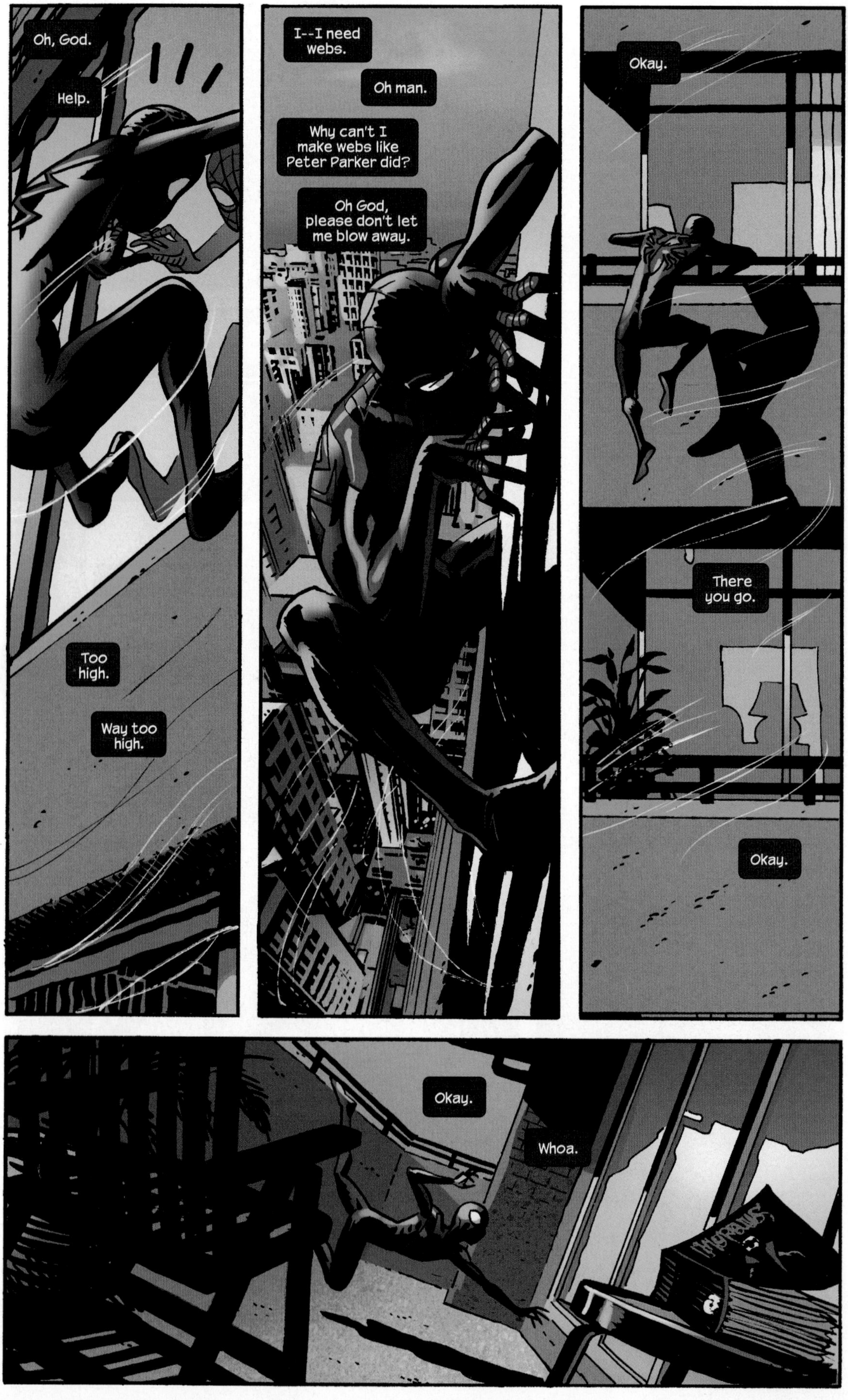
Oh, God.
Help.
Too high.
Way too high.
I--I need webs.
Oh man.
Why can't I make webs like Peter Parker did?
Oh God, please don't let me blow away.
Okay.
There you go.
Okay.
Okay.
Whoa.

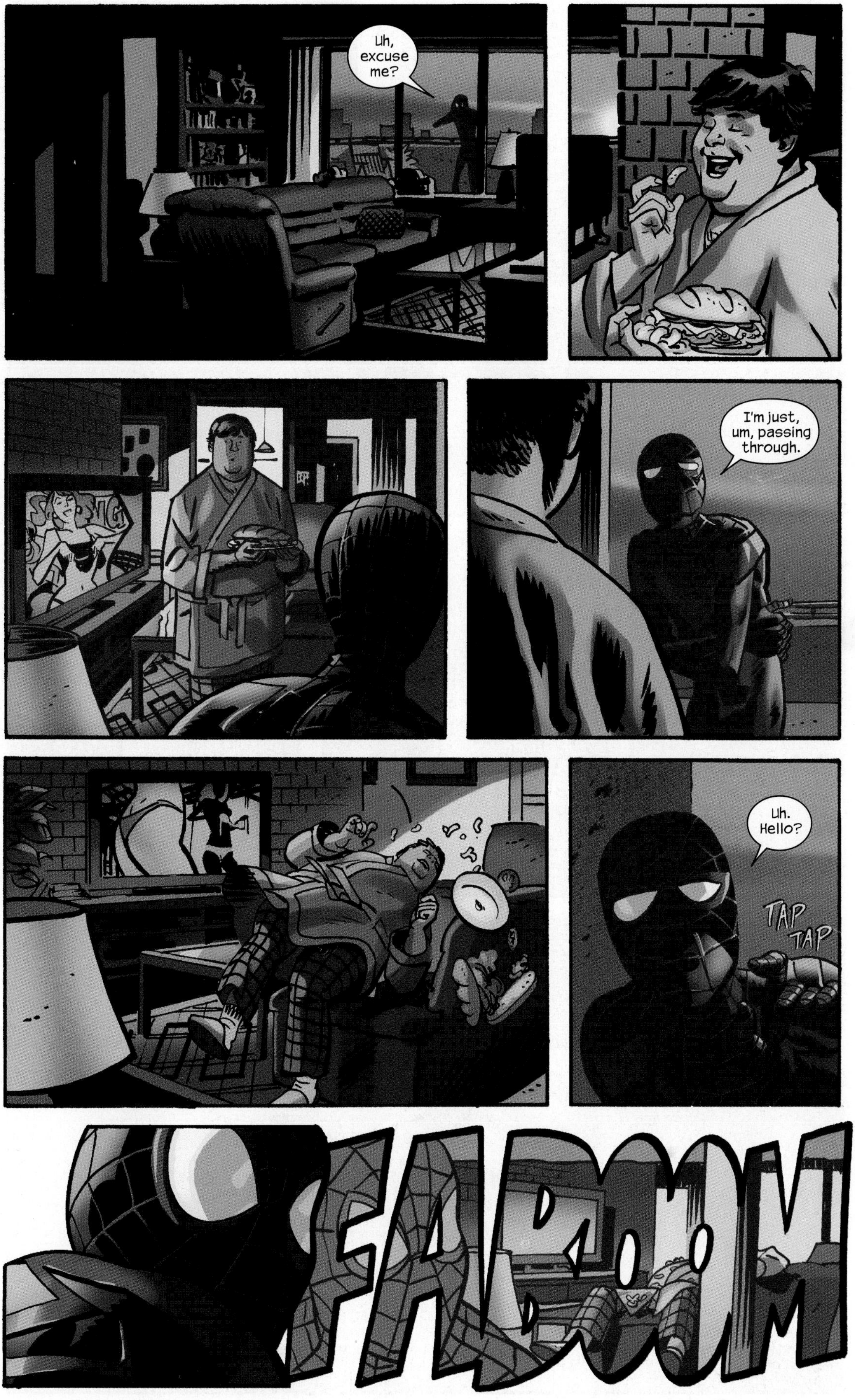
Uh, excuse me?
I'm just, um, passing through.
Uh. Hello?
TAP TAP
FADOOM

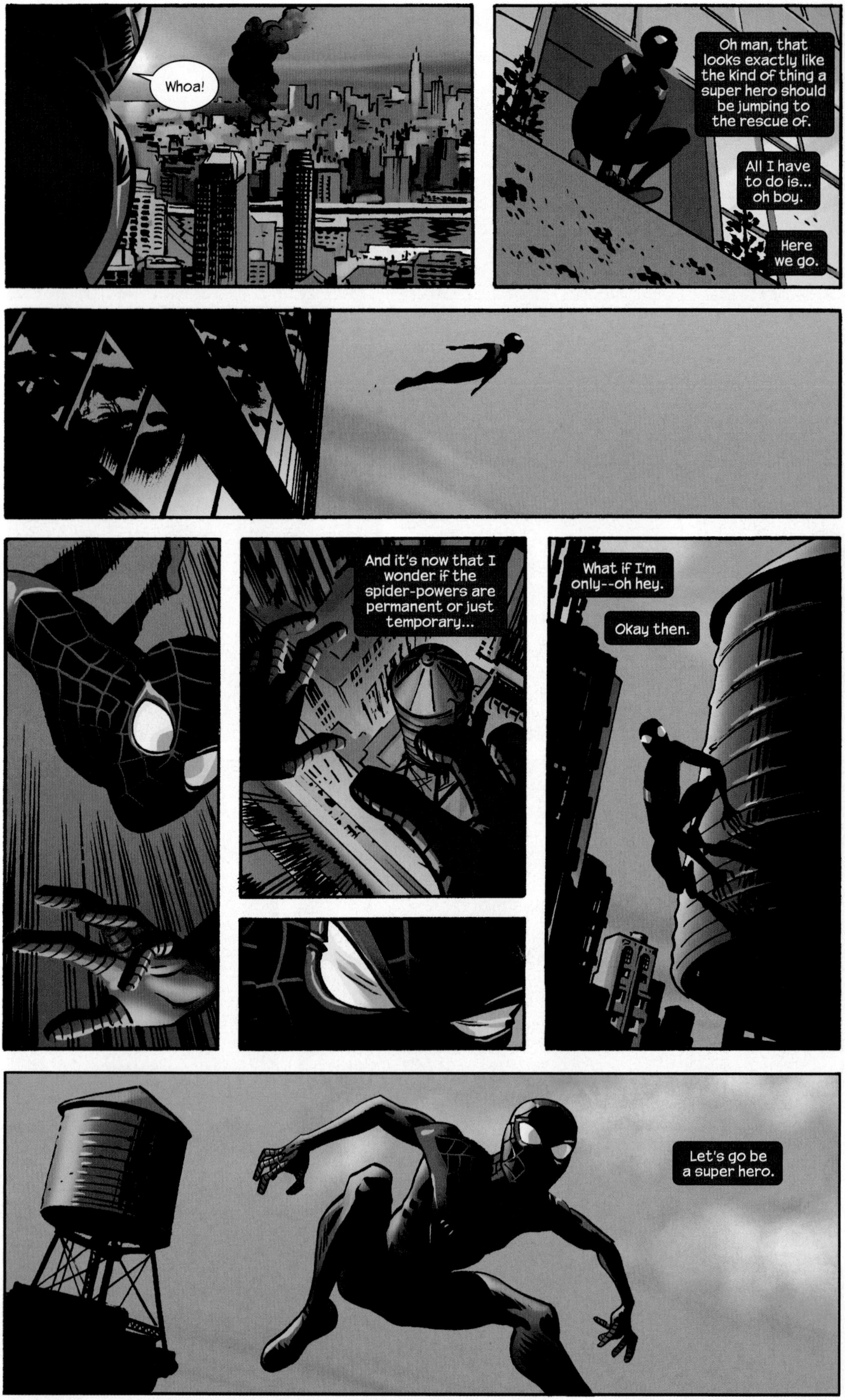

Whoa!
Oh man, that looks exactly like the kind of thing a super hero should be jumping to the rescue of.
All I have to do is... oh boy.
Here we go.
And it's now that I wonder if the spider-powers are permanent or just temporary...
What if I'm only--oh hey.
Okay then.
Let's go be a super hero.

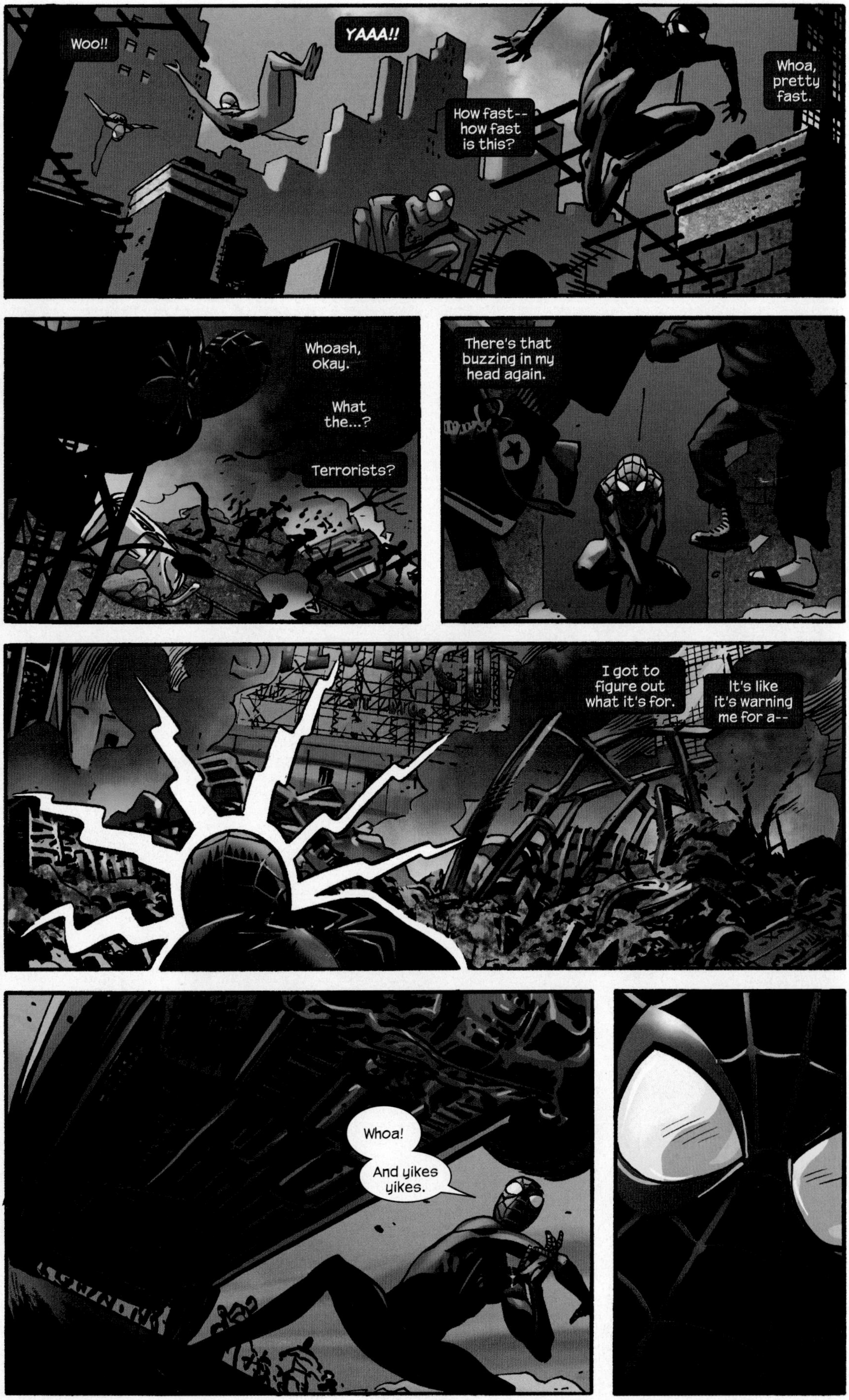
Woo!!
YAAA!!
How fast--
how fast
is this?
Whoa,
pretty
fast.
Whoash,
okay.
What
the...?
Terrorists?
There's that
buzzing in my
head again.
I got to
figure out
what it's for.
It's like
it's warning
me for a--
Whoa!
And yikes
yikes.

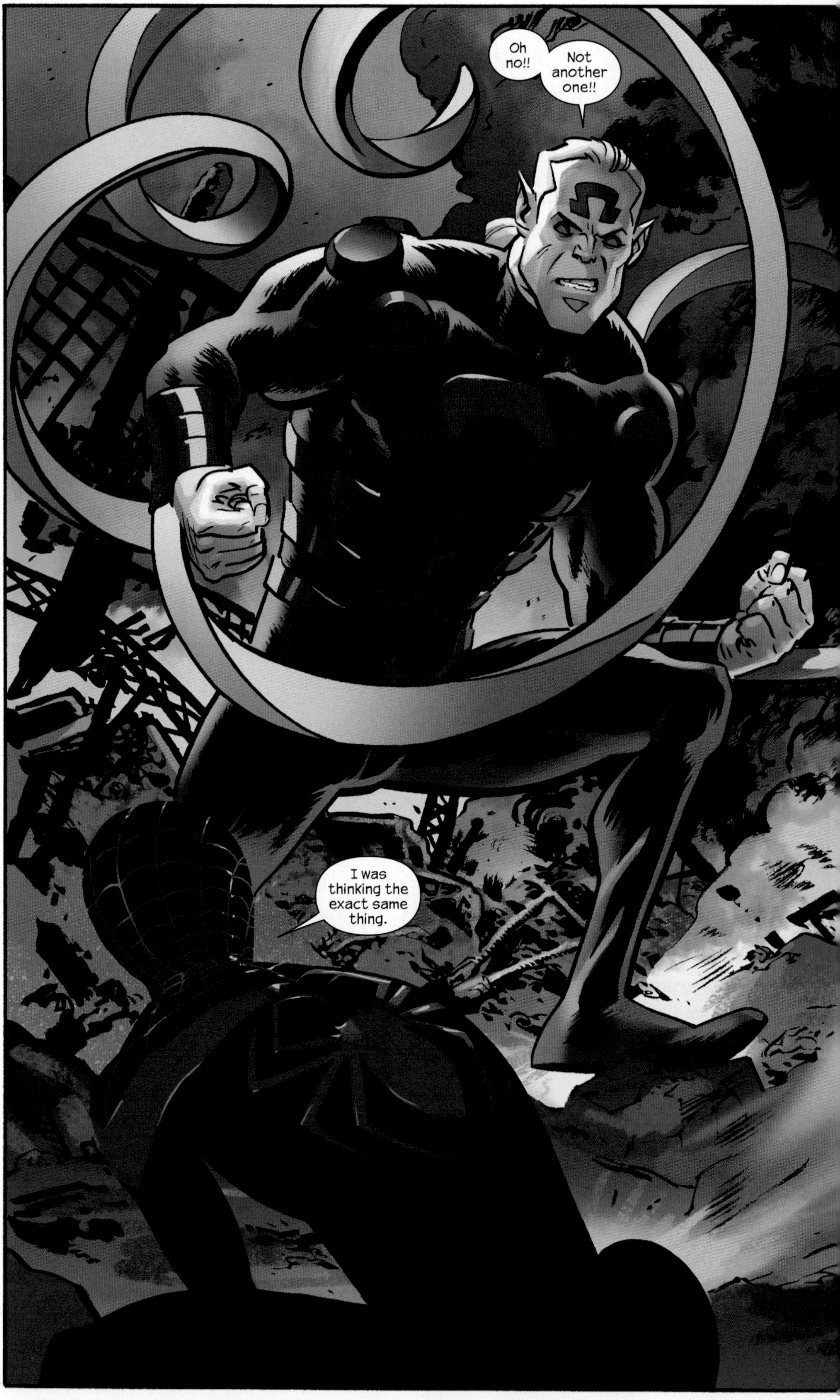
Oh no!!
Not another one!!
I was thinking the exact same thing.

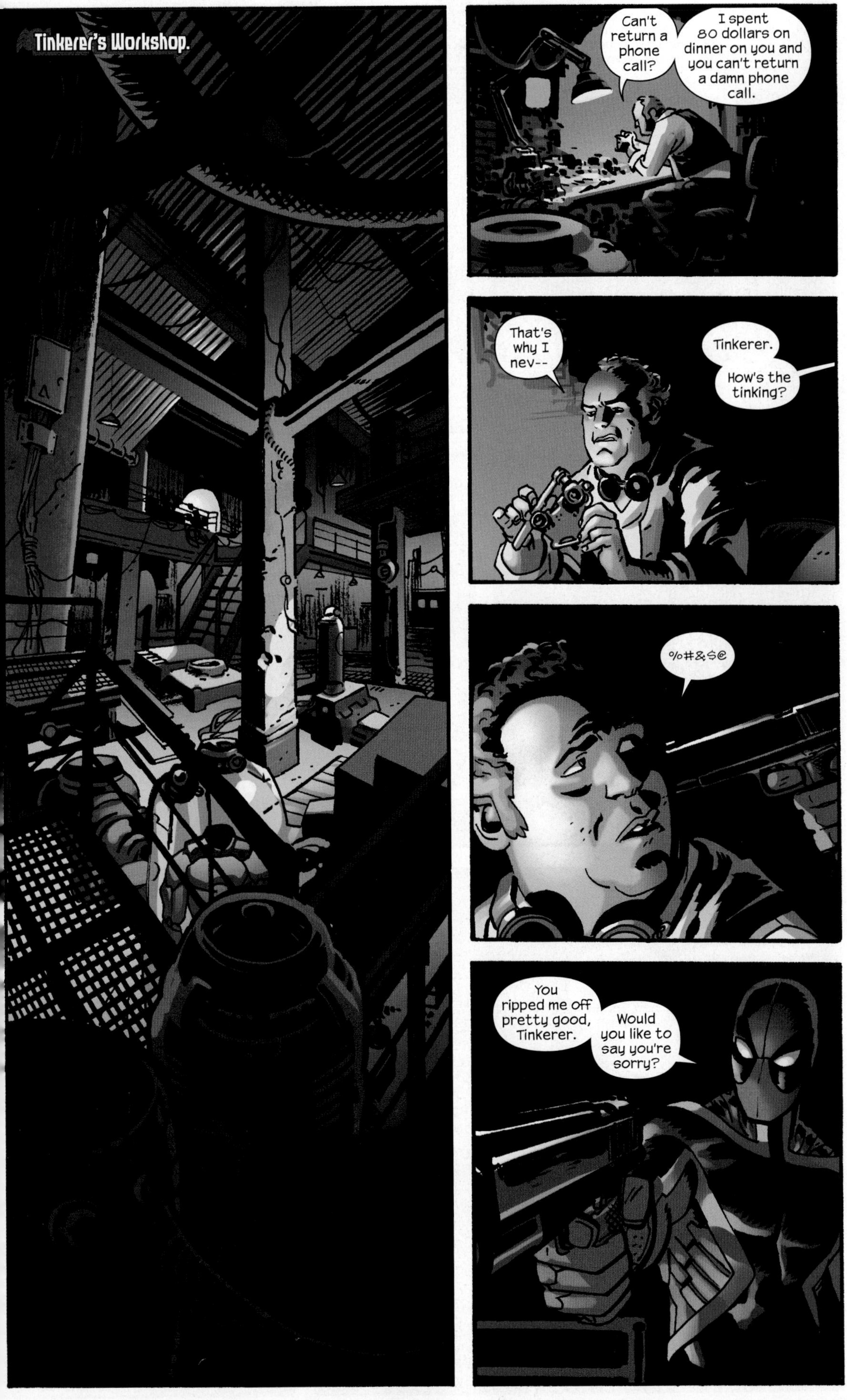
Tinkerer's Workshop.
Can't return a phone call?
I spent 80 dollars on dinner on you and you can't return a damn phone call.
That's why I nev--
Tinkerer.
How's the tinking?
%#&$@
You ripped me off pretty good, Tinkerer.
Would you like to say you're sorry?

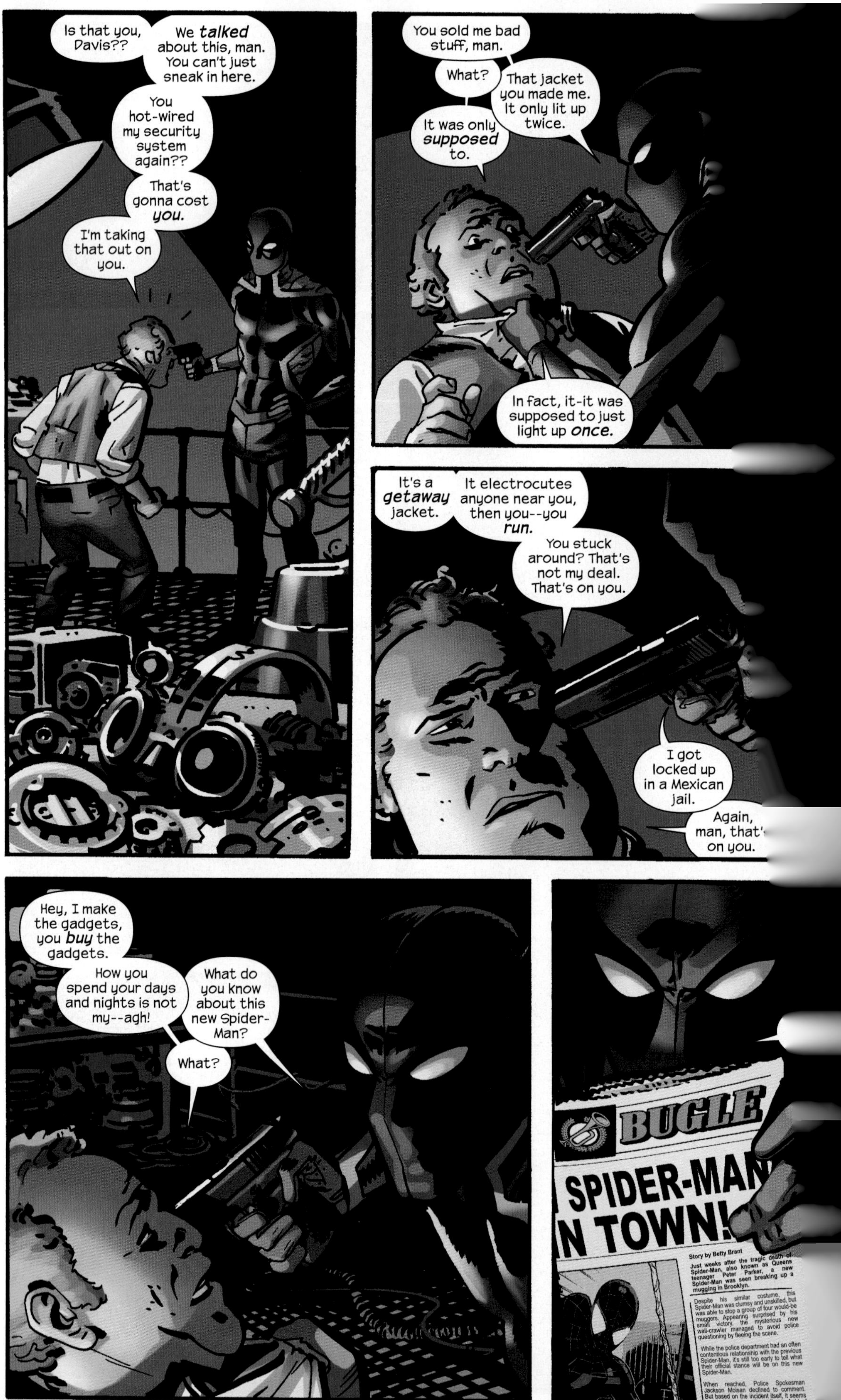
Is that you, Davis??
We *talked* about this, man. You can't just sneak in here.
You hot-wired my security system again??
That's gonna cost *you.*
I'm taking that out on you.
You sold me bad stuff, man.
What?
That jacket you made me. It only lit up twice.
It was only *supposed* to.
In fact, it-it was supposed to just light up *once.*
It's a *getaway* jacket.
It electrocutes anyone near you, then you--you *run.*
You stuck around? That's not my deal. That's on you.
I got locked up in a Mexican jail.
Again, man, that's on you.
Hey, I make the gadgets, you *buy* the gadgets.
How you spend your days and nights is not my--agh!
What do you know about this new Spider-Man?
What?
BUGLE
SPIDER-MAN
N TOWN!
Story by Betty Brant
Just weeks after the tragic death of Spider-Man, also known as Queens teenager Peter Parker, a new Spider-Man was seen breaking up a mugging in Brooklyn.
Despite his similar costume, this Spider-Man was clumsy and unskilled, but was able to stop a group of four would-be muggers. Appearing surprised by his small victory, the mysterious new wall-crawler managed to avoid police questioning by fleeing the scene.
While the police department had an often contentious relationship with the previous Spider-Man, it's still too early to tell what their official stance will be on this new Spider-Man.
When reached, Police Spokesman Jackson Moisan declined to comment. But based on the incident itself, it seems

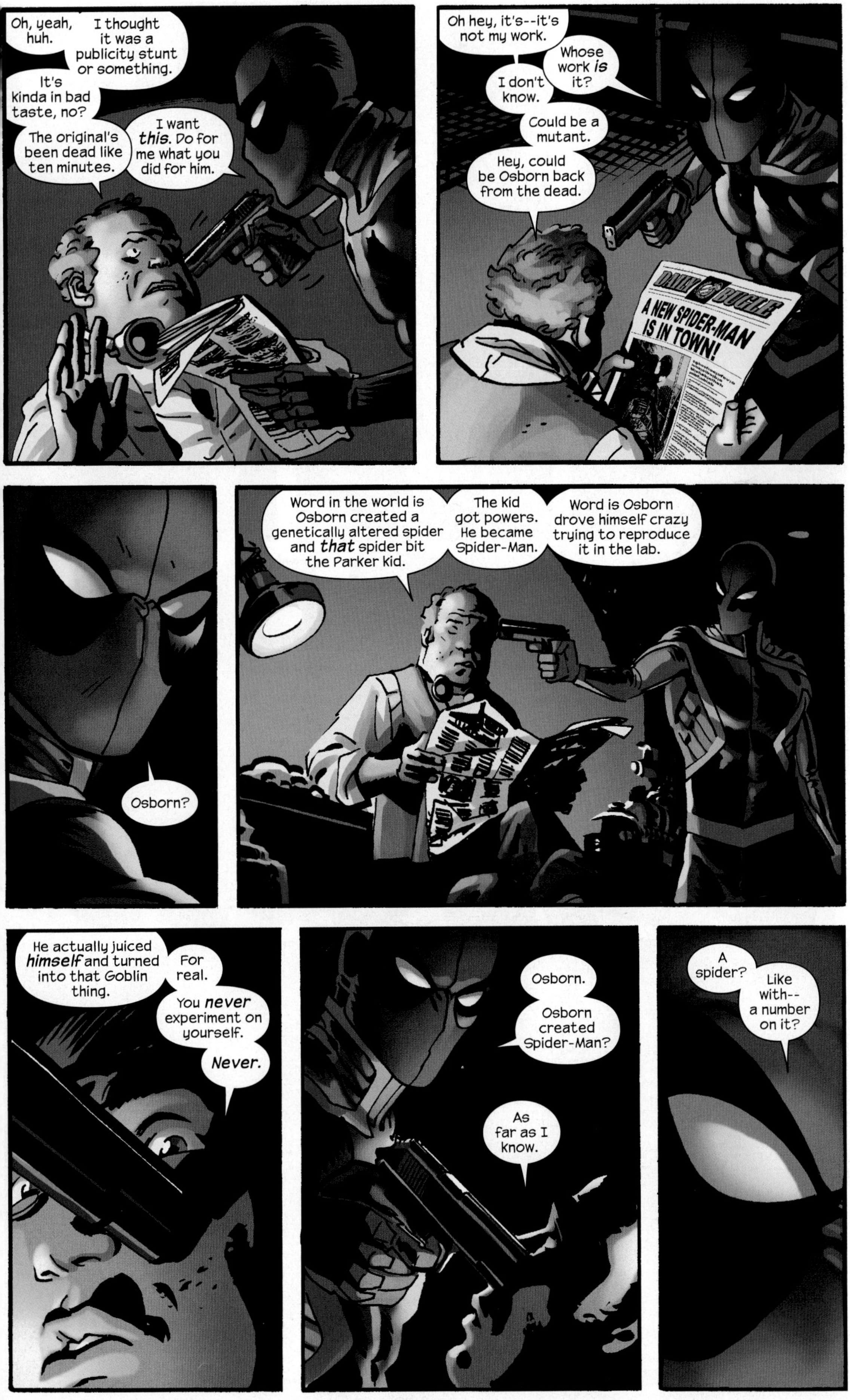

Oh, yeah, huh.
I thought it was a publicity stunt or something.
It's kinda in bad taste, no?
The original's been dead like ten minutes.
I want *this*. Do for me what you did for him.
Oh hey, it's--it's not my work.
Whose work *is* it?
I don't know.
Could be a mutant.
Hey, could be Osborn back from the dead.
DAILY BUGLE
A NEW SPIDER-MAN IS IN TOWN!
Osborn?
Word in the world is Osborn created a genetically altered spider and *that* spider bit the Parker kid.
The kid got powers. He became Spider-Man.
Word is Osborn drove himself crazy trying to reproduce it in the lab.
He actually juiced *himself* and turned into that Goblin thing.
For real.
You *never* experiment on yourself.
Never.
Osborn.
Osborn created Spider-Man?
As far as I know.
A spider?
Like with-- a number on it?

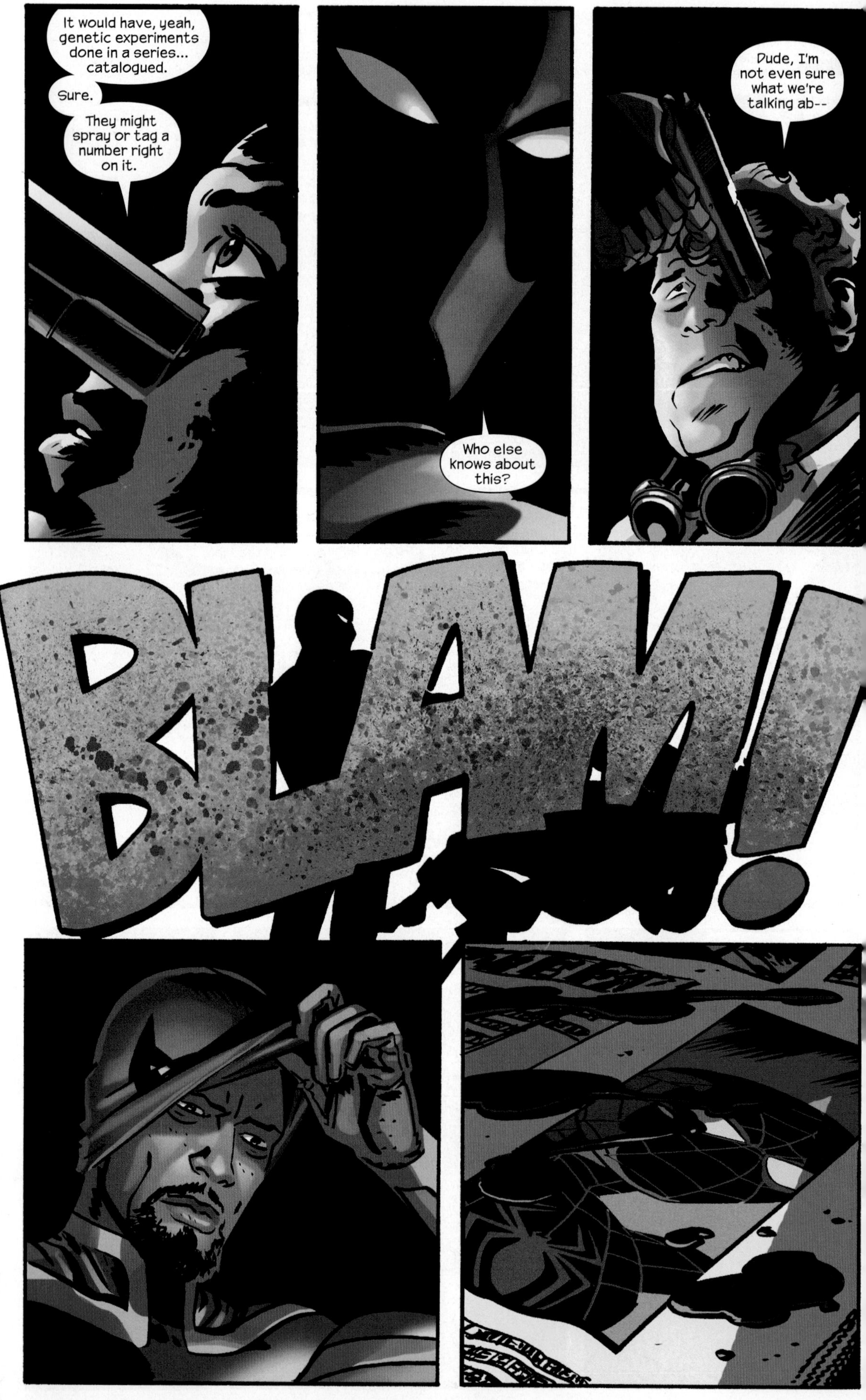
It would have, yeah, genetic experiments done in a series... catalogued.
Sure.
They might spray or tag a number right on it.
Who else knows about this?
Dude, I'm not even sure what we're talking ab--
BLAM!

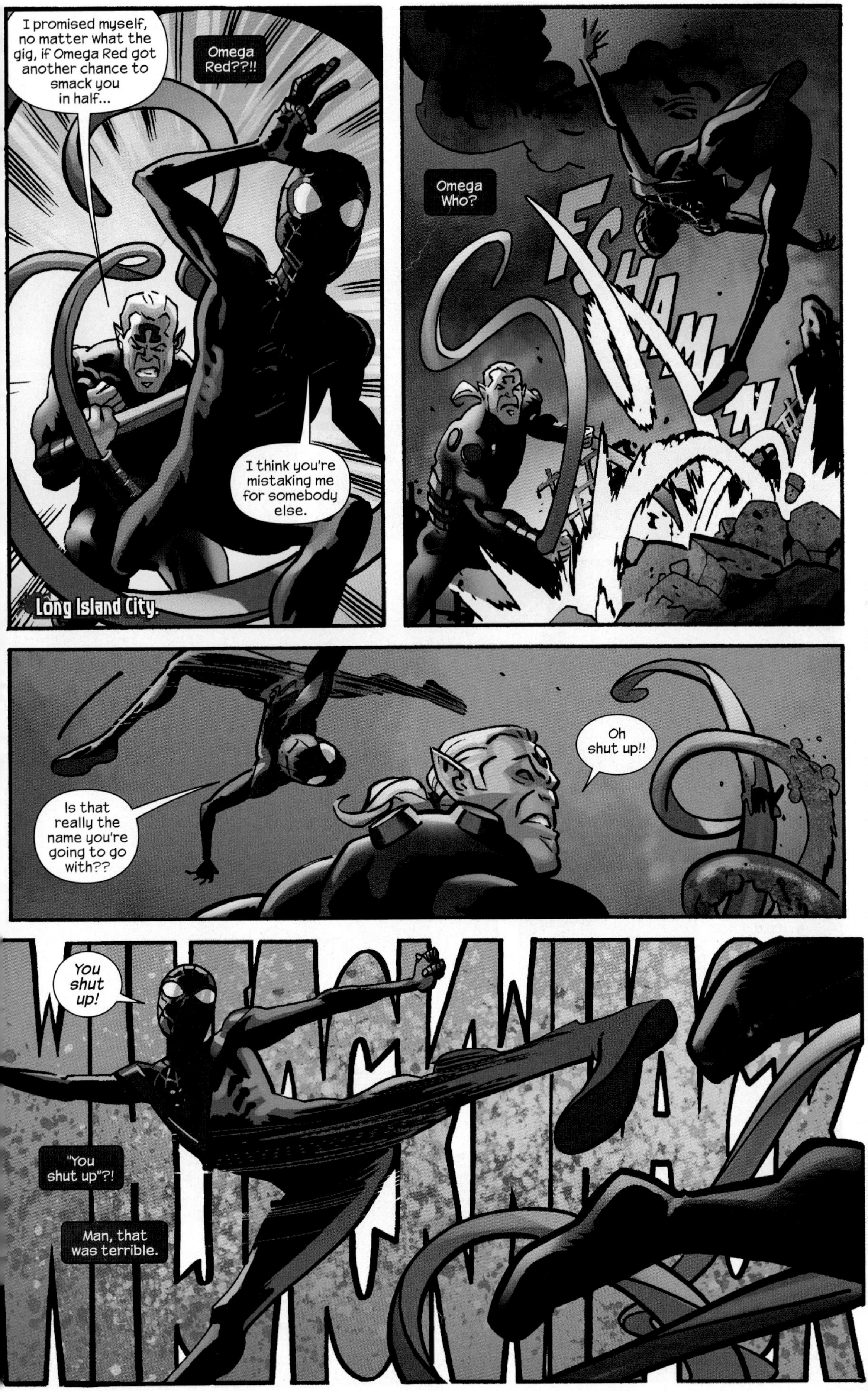
I promised myself, no matter what the gig, if Omega Red got another chance to smack you in half...
Omega Red??!!
I think you're mistaking me for somebody else.
Long Island City.
Omega Who?
FSHAMWN!
Is that really the name you're going to go with??
Oh shut up!!
You shut up!
"You shut up"?!
Man, that was terrible.

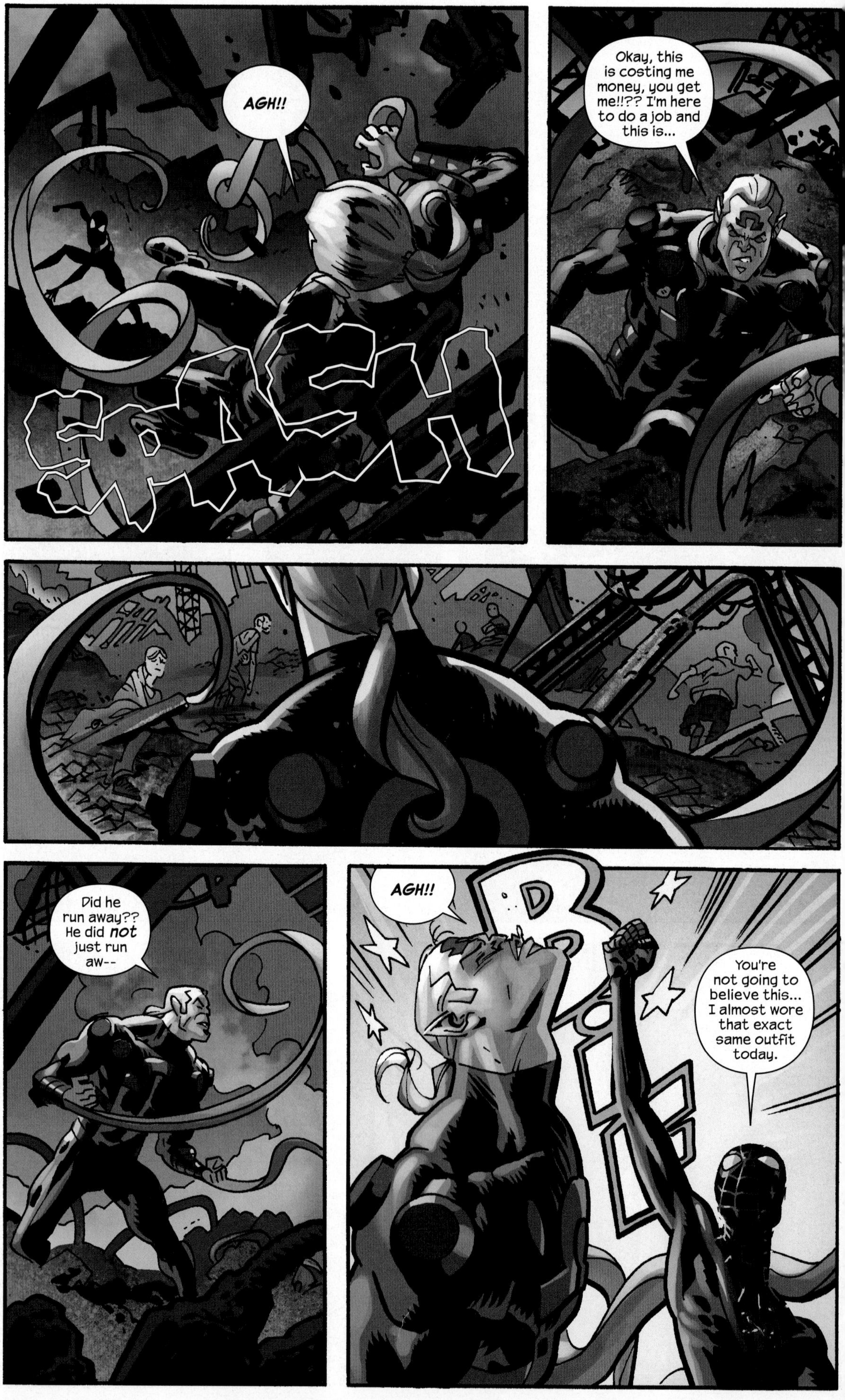
AGH!!
SPASH
Okay, this is costing me money, you get me!!?? I'm here to do a job and this is...
Did he run away?? He did *not* just run aw--
AGH!!
You're not going to believe this... I almost wore that exact same outfit today.

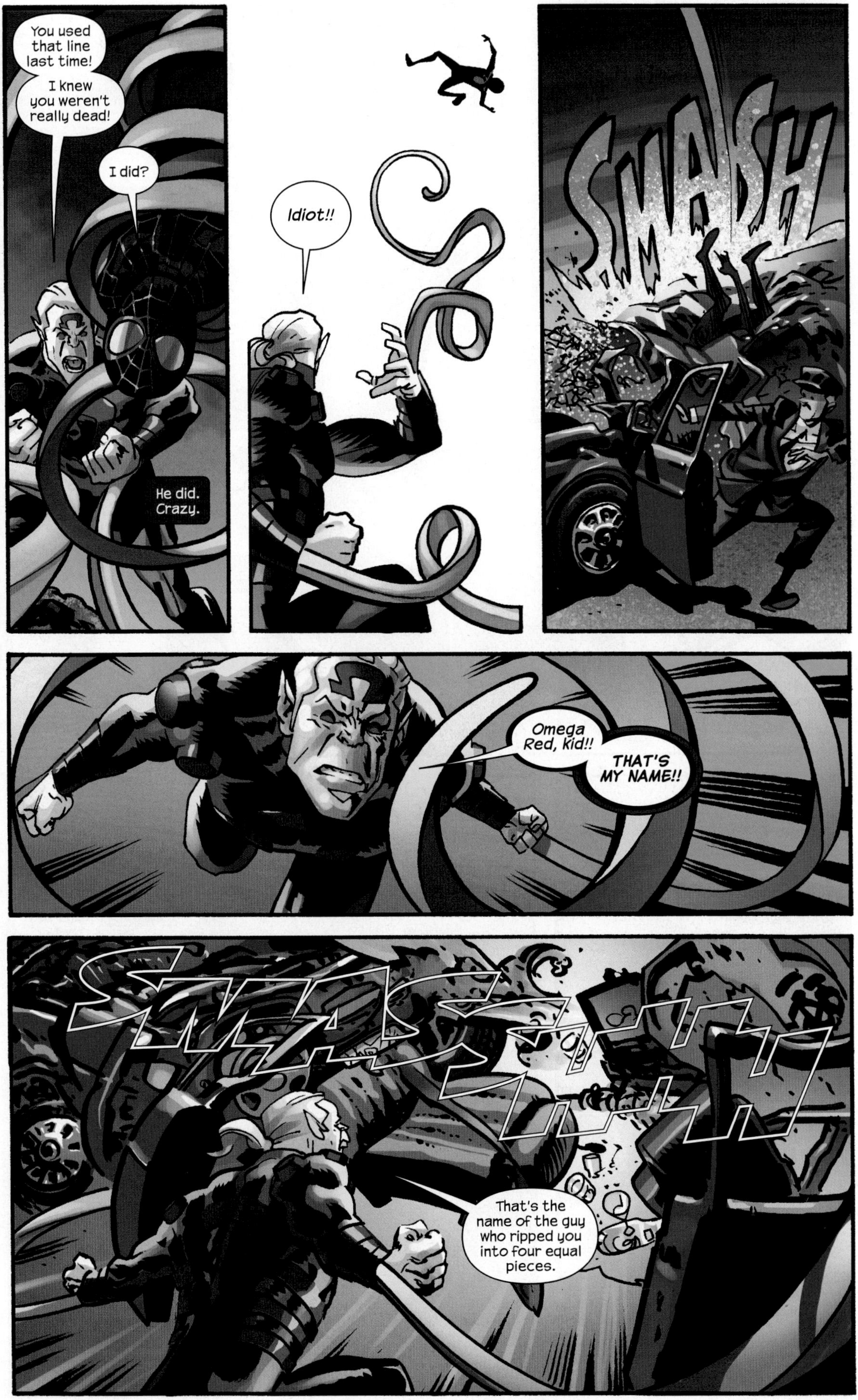
You used that line last time!
I knew you weren't really dead!
I did?
He did. Crazy.
Idiot!!
SMASH
Omega Red, kid!!
THAT'S MY NAME!!
SMASH
That's the name of the guy who ripped you into four equal pieces.

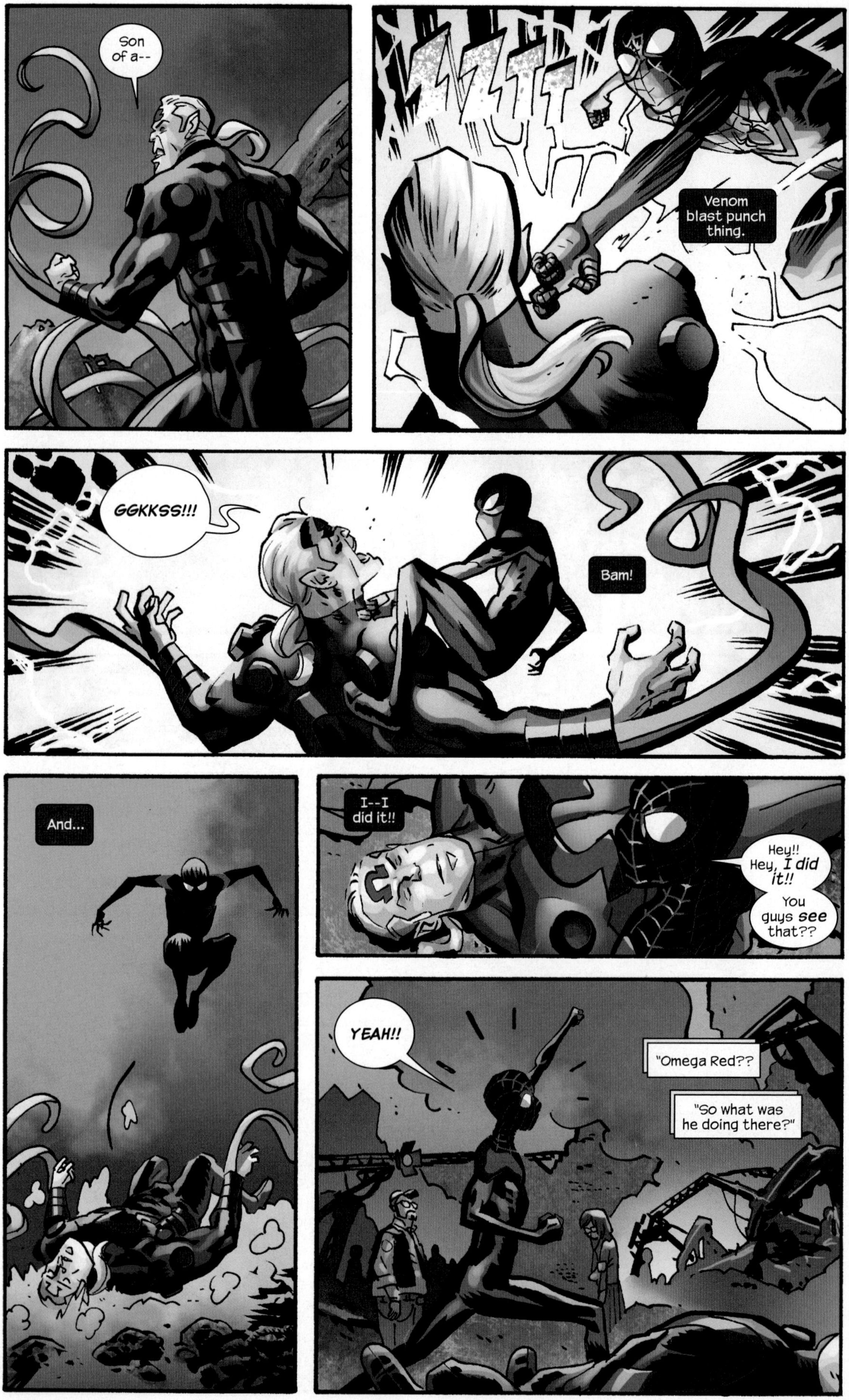
Son of a--
Venom blast punch thing.
GGKKSS!!!
Bam!
And...
I--I did it!!
Hey!! Hey, I did it!!
You guys see that??
YEAH!!
"Omega Red??
"So what was he doing there?"

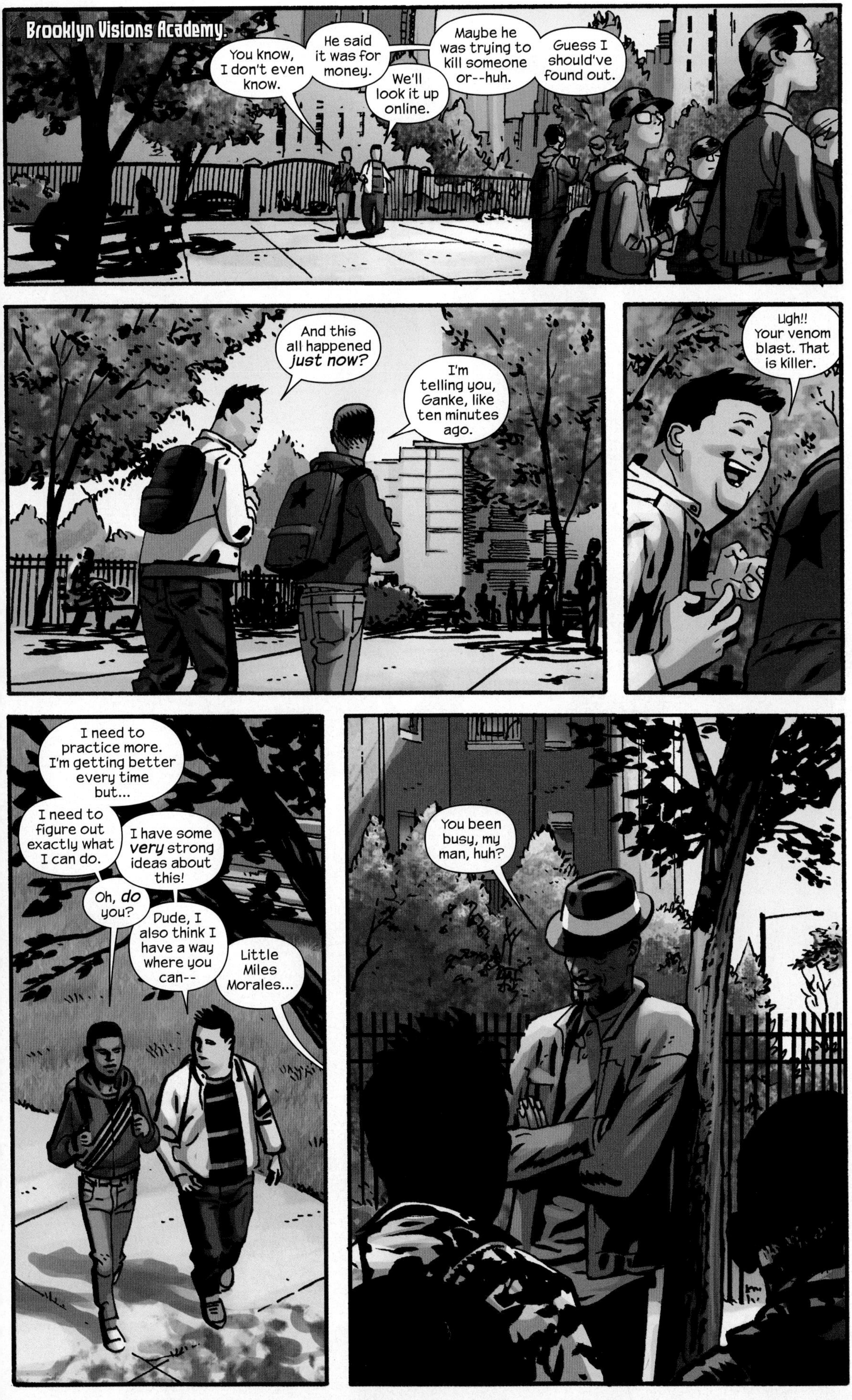
Brooklyn Visions Academy.
You know, I don't even know.
He said it was for money.
We'll look it up online.
Maybe he was trying to kill someone or--huh.
Guess I should've found out.
And this all happened *just now?*
I'm telling you, Ganke, like ten minutes ago.
Ugh!! Your venom blast. That is killer.
I need to practice more. I'm getting better every time but...
I need to figure out exactly what I can do.
I have some *very* strong ideas about this!
Oh, *do* you?
Dude, I also think I have a way where you can--
Little Miles Morales...
You been busy, my man, huh?

8

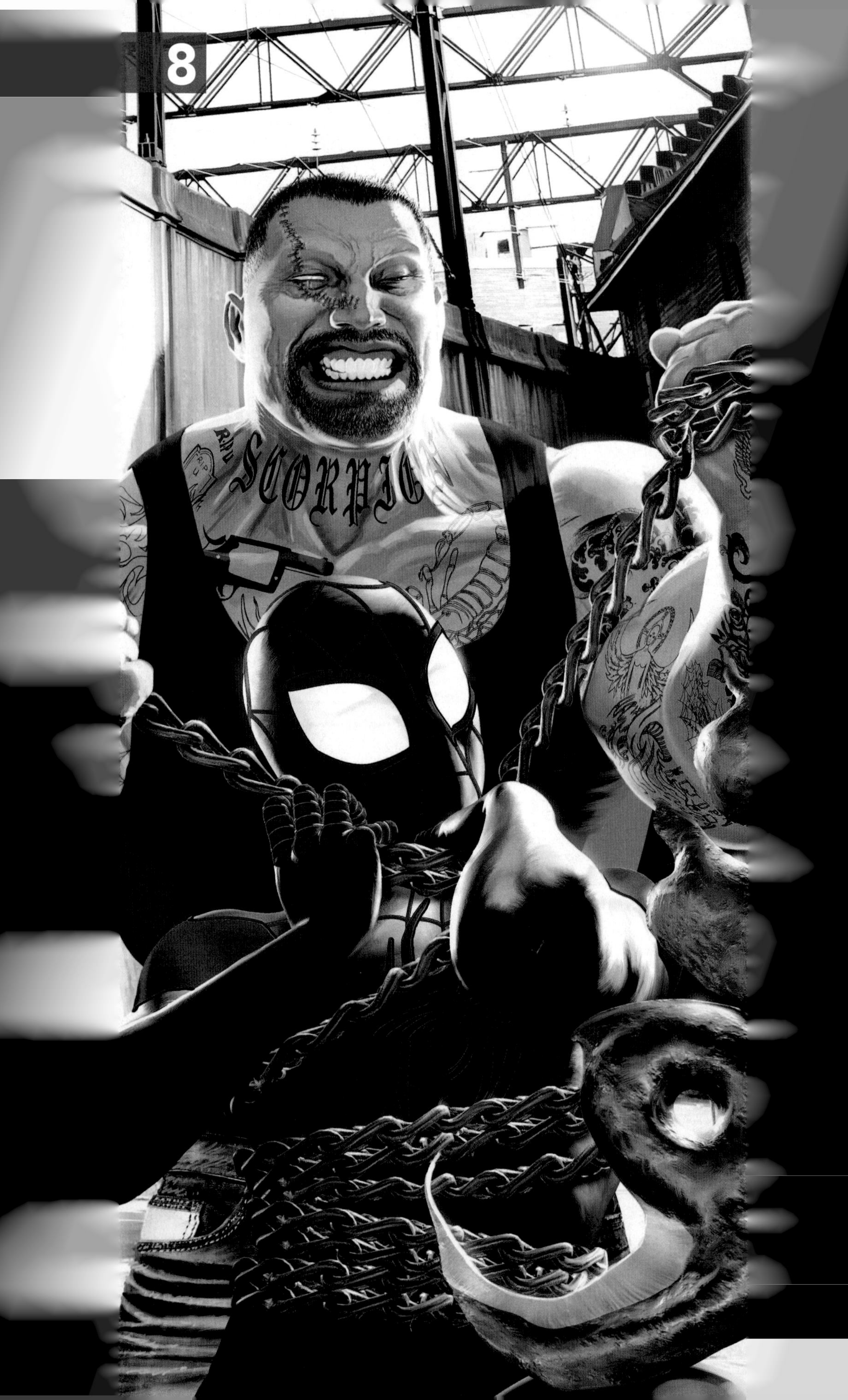

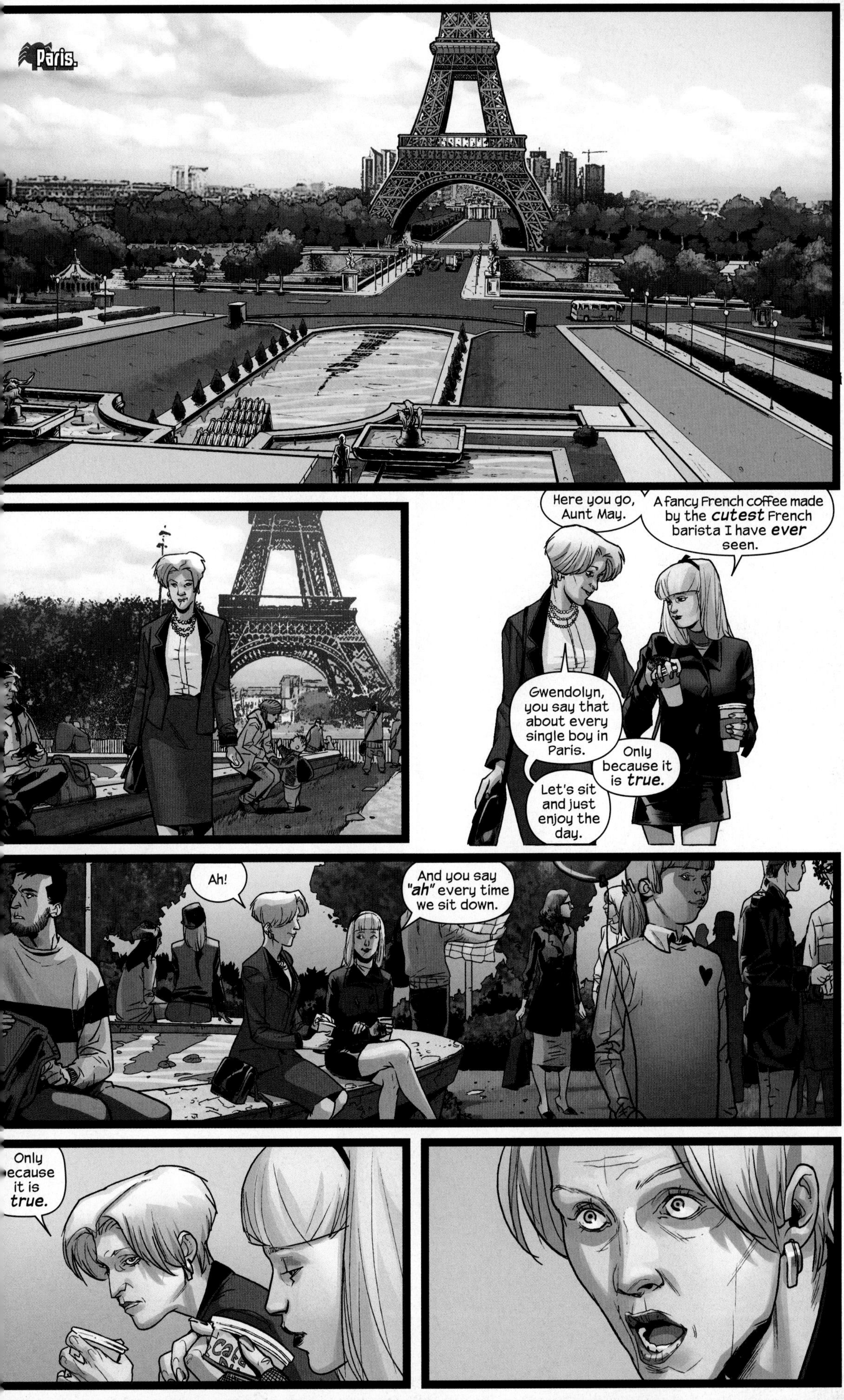
Paris.
Here you go, Aunt May.
A fancy French coffee made by the cutest French barista I have ever seen.
Gwendolyn, you say that about every single boy in Paris.
Only because it is true.
Let's sit and just enjoy the day.
Ah!
And you say "ah" every time we sit down.
Only ecause it is true.

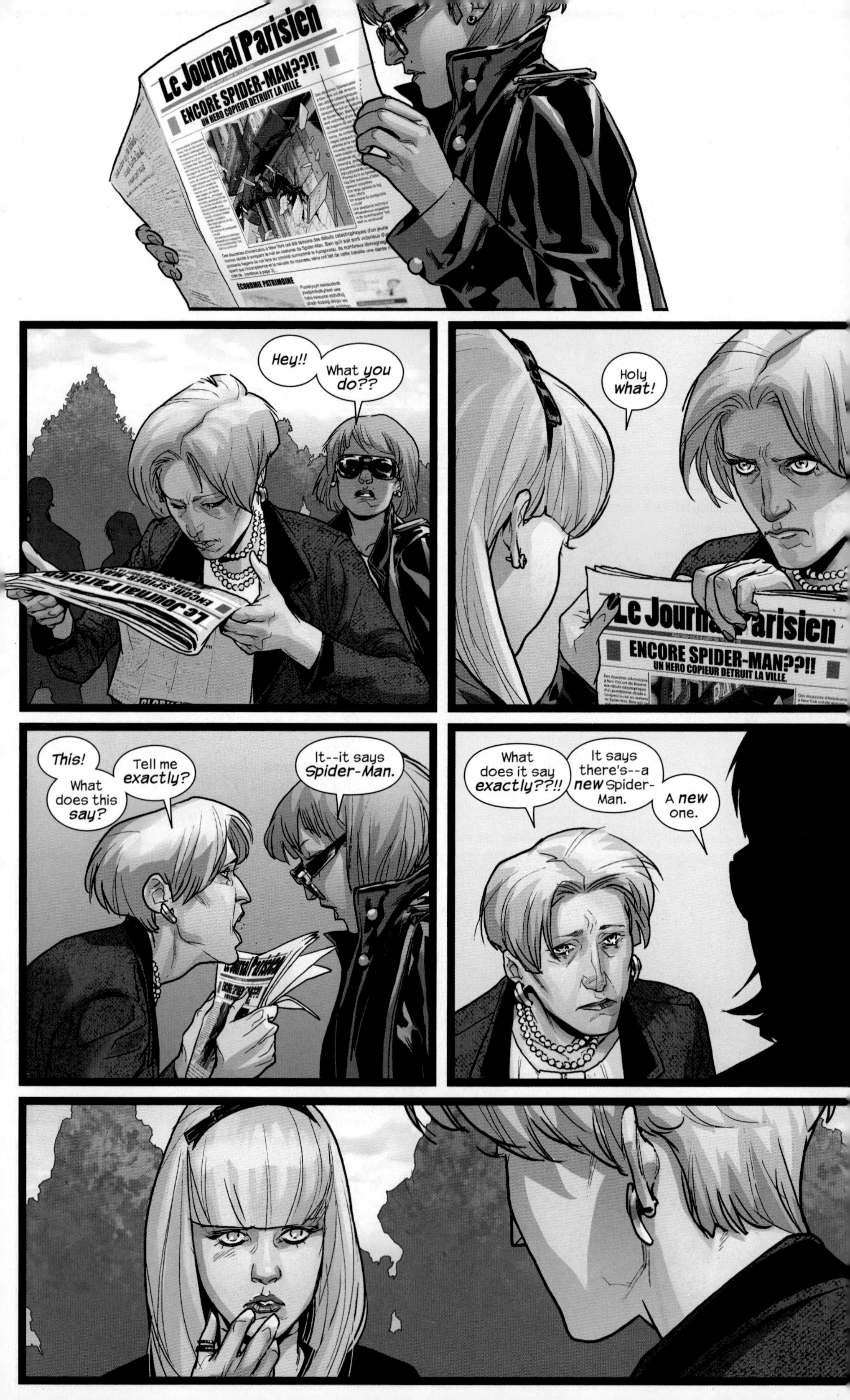
Le Journal Parisien
ENCORE SPIDER-MAN??!!
UN HERO COPIEUR DETRUIT LA VILLE.
ÉCONOMIE PATRIMOINE
Hey!!
What you do??
Holy what!
Le Journal Parisien
ENCORE SPIDER-MAN??!!
UN HERO COPIEUR DETRUIT LA VILLE.
This! What does this say?
Tell me exactly?
It--it says Spider-Man.
What does it say exactly??!!
It says there's--a new Spider-Man.
A new one.

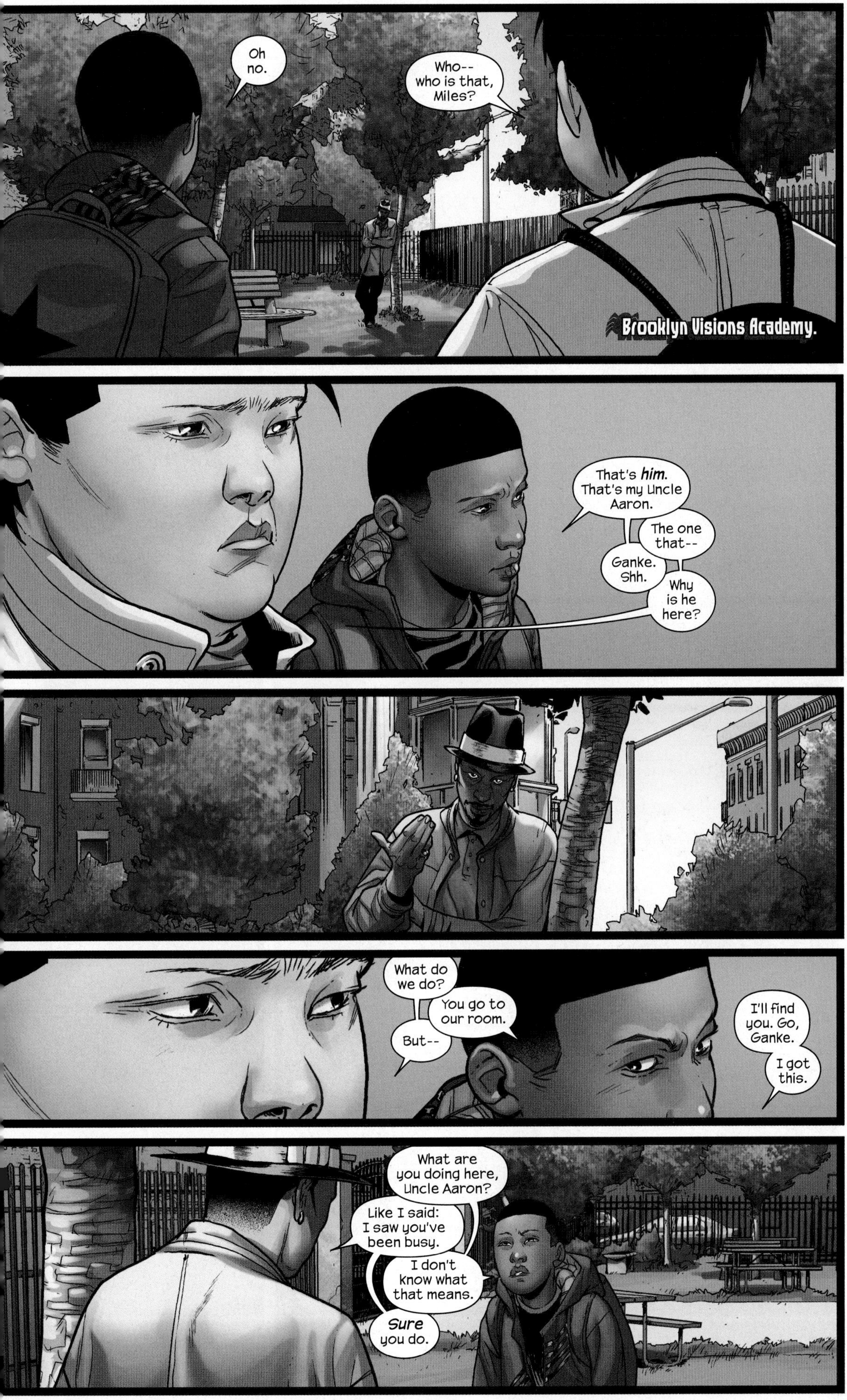
Oh no.
Who-- who is that, Miles?
Brooklyn Visions Academy.
That's *him*. That's my Uncle Aaron.
The one that--
Ganke. Shh.
Why is he here?
What do we do?
You go to our room.
But--
I'll find you. Go, Ganke.
I got this.
What are you doing here, Uncle Aaron?
Like I said: I saw you've been busy.
I don't know what that means.
Sure you do.

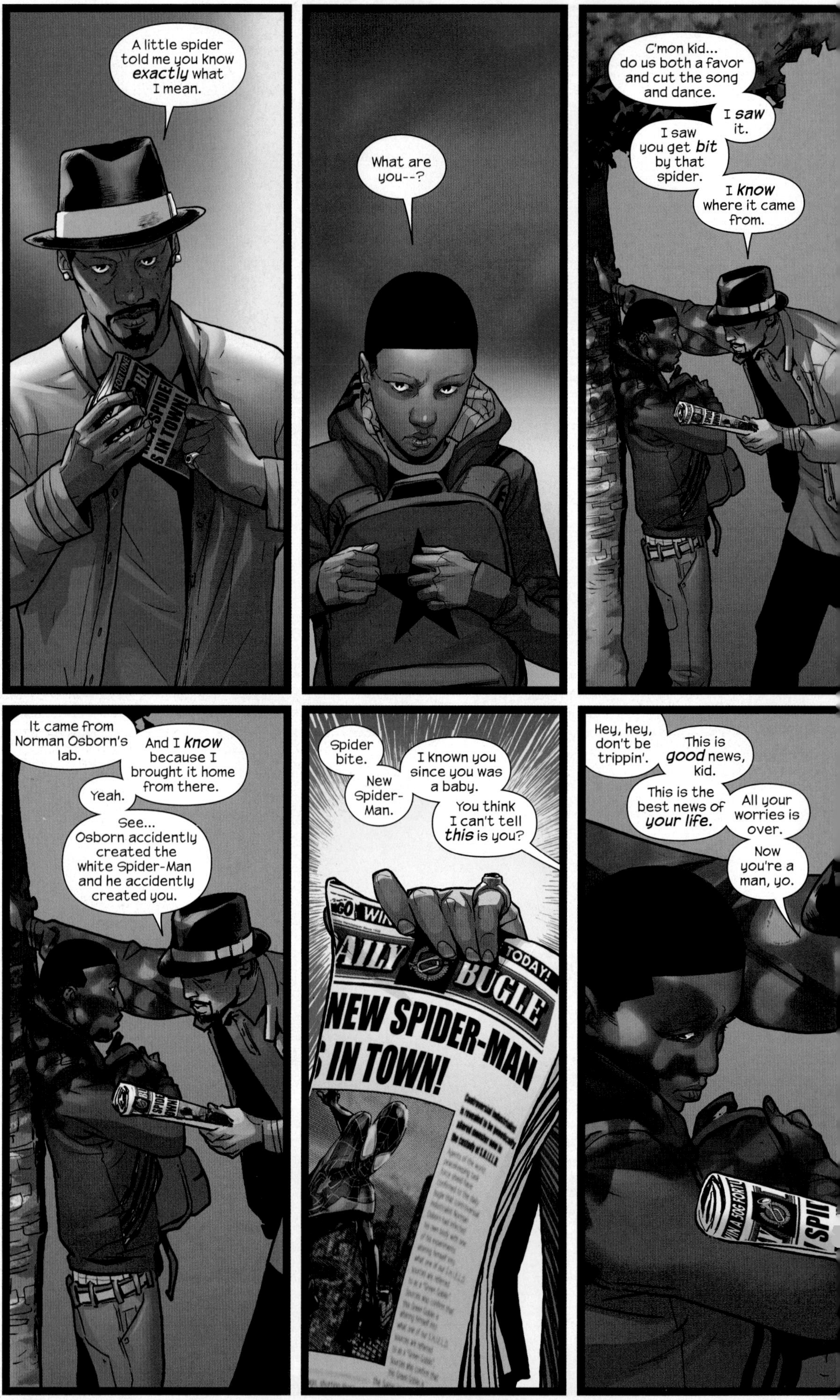
A little spider told me you know *exactly* what I mean.
What are you--?
C'mon kid... do us both a favor and cut the song and dance.
I *saw* it.
I saw you get *bit* by that spider.
I *know* where it came from.
It came from Norman Osborn's lab.
And I *know* because I brought it home from there.
Yeah.
See... Osborn accidently created the white Spider-Man and he accidently created you.
Spider bite.
New Spider-Man.
I known you since you was a baby.
You think I can't tell *this* is you?
DAILY BUGLE
TODAY!
NEW SPIDER-MAN IS IN TOWN!
Hey, hey, don't be trippin'.
This is *good* news, kid.
This is the best news of *your life.*
All your worries is over.
Now you're a man, yo.

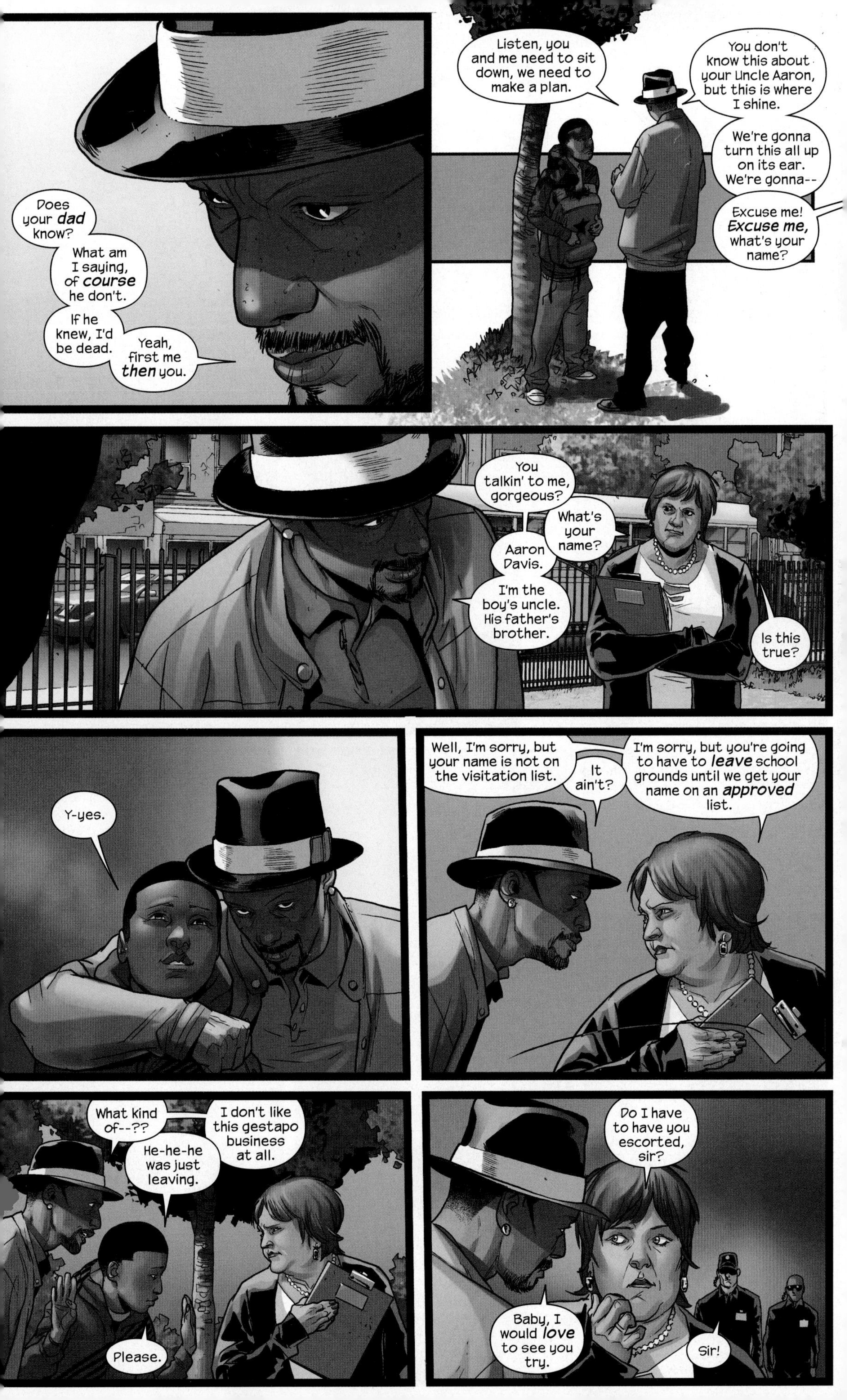

Does your *dad* know?
What am I saying, of *course* he don't.
If he knew, I'd be dead.
Yeah, first me *then* you.
Listen, you and me need to sit down, we need to make a plan.
You don't know this about your Uncle Aaron, but this is where I shine.
We're gonna turn this all up on its ear. We're gonna--
Excuse me! ***Excuse me,*** what's your name?
You talkin' to me, gorgeous?
What's your name?
Aaron Davis.
I'm the boy's uncle. His father's brother.
Is this true?
Y-yes.
Well, I'm sorry, but your name is not on the visitation list.
It ain't?
I'm sorry, but you're going to have to *leave* school grounds until we get your name on an *approved* list.
What kind of--??
I don't like this gestapo business at all.
He-he-he was just leaving.
Please.
Do I have to have you escorted, sir?
Baby, I would *love* to see you try.
Sir!

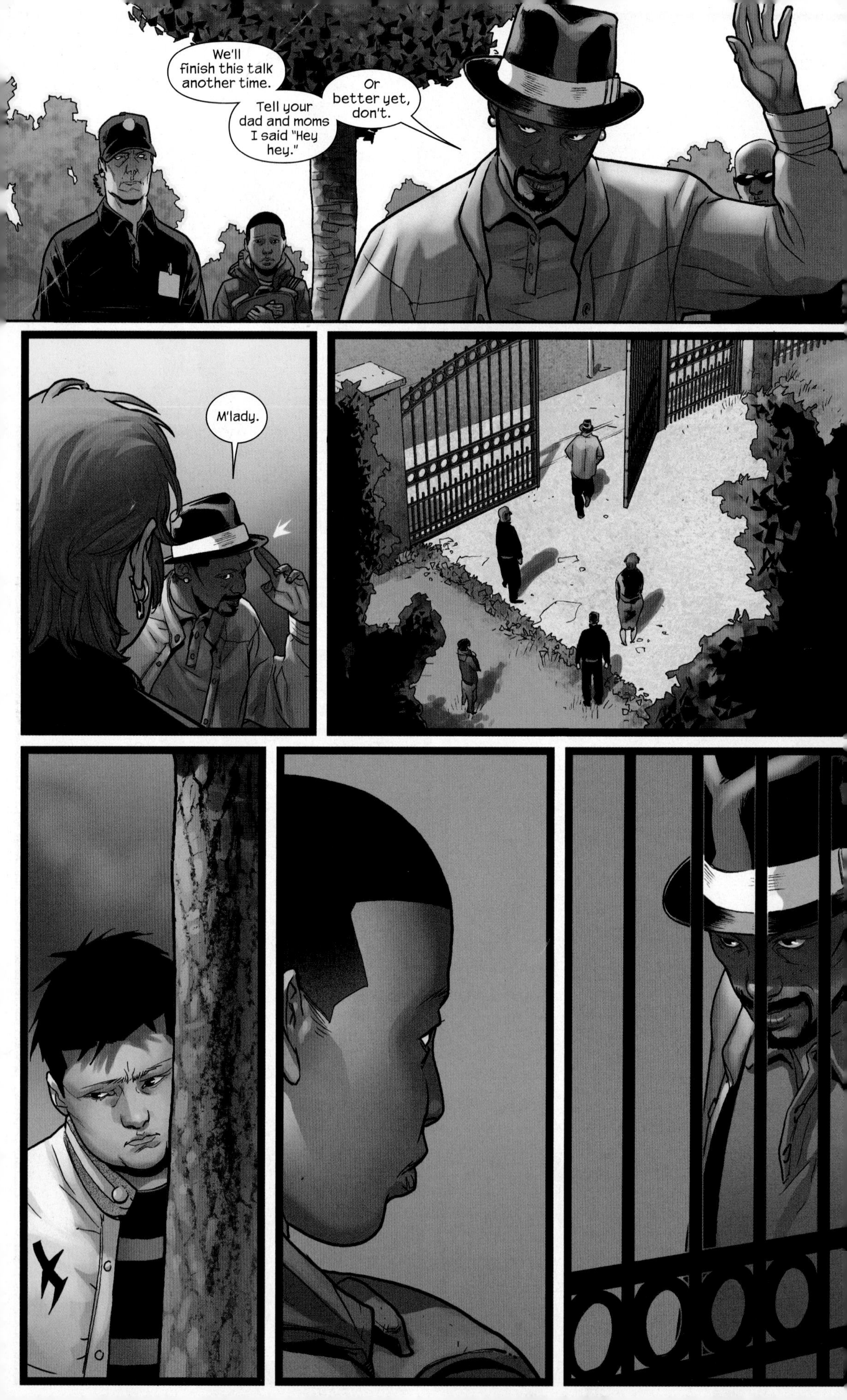

We'll finish this talk another time.
Tell your dad and moms I said "Hey hey."
Or better yet, don't.
M'lady.

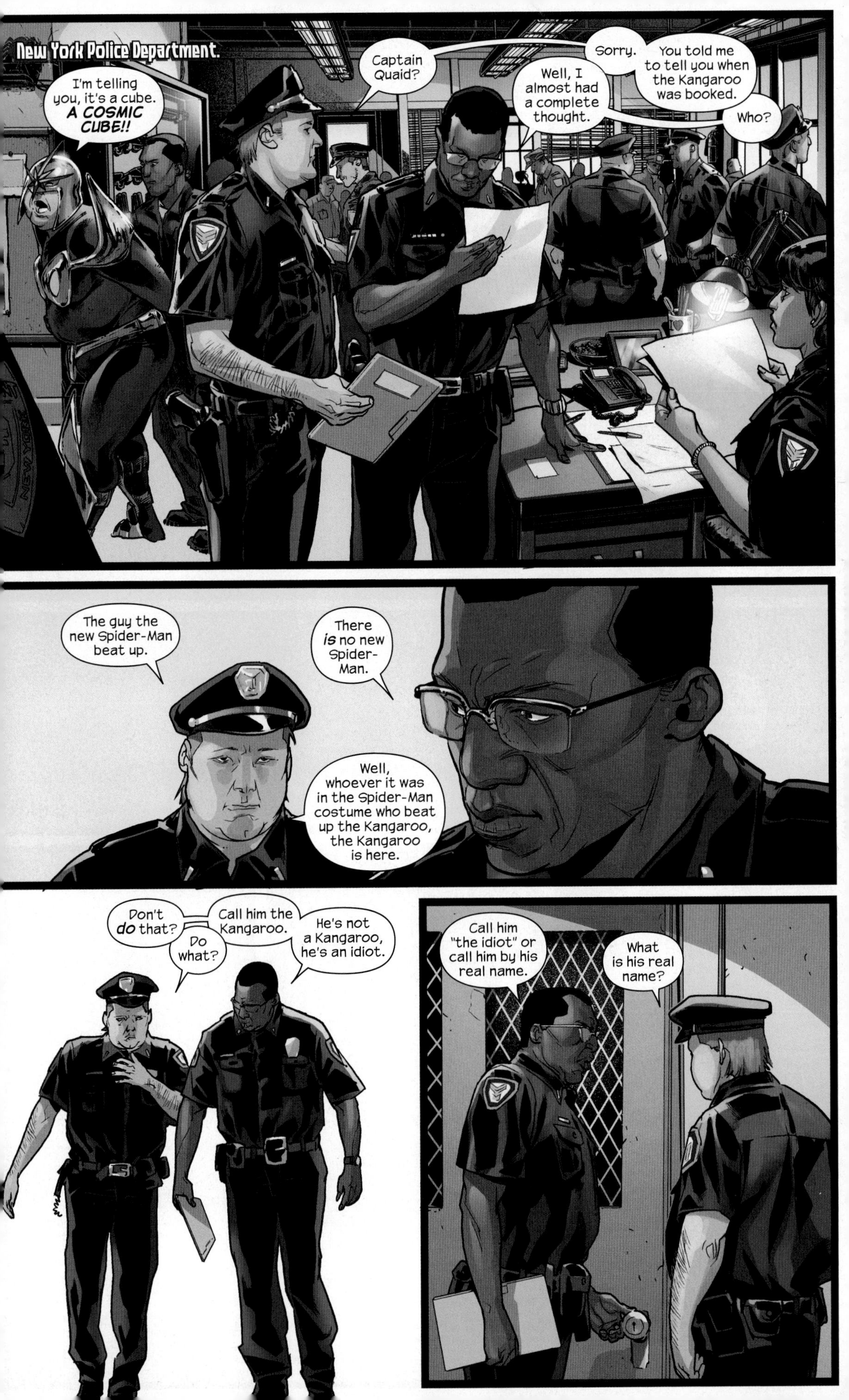

New York Police Department.
I'm telling you, it's a cube. A COSMIC CUBE!!
Captain Quaid?
Sorry.
You told me to tell you when the Kangaroo was booked.
Well, I almost had a complete thought.
Who?
The guy the new Spider-Man beat up.
There *is* no new Spider-Man.
Well, whoever it was in the Spider-Man costume who beat up the Kangaroo, the Kangaroo is here.
Don't *do* that?
Do what?
Call him the Kangaroo.
He's not a Kangaroo, he's an idiot.
Call him "the idiot" or call him by his real name.
What is his real name?

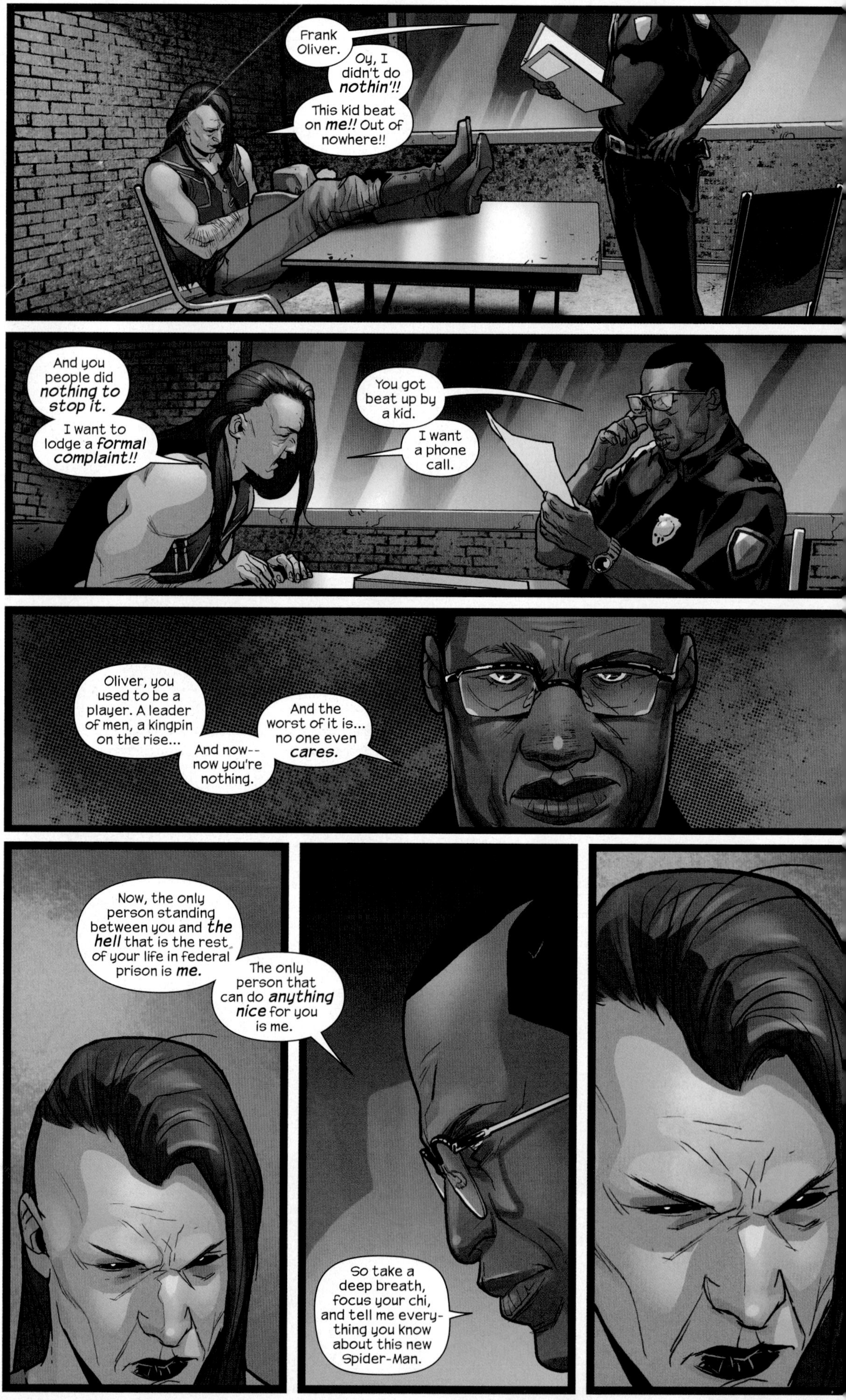
Frank Oliver.
Oy, I didn't do *nothin'!!*
This kid beat on *me!!* Out of nowhere!!
And you people did *nothing to stop it.*
I want to lodge a *formal complaint!!*
You got beat up by a kid.
I want a phone call.
Oliver, you used to be a player. A leader of men, a kingpin on the rise...
And now-- now you're nothing.
And the worst of it is... no one even *cares.*
Now, the only person standing between you and *the hell* that is the rest of your life in federal prison is *me.*
The only person that can do *anything nice* for you is me.
So take a deep breath, focus your chi, and tell me every-thing you know about this new Spider-Man.

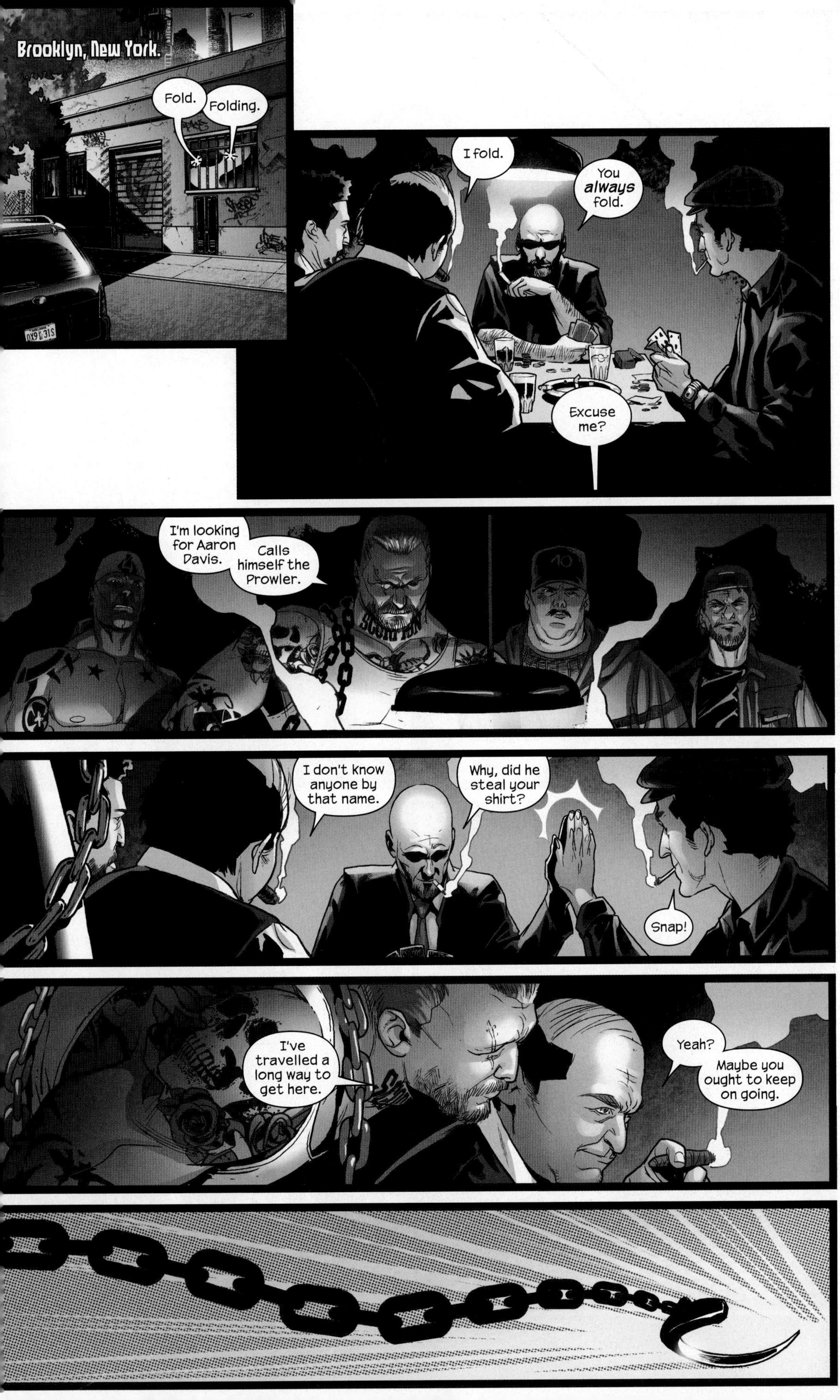
Brooklyn, New York.
Fold.
Folding.
I fold.
You *always* fold.
Excuse me?
I'm looking for Aaron Davis.
Calls himself the Prowler.
I don't know anyone by that name.
Why, did he steal your shirt?
Snap!
I've travelled a long way to get here.
Yeah?
Maybe you ought to keep on going.

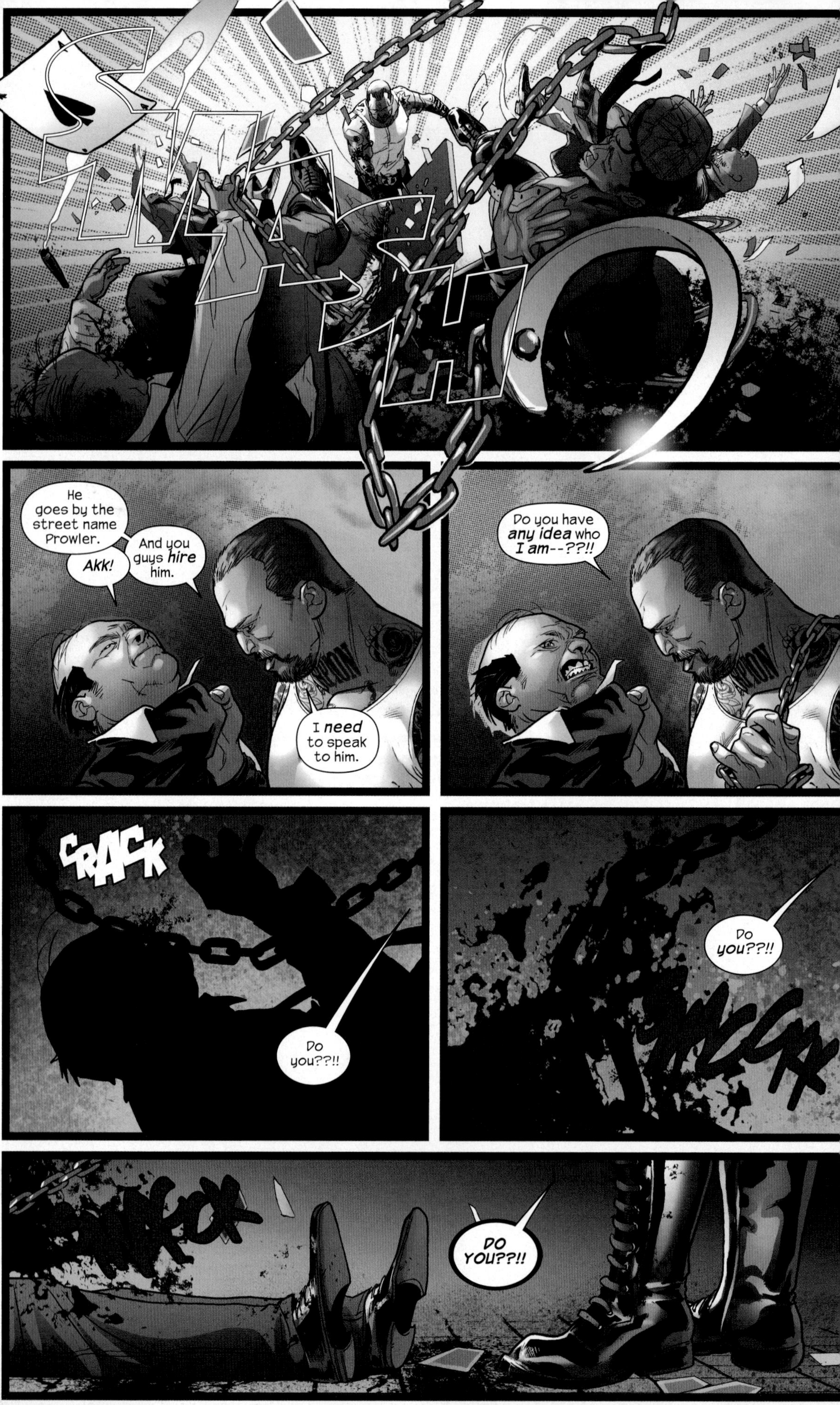
He goes by the street name Prowler.
Akk!
And you guys hire him.
I need to speak to him.
Do you have any idea who I am--??!!
CRACK
Do you??!!
Do you??!!
DO YOU??!!

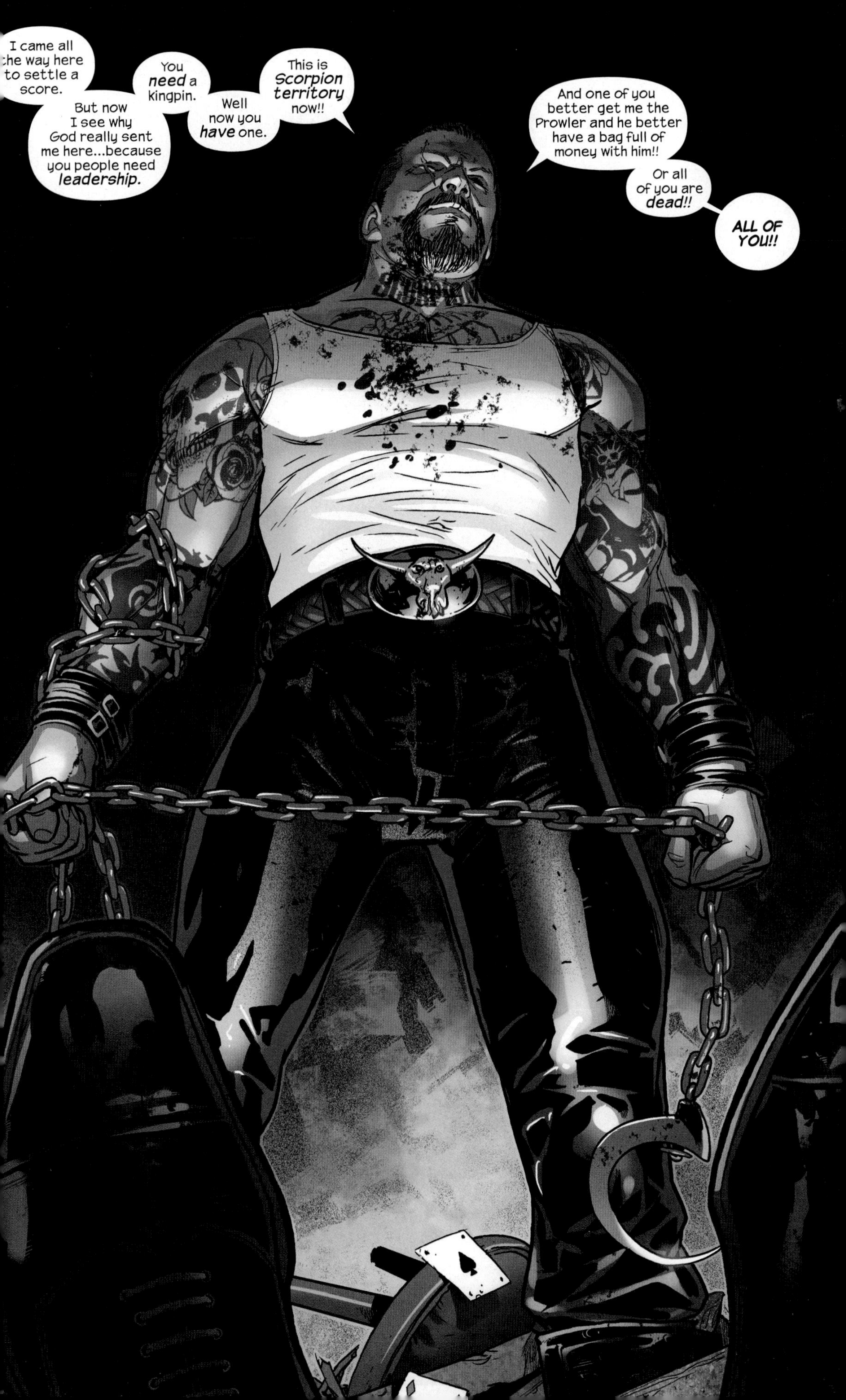
I came all the way here to settle a score.
But now I see why God really sent me here...because you people need leadership.
You need a kingpin.
Well now you have one.
This is Scorpion territory now!!
And one of you better get me the Prowler and he better have a bag full of money with him!!
Or all of you are dead!!
ALL OF YOU!!

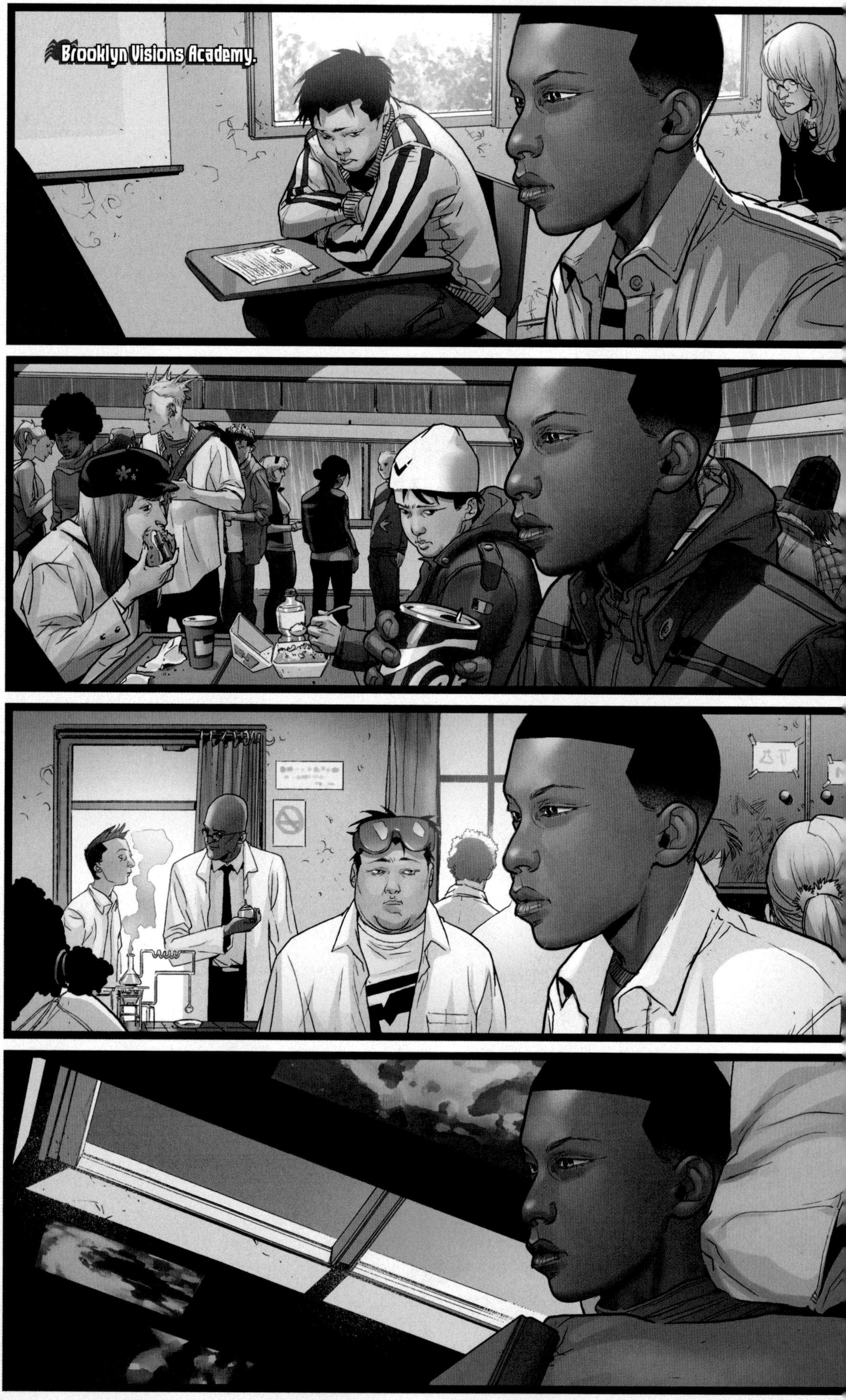
Brooklyn Visions Academy.

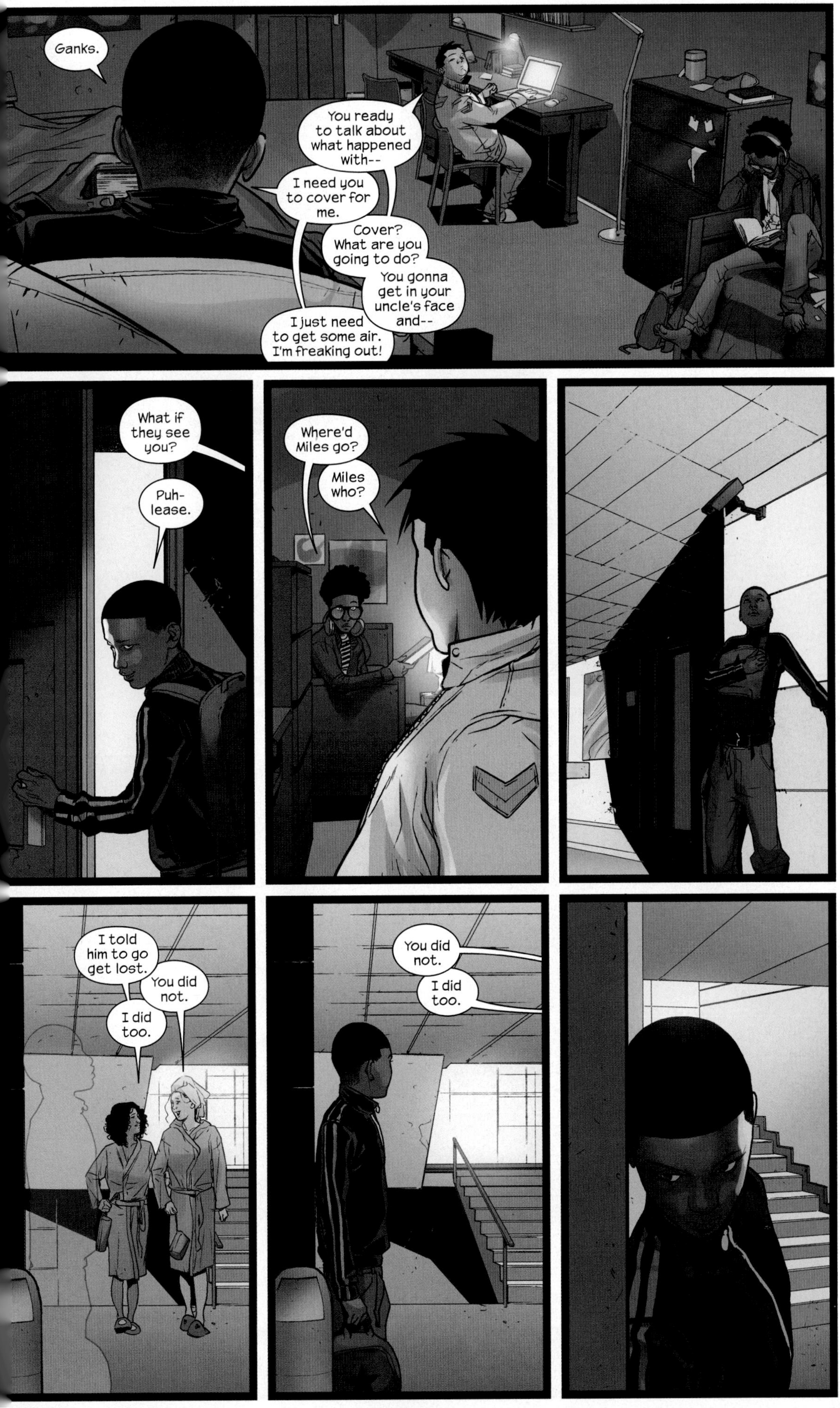

Ganks.
You ready to talk about what happened with--
I need you to cover for me.
Cover? What are you going to do?
You gonna get in your uncle's face and--
I just need to get some air. I'm freaking out!
What if they see you?
Puh-lease.
Where'd Miles go?
Miles who?
I told him to go get lost.
You did not.
I did too.
You did not.
I did too.

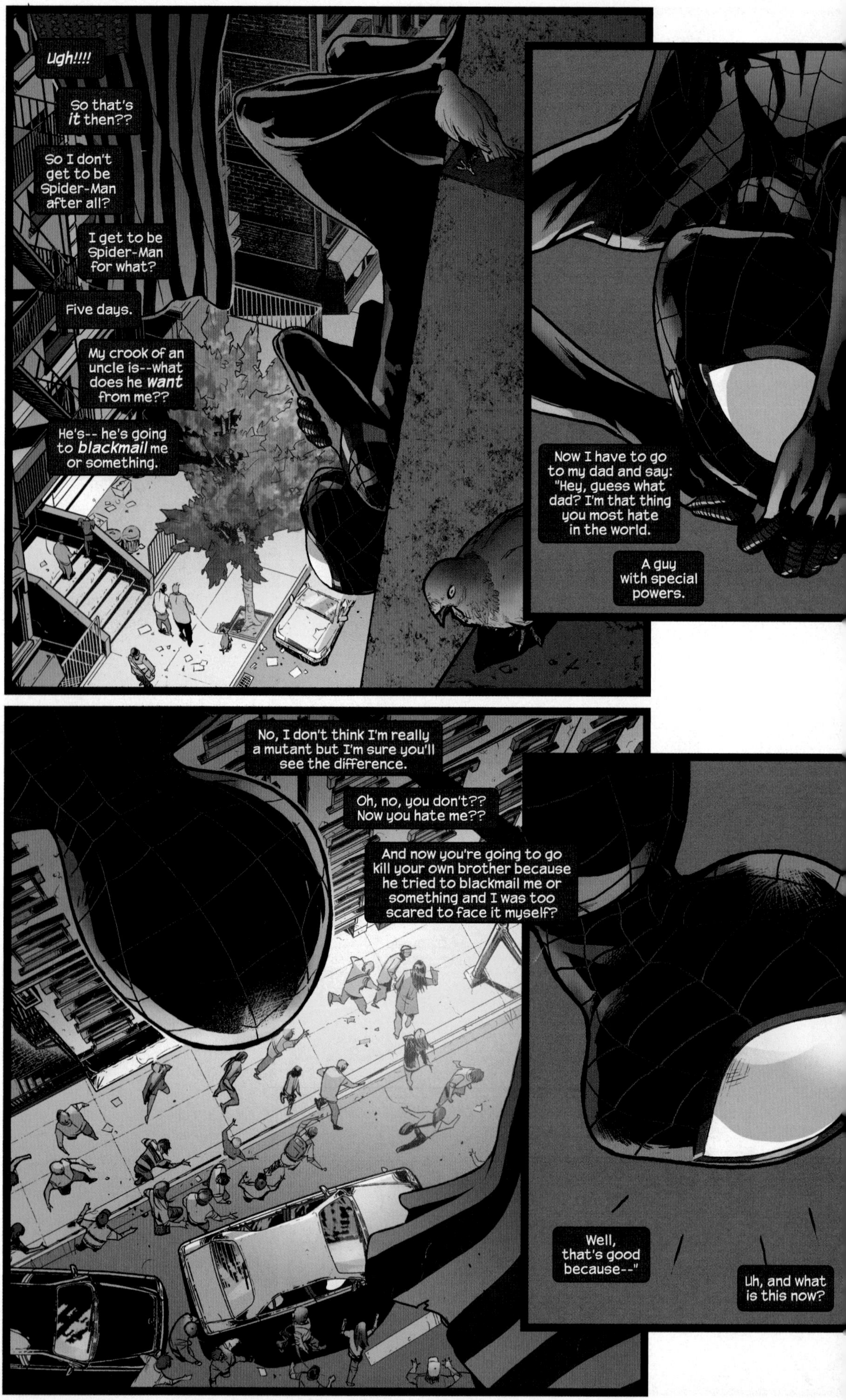
Ugh!!!!
So that's it then??
So I don't get to be Spider-Man after all?
I get to be Spider-Man for what?
Five days.
My crook of an uncle is--what does he want from me??
He's-- he's going to blackmail me or something.
Now I have to go to my dad and say: "Hey, guess what dad? I'm that thing you most hate in the world.
A guy with special powers.
No, I don't think I'm really a mutant but I'm sure you'll see the difference.
Oh, no, you don't?? Now you hate me??
And now you're going to go kill your own brother because he tried to blackmail me or something and I was too scared to face it myself?
Well, that's good because--"
Uh, and what is this now?

Huh.

What is this?

A hoop?

Is there a truck spill or a--??

FIIZZZZZZ

Whoa!!

Wait, wait, I know this one.

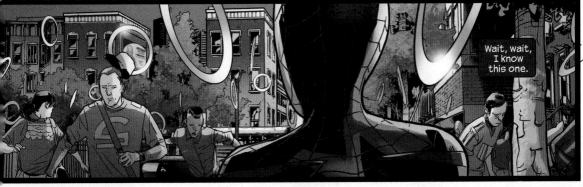

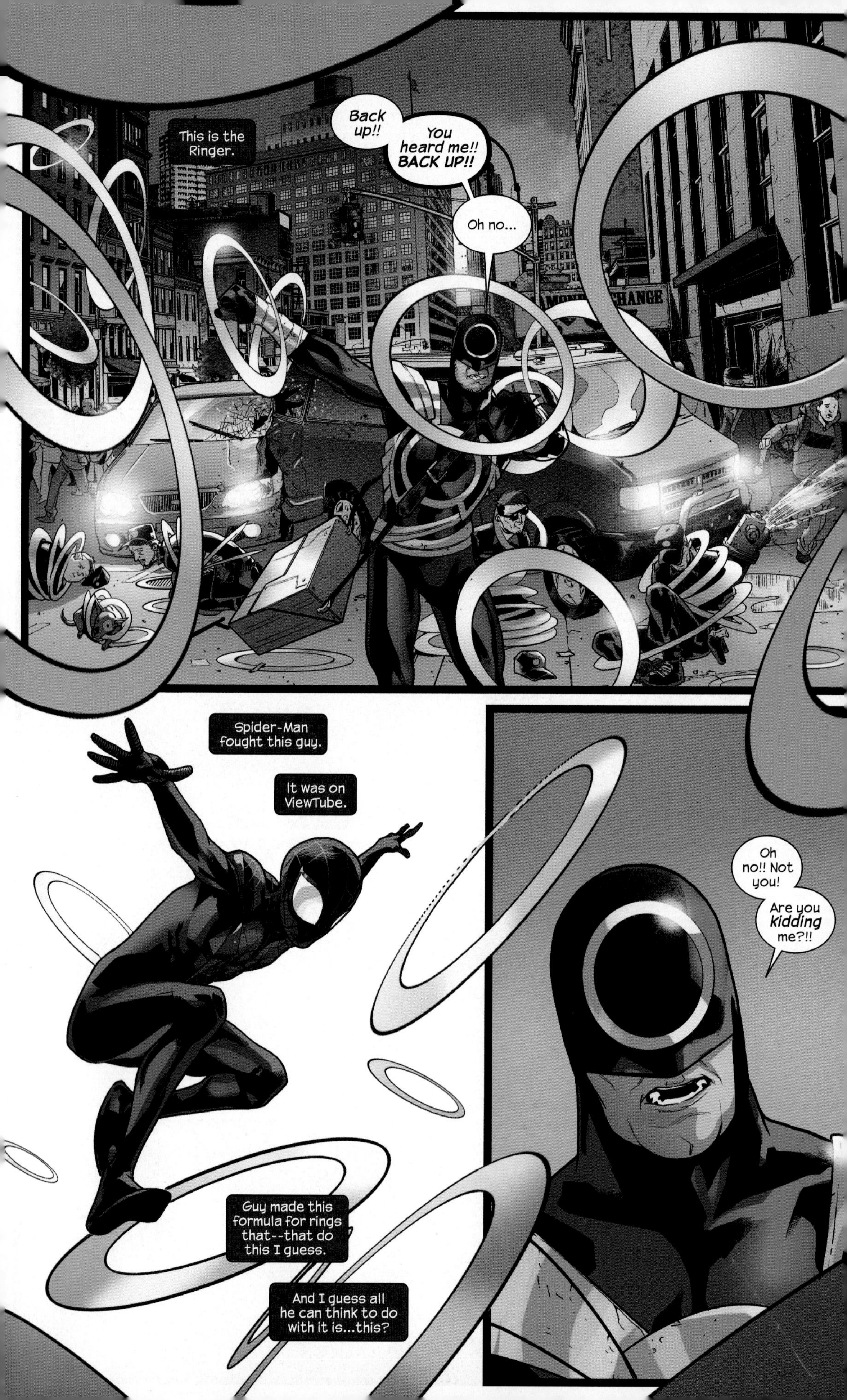

This is the Ringer.
Back up!!
You heard me!! BACK UP!!
Oh no...
Spider-Man fought this guy.
It was on ViewTube.
Oh no!! Not you!
Are you *kidding* me?!!
Guy made this formula for rings that--that do this I guess.
And I guess all he can think to do with it is...this?

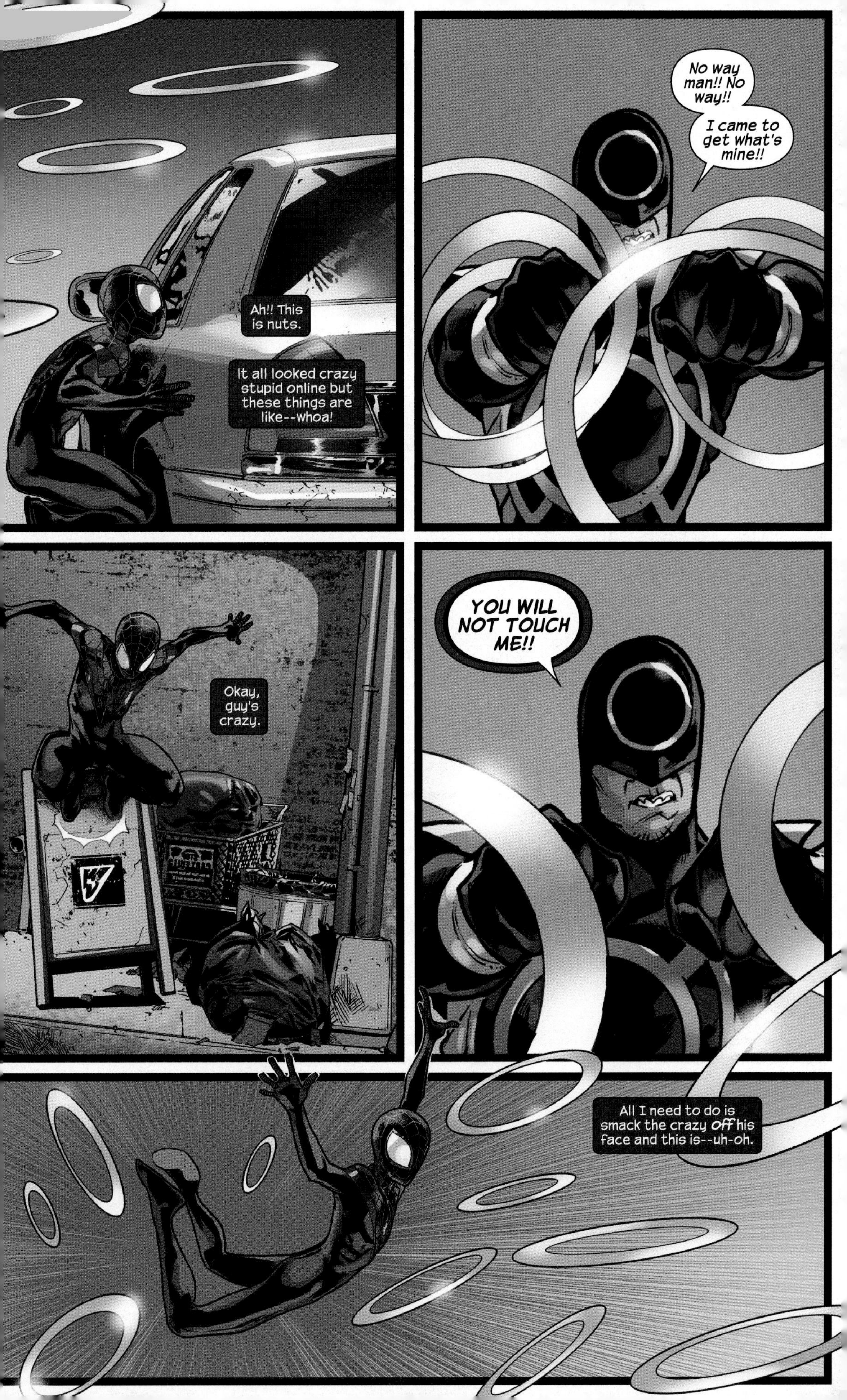
Ah!! This is nuts.
It all looked crazy stupid online but these things are like--whoa!
No way man!! No way!!
I came to get what's mine!!
Okay, guy's crazy.
YOU WILL NOT TOUCH ME!!
All I need to do is smack the crazy *off* his face and this is--uh-oh.

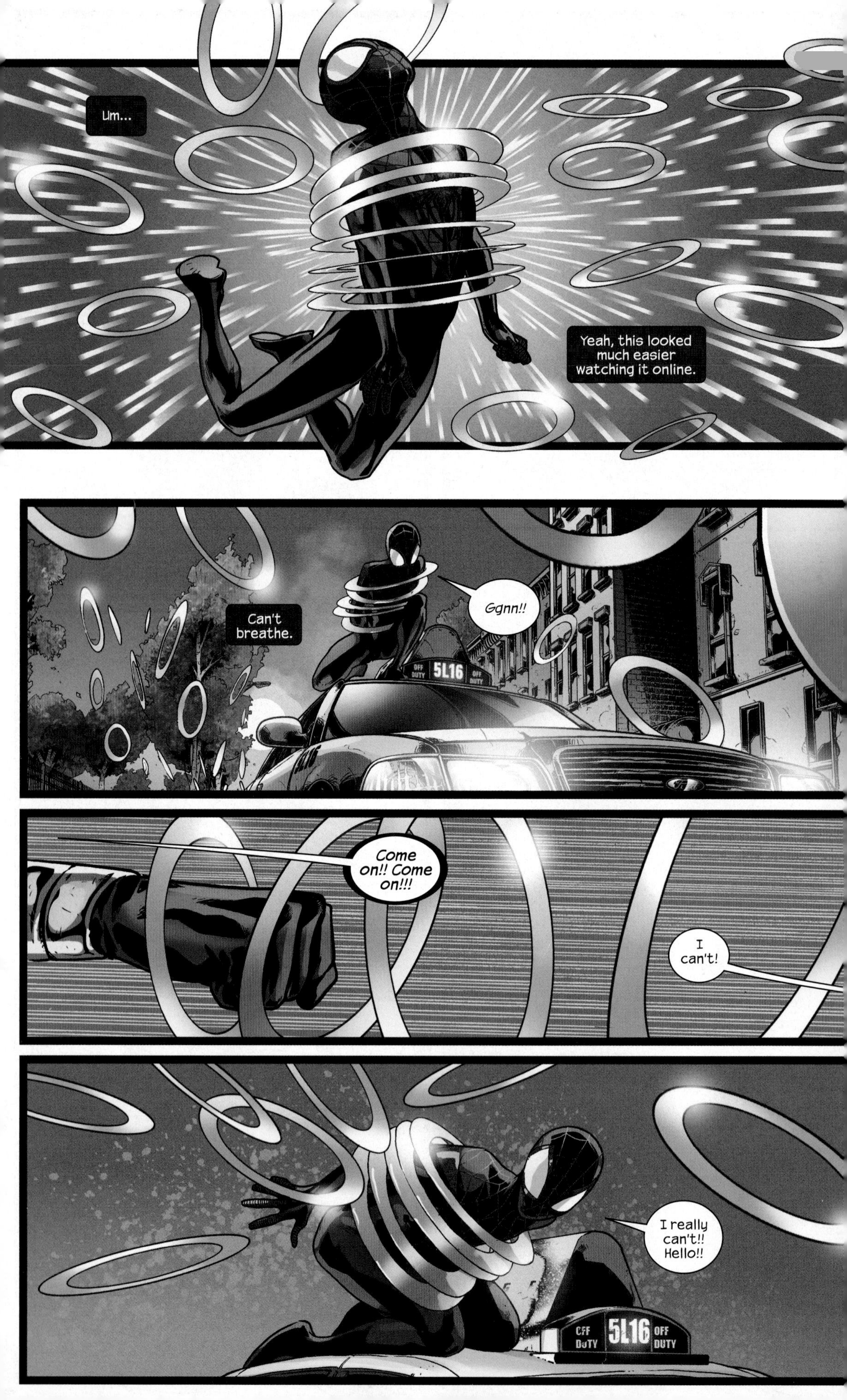
Um...
Yeah, this looked much easier watching it online.
Can't breathe.
Ggnn!!
OFF DUTY 5L16 OFF DUTY
Come on!! Come on!!!
I can't!
I really can't!! Hello!!
OFF DUTY 5L16 OFF DUTY

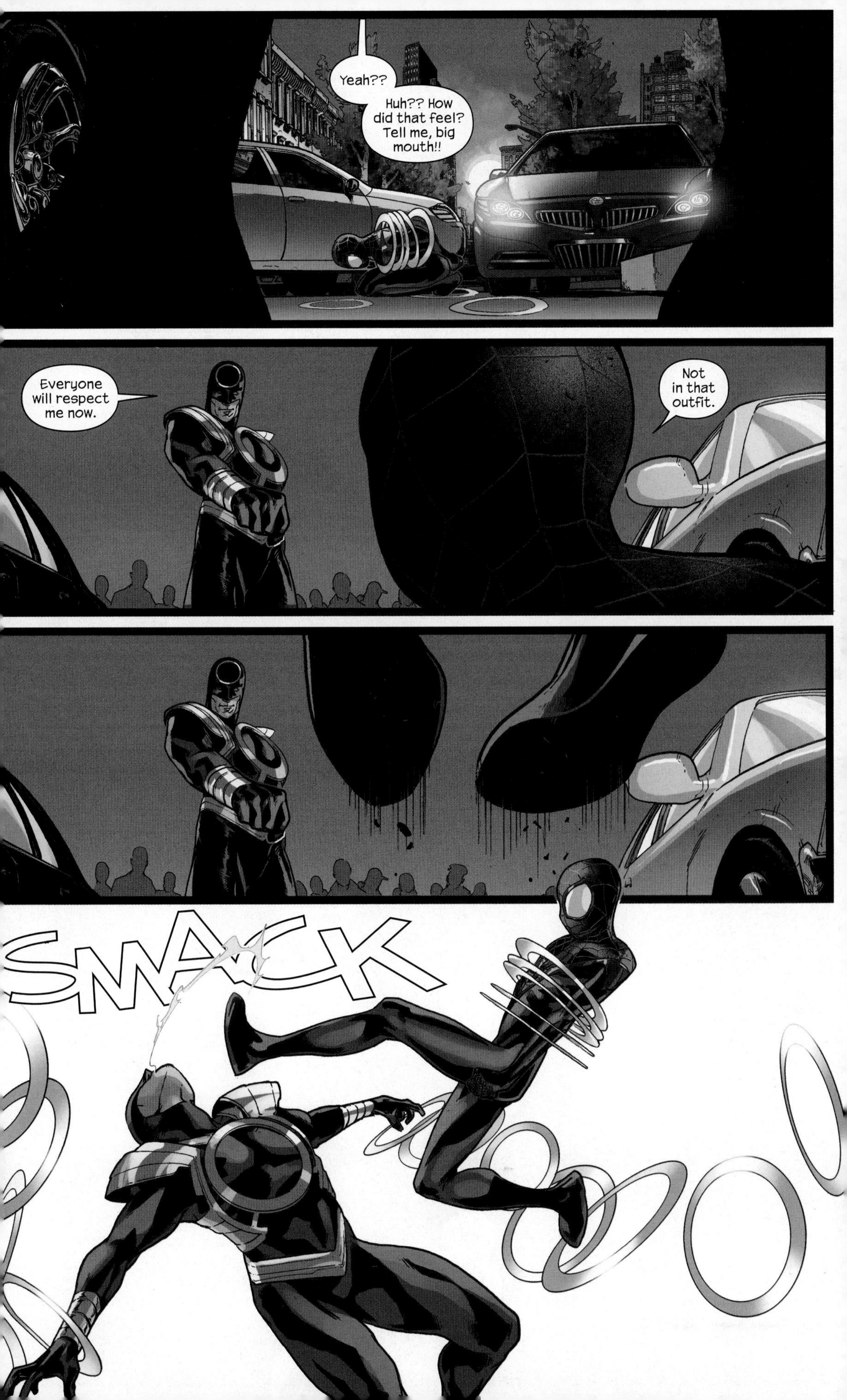
Yeah??
Huh?? How did that feel? Tell me, big mouth!!
Everyone will respect me now.
Not in that outfit.
SMACK

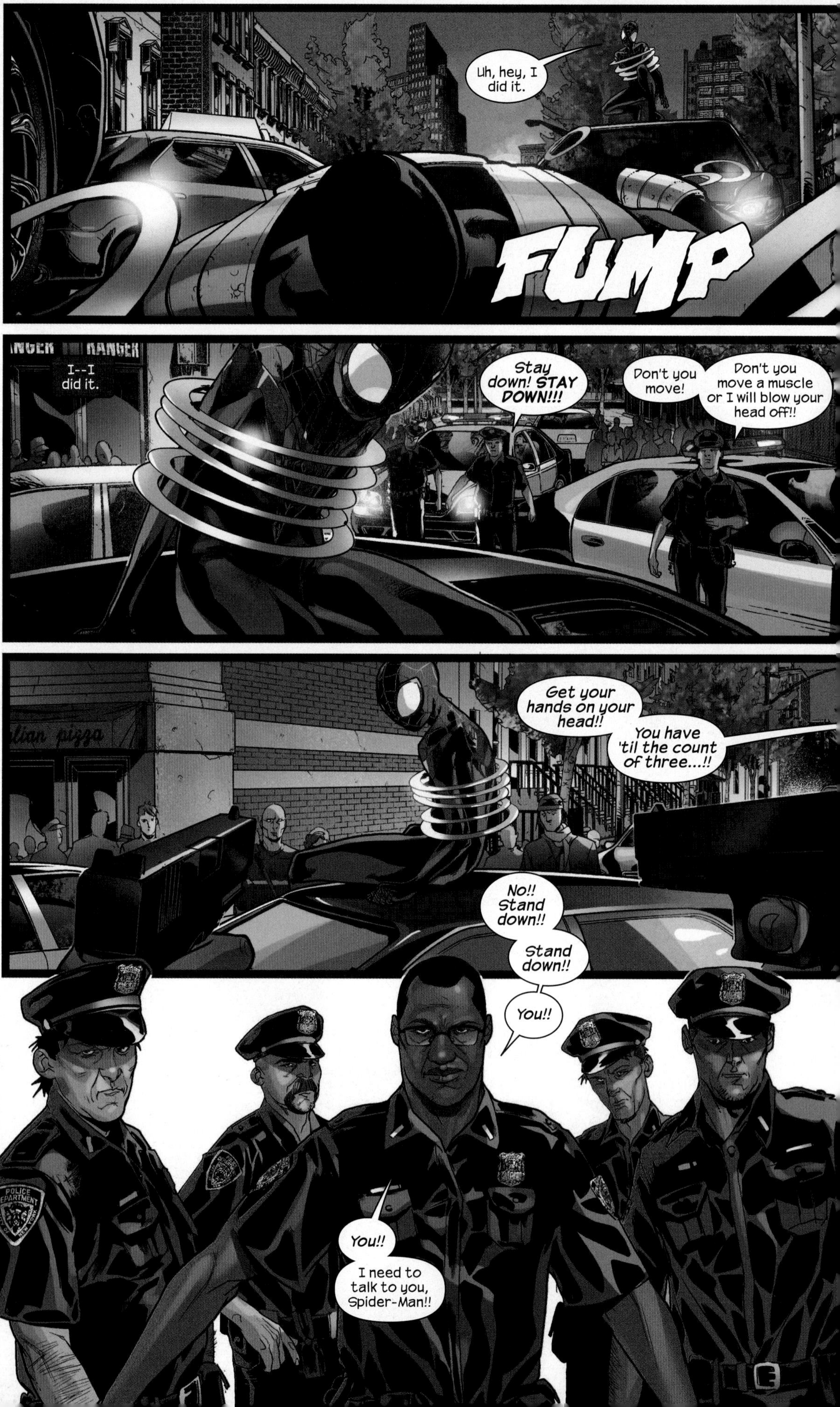
Uh, hey, I did it.
FUMP
ANGER RANGER
I--I did it.
Stay down! STAY DOWN!!!
Don't you move!
Don't you move a muscle or I will blow your head off!!
alian pizza
Get your hands on your head!!
You have 'til the count of three...!!
No!! Stand down!!
Stand down!!
You!!
POLICE DEPARTMENT CITY OF NEW YORK
You!!
I need to talk to you, Spider-Man!!

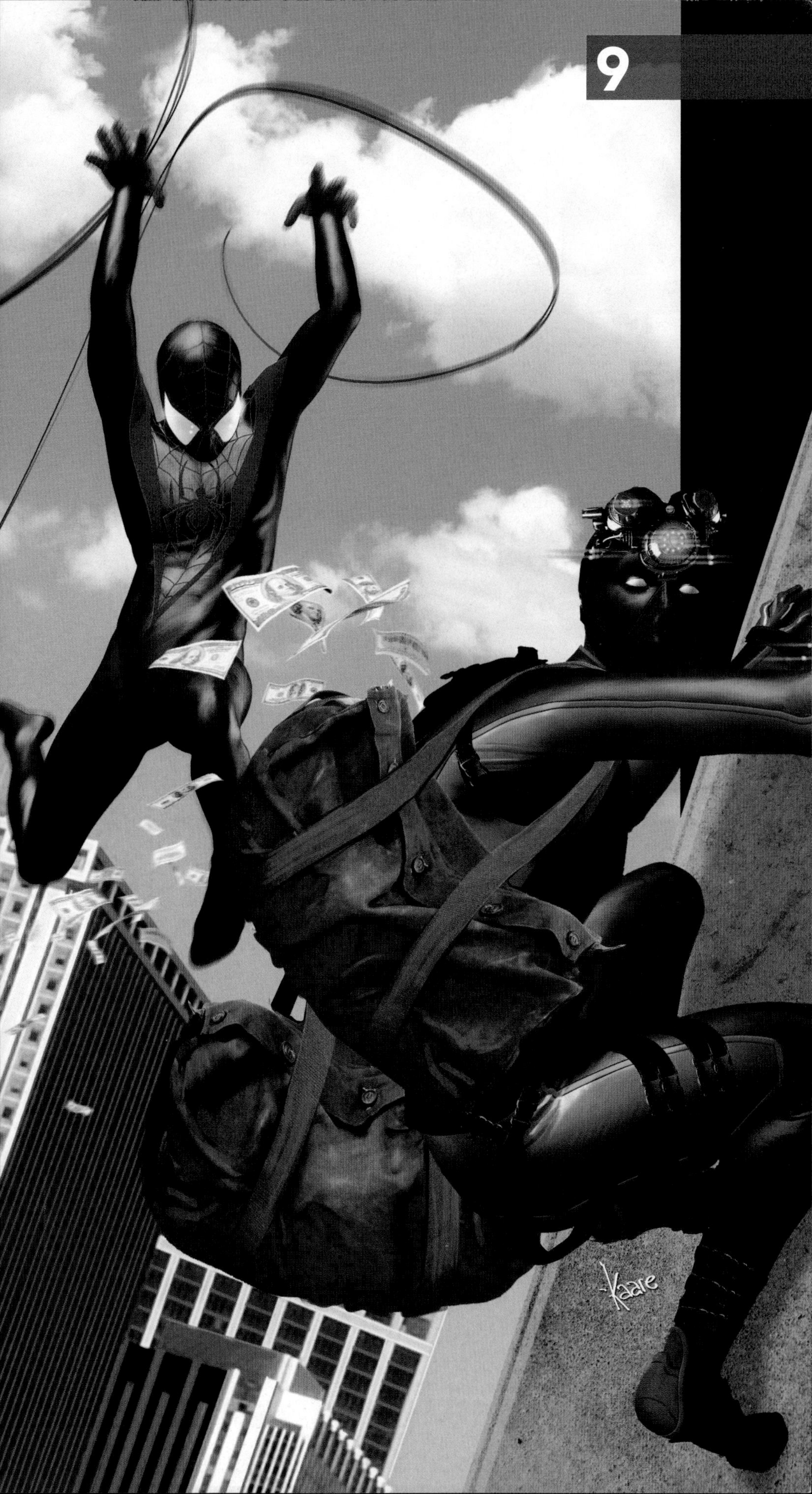
9
Kaare

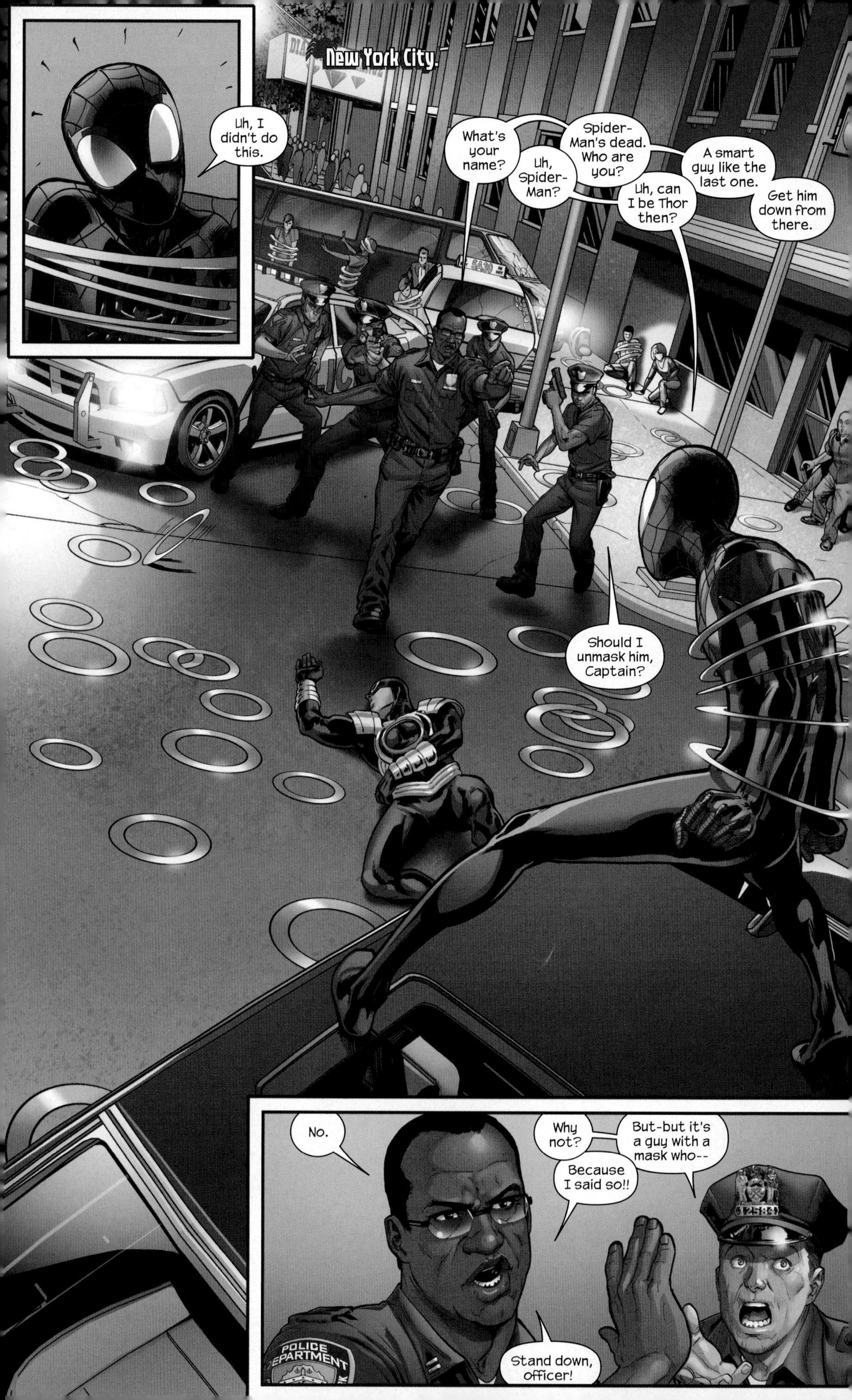
Uh, I didn't do this.
New York City.
What's your name?
Uh, Spider-Man?
Spider-Man's dead. Who are you?
Uh, can I be Thor then?
A smart guy like the last one.
Get him down from there.
Should I unmask him, Captain?
No.
Why not?
But-but it's a guy with a mask who--
Because I said so!!
Stand down, officer!
POLICE DEPARTMENT

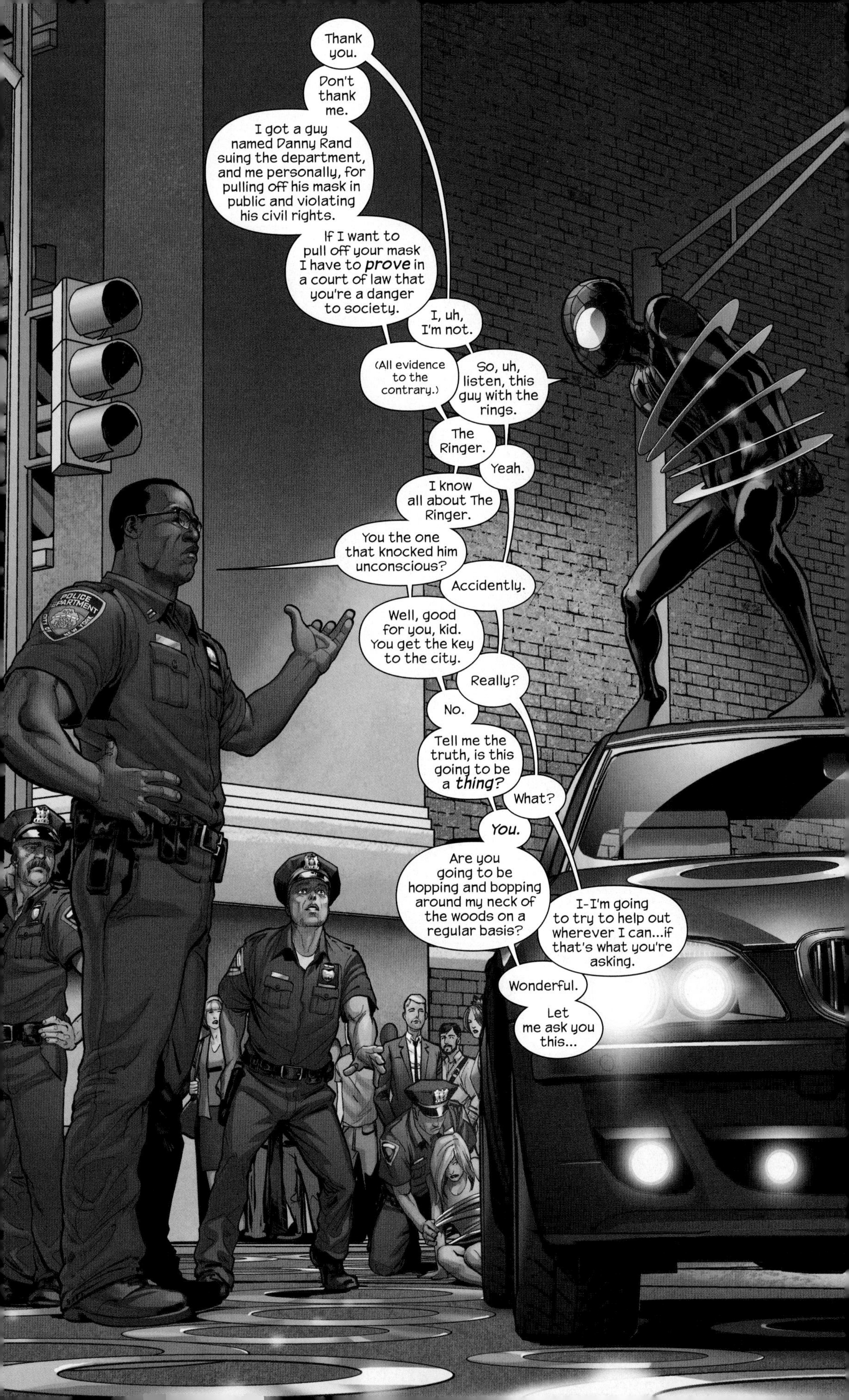
Thank you.
Don't thank me.
I got a guy named Danny Rand suing the department, and me personally, for pulling off his mask in public and violating his civil rights.
If I want to pull off your mask I have to *prove* in a court of law that you're a danger to society.
I, uh, I'm not.
(All evidence to the contrary.)
So, uh, listen, this guy with the rings.
The Ringer.
Yeah.
I know all about The Ringer.
You the one that knocked him unconscious?
Accidently.
Well, good for you, kid. You get the key to the city.
Really?
No.
Tell me the truth, is this going to be a *thing?*
What?
You.
Are you going to be hopping and bopping around my neck of the woods on a regular basis?
I-I'm going to try to help out wherever I can...if that's what you're asking.
Wonderful.
Let me ask you this...

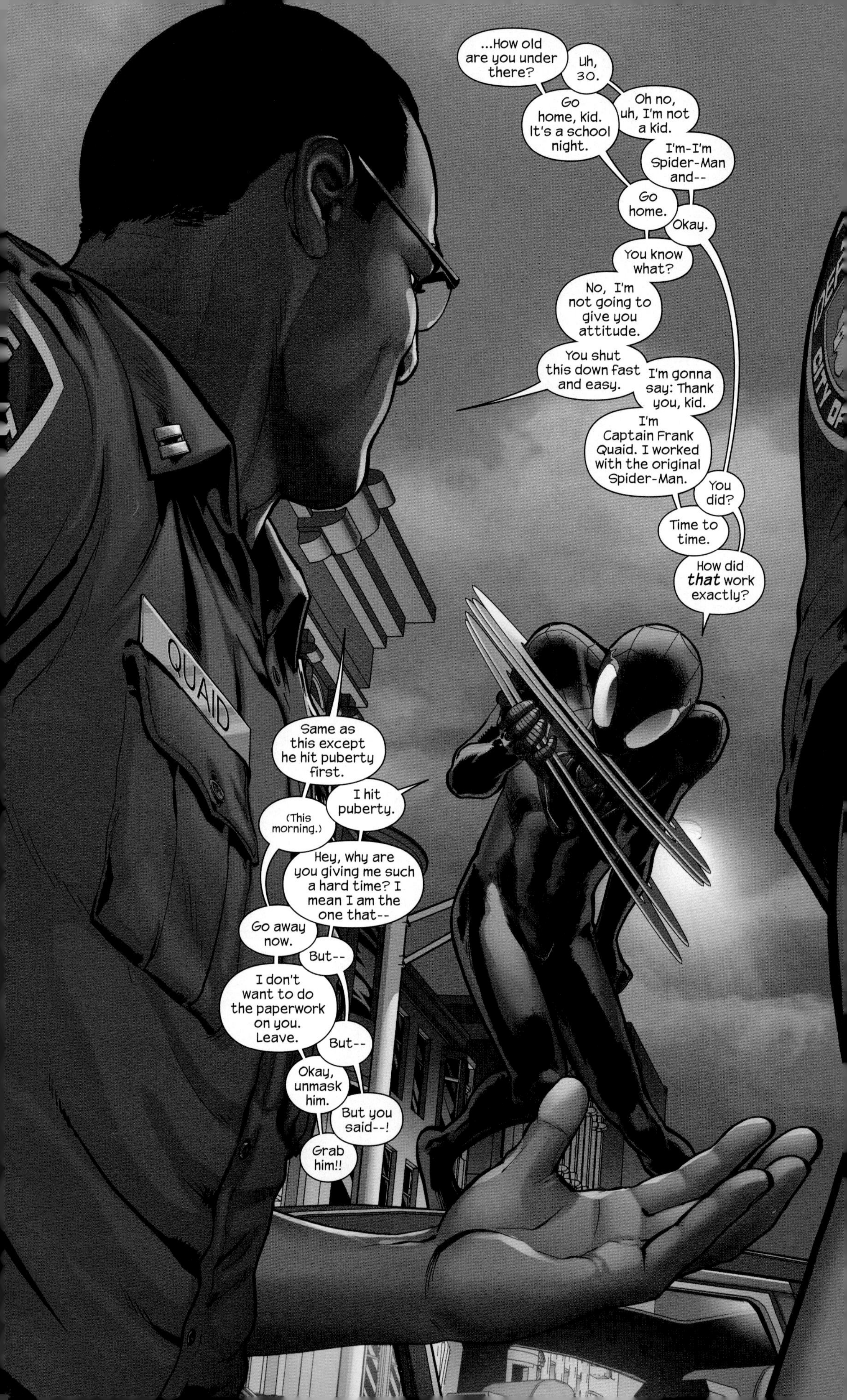
...How old are you under there?
Uh, 30.
Go home, kid. It's a school night.
Oh no, uh, I'm not a kid.
I'm-I'm Spider-Man and--
Go home.
Okay.
You know what?
No, I'm not going to give you attitude.
You shut this down fast and easy.
I'm gonna say: Thank you, kid.
I'm Captain Frank Quaid. I worked with the original Spider-Man.
You did?
Time to time.
How did *that* work exactly?
QUAID
Same as this except he hit puberty first.
I hit puberty.
(This morning.)
Hey, why are you giving me such a hard time? I mean I am the one that--
Go away now.
But--
I don't want to do the paperwork on you. Leave.
But--
Okay, unmask him.
But you said--!
Grab him!!

Come on!!

Were you serious?

No.

Just wanted him to get out of here.

Can't believe there's another one.

Kid has no idea what he's doing.

How is there another one?

Hey, idiot.

You're under arrest.

You have the right to remain silent.

POLICE DEPARTMENT CITY OF NEW YORK

Oh, come on!

Aaghh!!

ZZTTT

Anyway... you have the right to remain silent.

And I *truly* hope you do.

Bff!!!...

Yeah, well, you *still* have the right to remain silent.

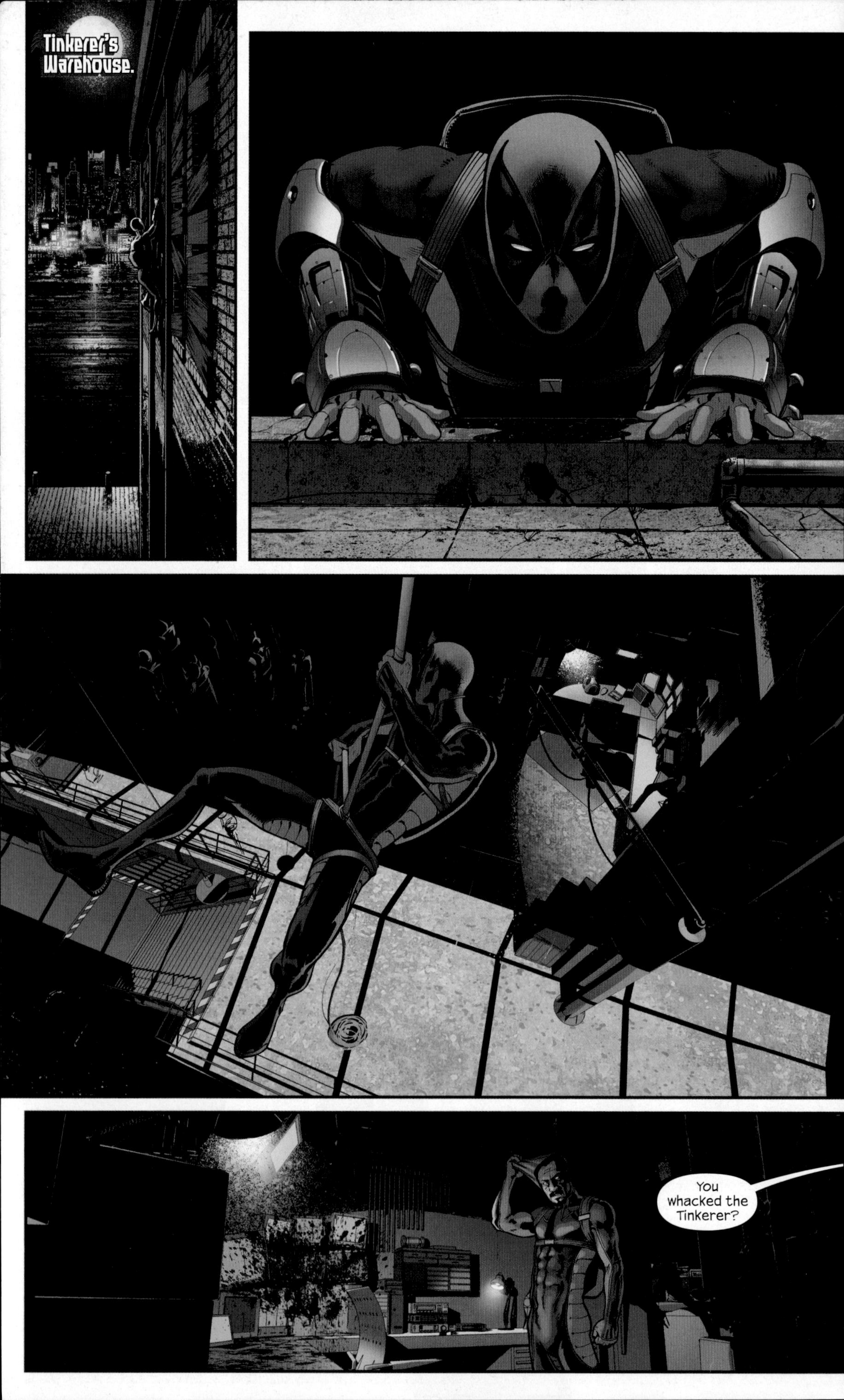
Tinkerer's Warehouse.
You whacked the Tinkerer?

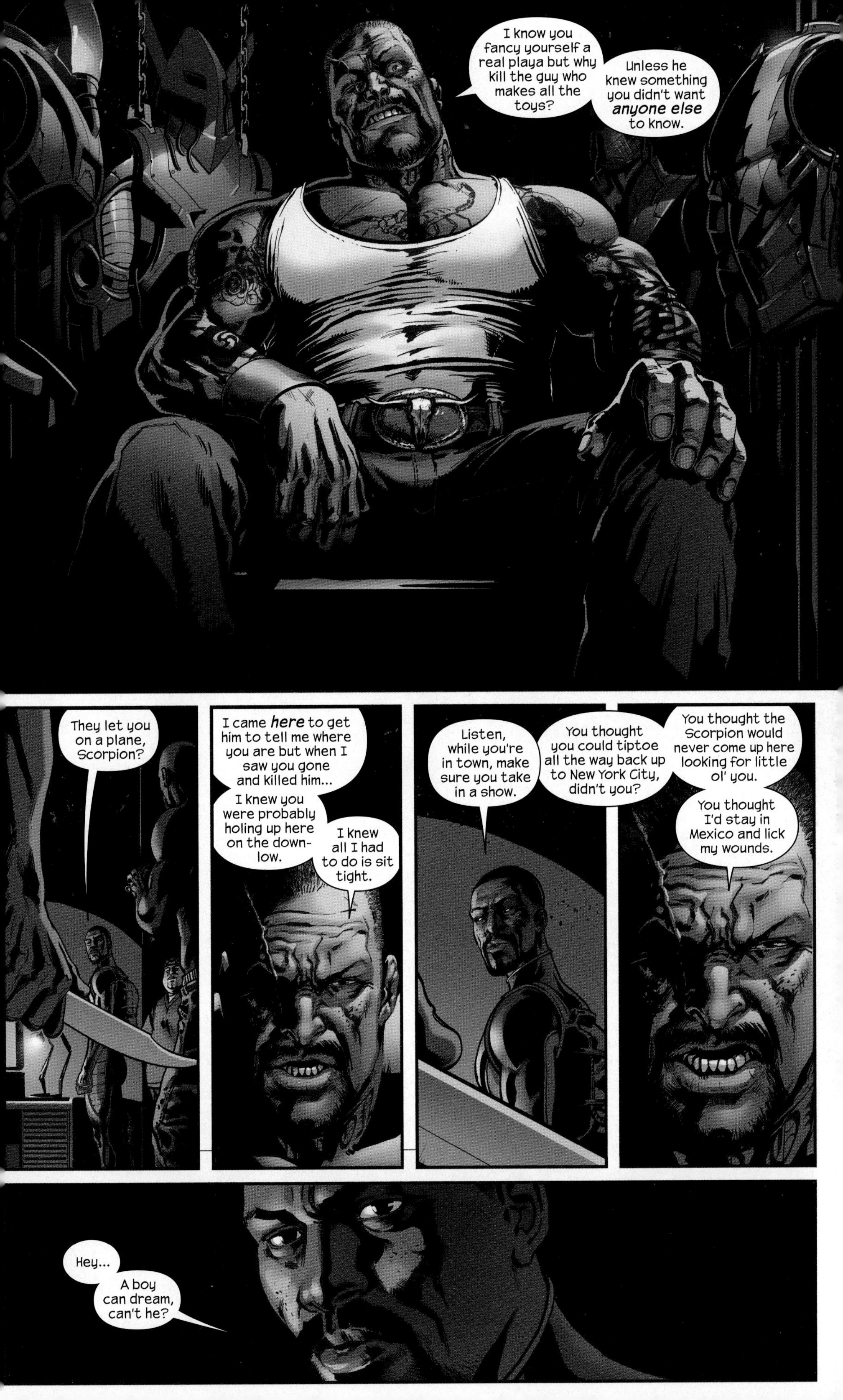

I know you fancy yourself a real playa but why kill the guy who makes all the toys?
Unless he knew something you didn't want *anyone else* to know.
They let you on a plane, Scorpion?
I came *here* to get him to tell me where you are but when I saw you gone and killed him...
I knew you were probably holing up here on the down-low.
I knew all I had to do is sit tight.
Listen, while you're in town, make sure you take in a show.
You thought you could tiptoe all the way back up to New York City, didn't you?
You thought the Scorpion would never come up here looking for little ol' you.
You thought I'd stay in Mexico and lick my wounds.
Hey...
A boy can dream, can't he?

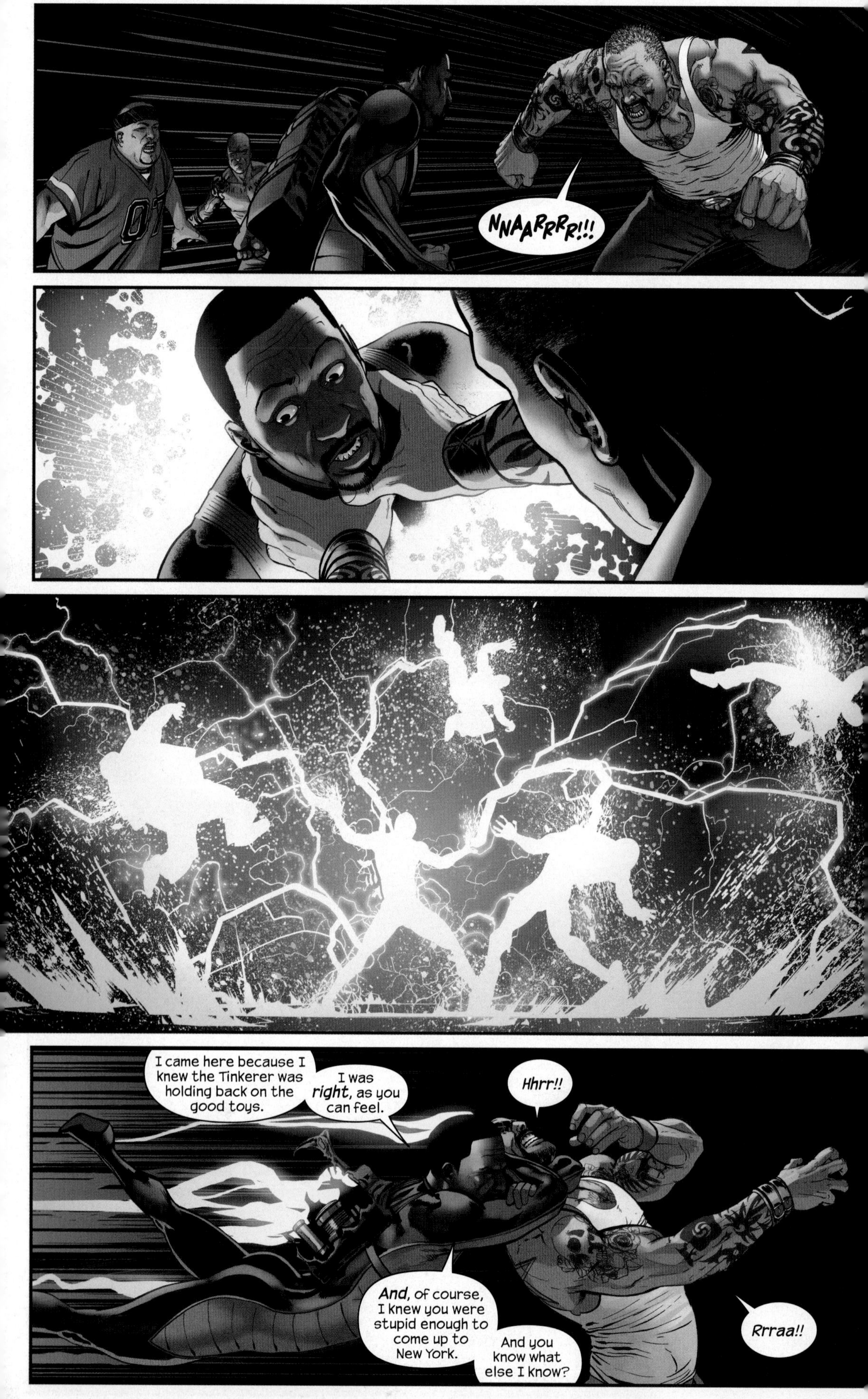
NNAARRRR!!!
I came here because I knew the Tinkerer was holding back on the good toys.
I was right, as you can feel.
Hhrr!!
And, of course, I knew you were stupid enough to come up to New York.
And you know what else I know?
Rrraa!!

This!!

CRAASSHH

CRASH

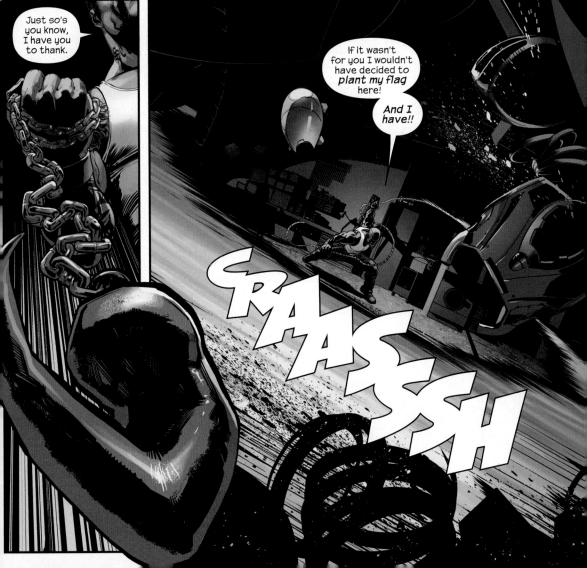

Just so's you know, I have you to thank.

If it wasn't for you I wouldn't have decided to *plant my flag* here!

And I have!!

CRAASSH

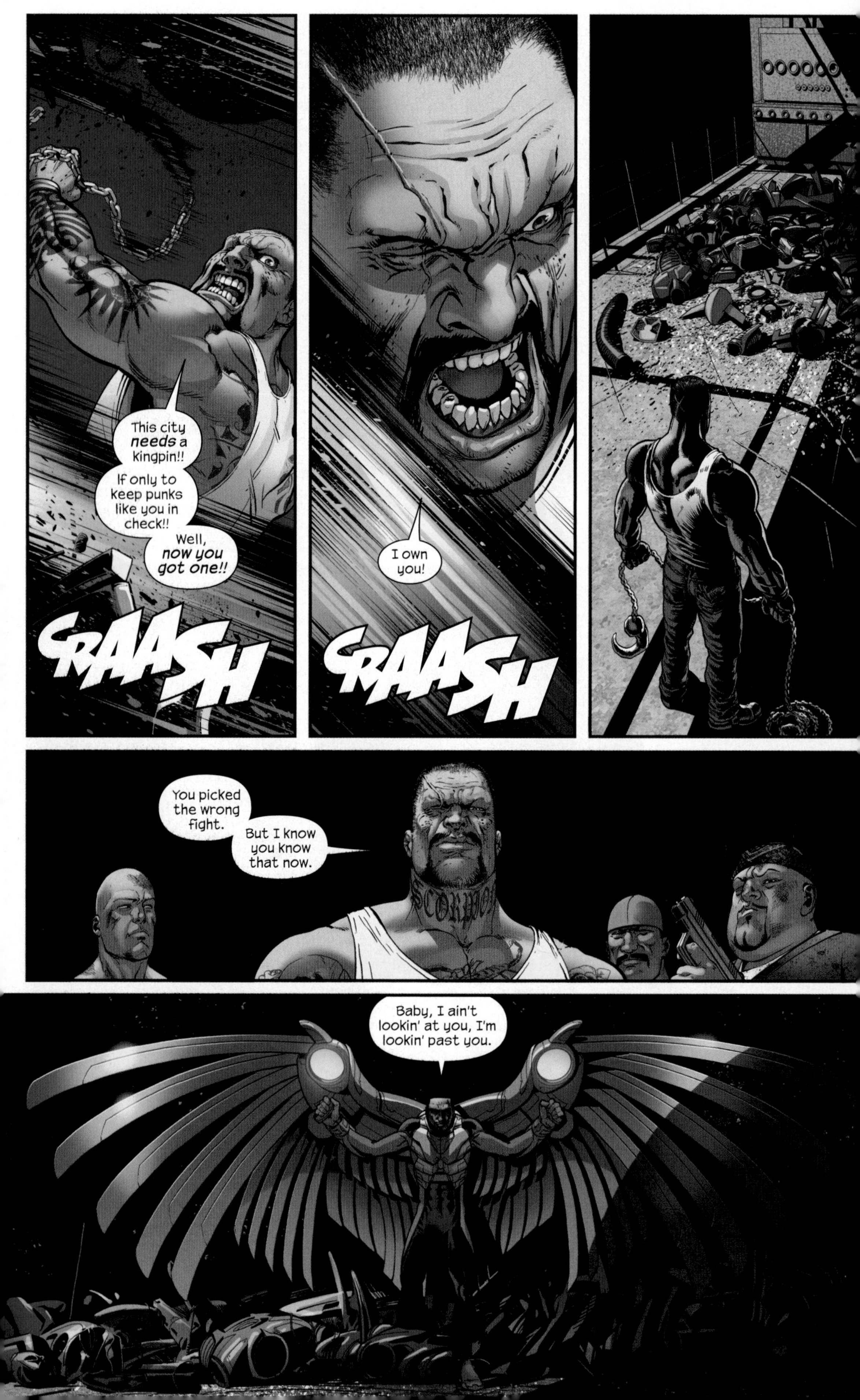
This city *needs* a kingpin!!
If only to keep punks like you in check!!
Well, *now you got one!!*
CRAASH
I own you!
CRAASH
You picked the wrong fight.
But I know you know that now.
SCORPION
Baby, I ain't lookin' at you, I'm lookin' past you.

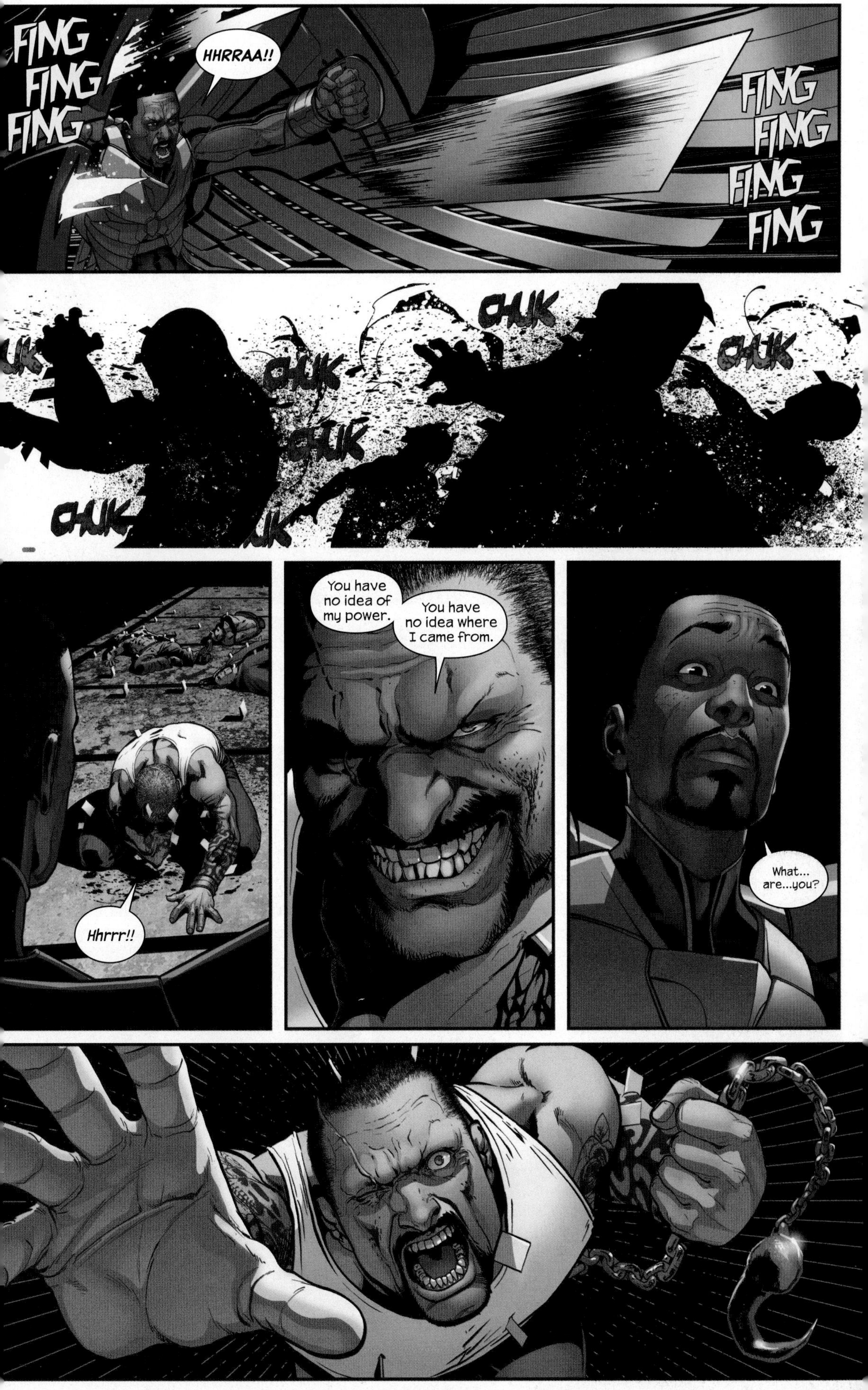
FING FING FING
HHRRAA!!
FING FING FING FING
CHUK
CHUK
CHUK
CHUK
CHUK
CHUK
Hhrrr!!
You have no idea of my power.
You have no idea where I came from.
What... are...you?

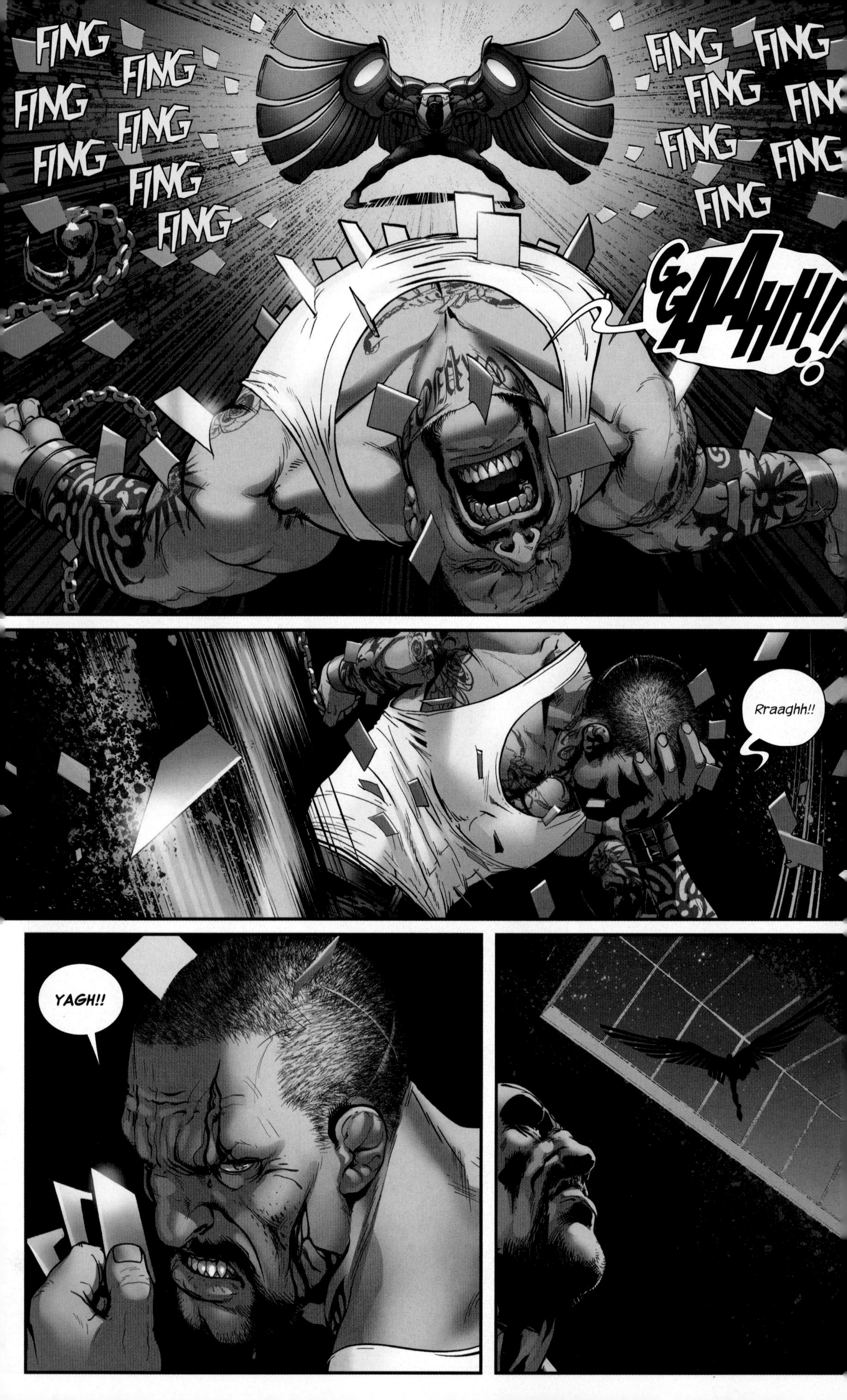
FING
FING
FING
FING
FING
FING
FING
FING
FING
FING
FING
FING
FING
FING
FING
GGAAHHH!!
Rraaghh!!
YAGH!!

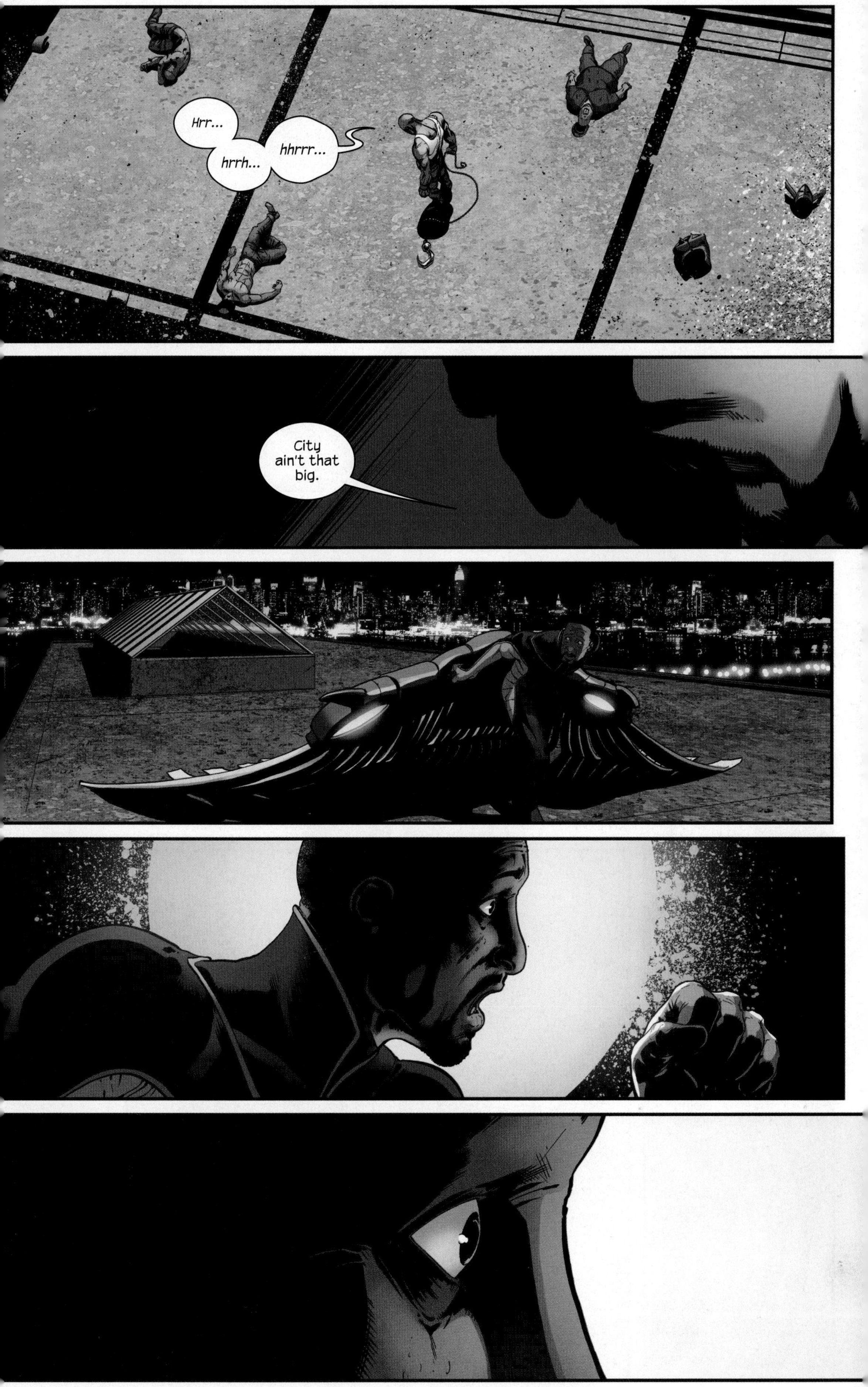
Hrr...
hrrh...
hhrrr...
City ain't that big.

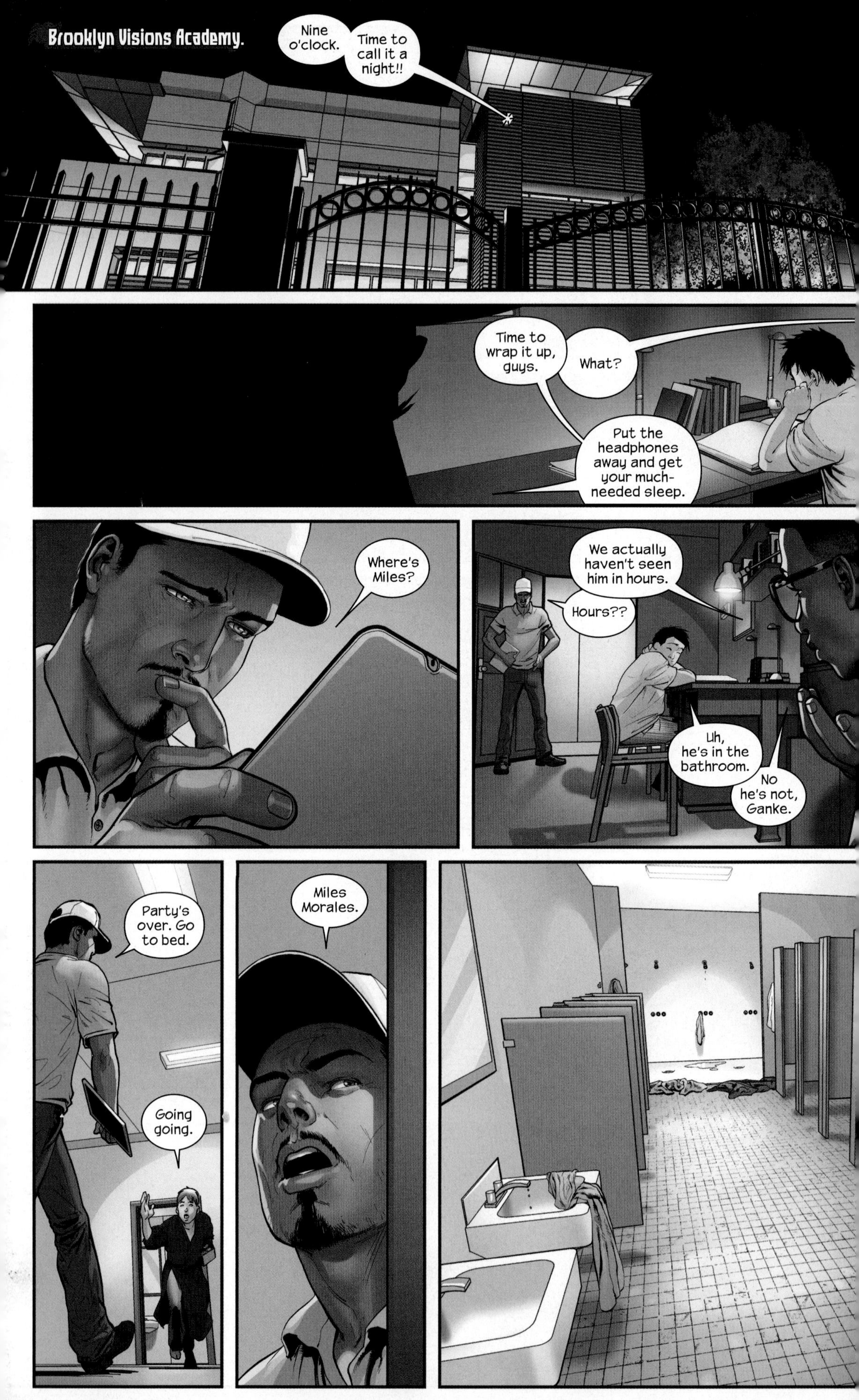
Brooklyn Visions Academy.
Nine o'clock.
Time to call it a night!!
Time to wrap it up, guys.
What?
Put the headphones away and get your much-needed sleep.
Where's Miles?
We actually haven't seen him in hours.
Hours??
Uh, he's in the bathroom.
No he's not, Ganke.
Party's over. Go to bed.
Going going.
Miles Morales.

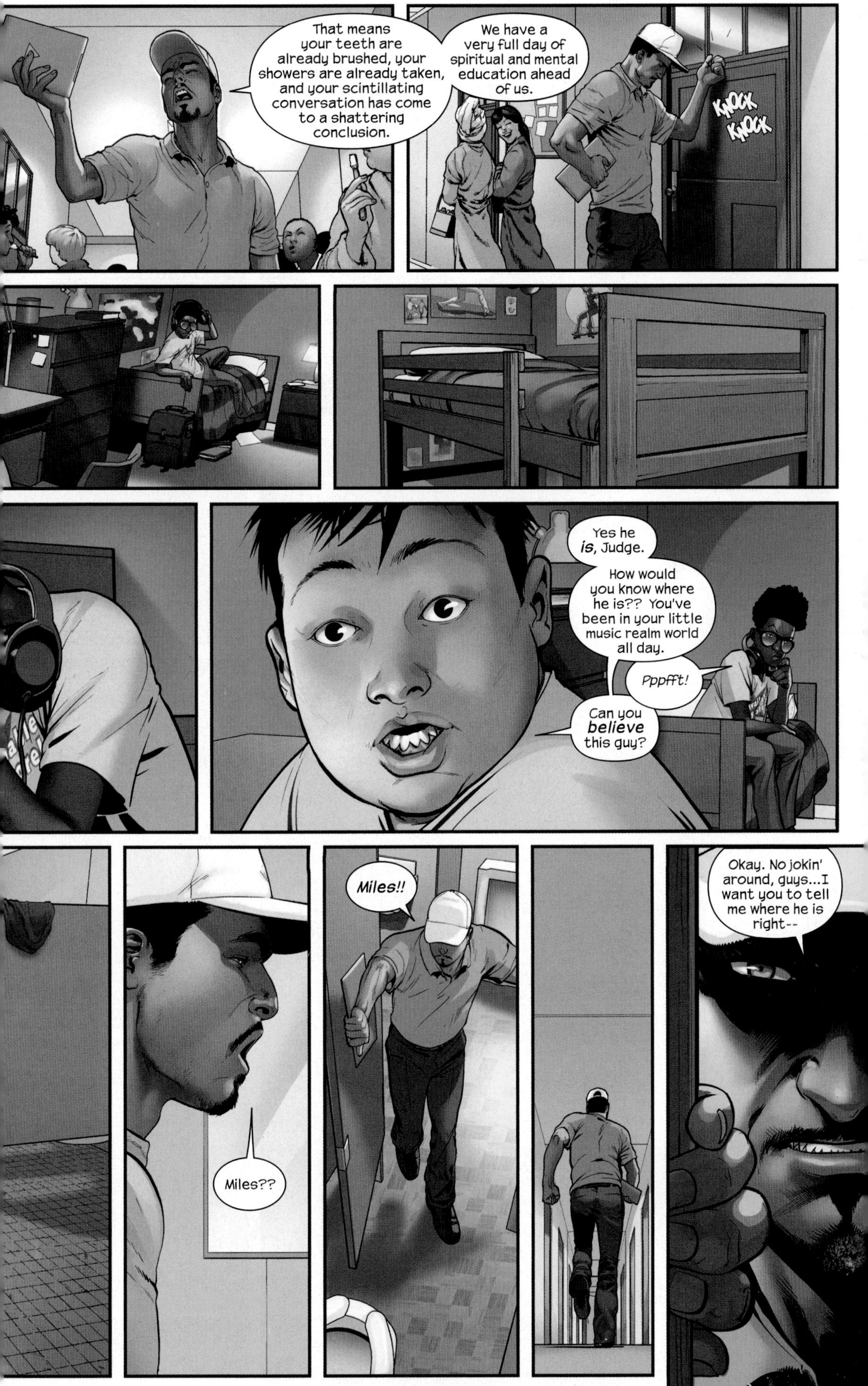
That means your teeth are already brushed, your showers are already taken, and your scintillating conversation has come to a shattering conclusion.
We have a very full day of spiritual and mental education ahead of us.
KNOCK KNOCK
Yes he is, Judge.
How would you know where he is?? You've been in your little music realm world all day.
Pppfft!
Can you believe this guy?
Miles??
Miles!!
Okay. No jokin' around, guys...I want you to tell me where he is right--

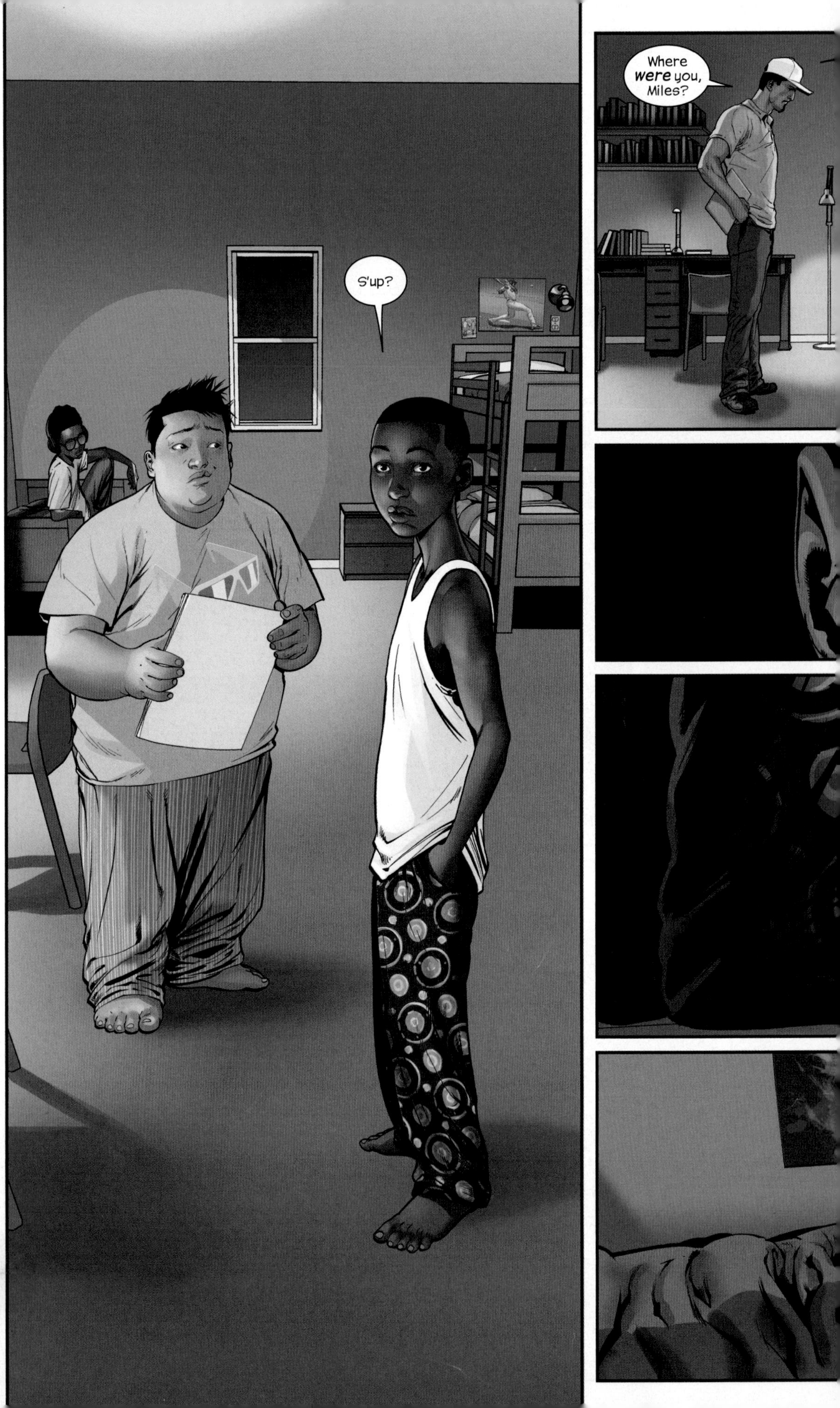
S'up?
Where *were* you, Miles?

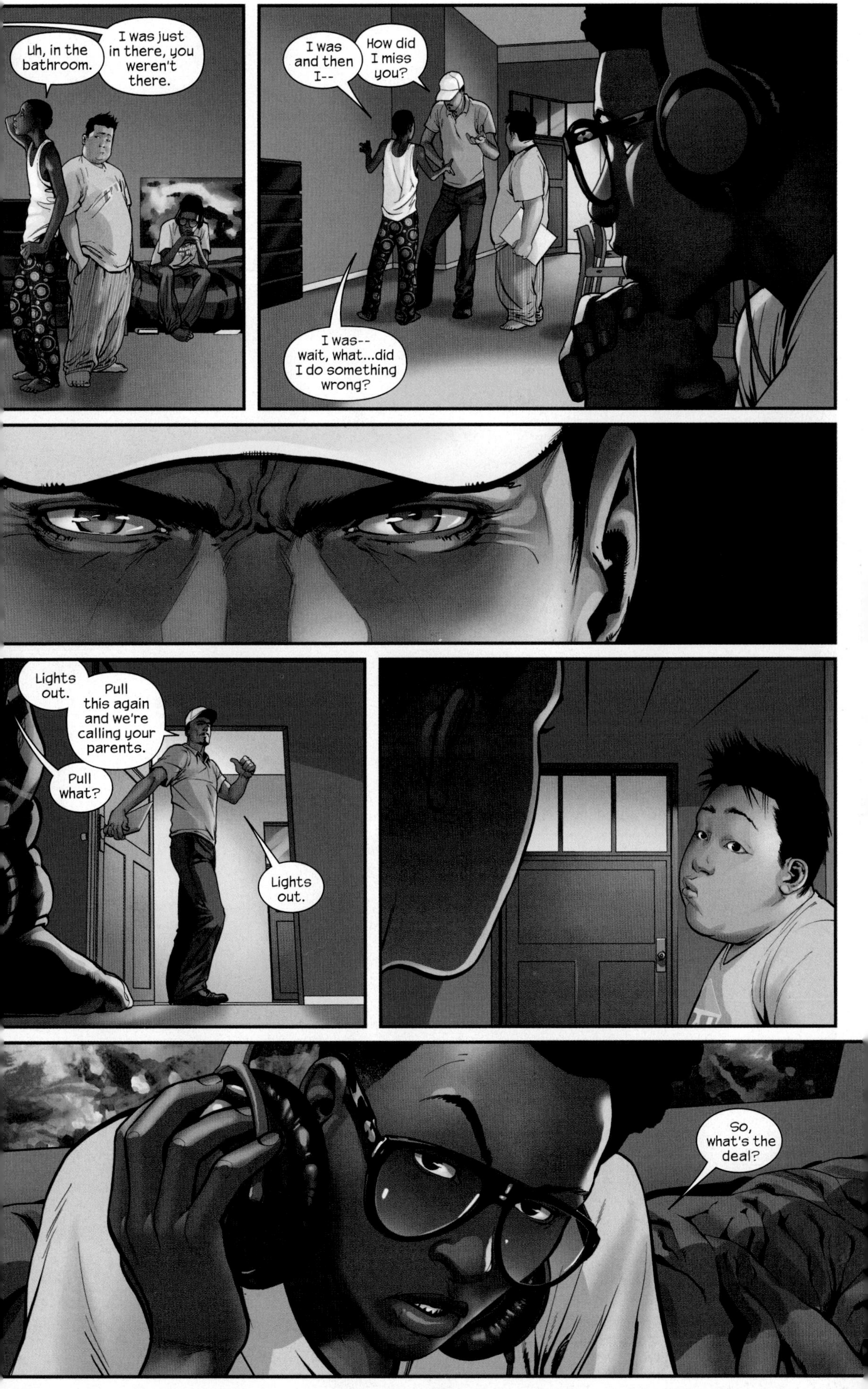
Uh, in the bathroom.
I was just in there, you weren't there.
I was and then I--
How did I miss you?
I was-- wait, what...did I do something wrong?
Lights out.
Pull this again and we're calling your parents.
Pull what?
Lights out.
So, what's the deal?

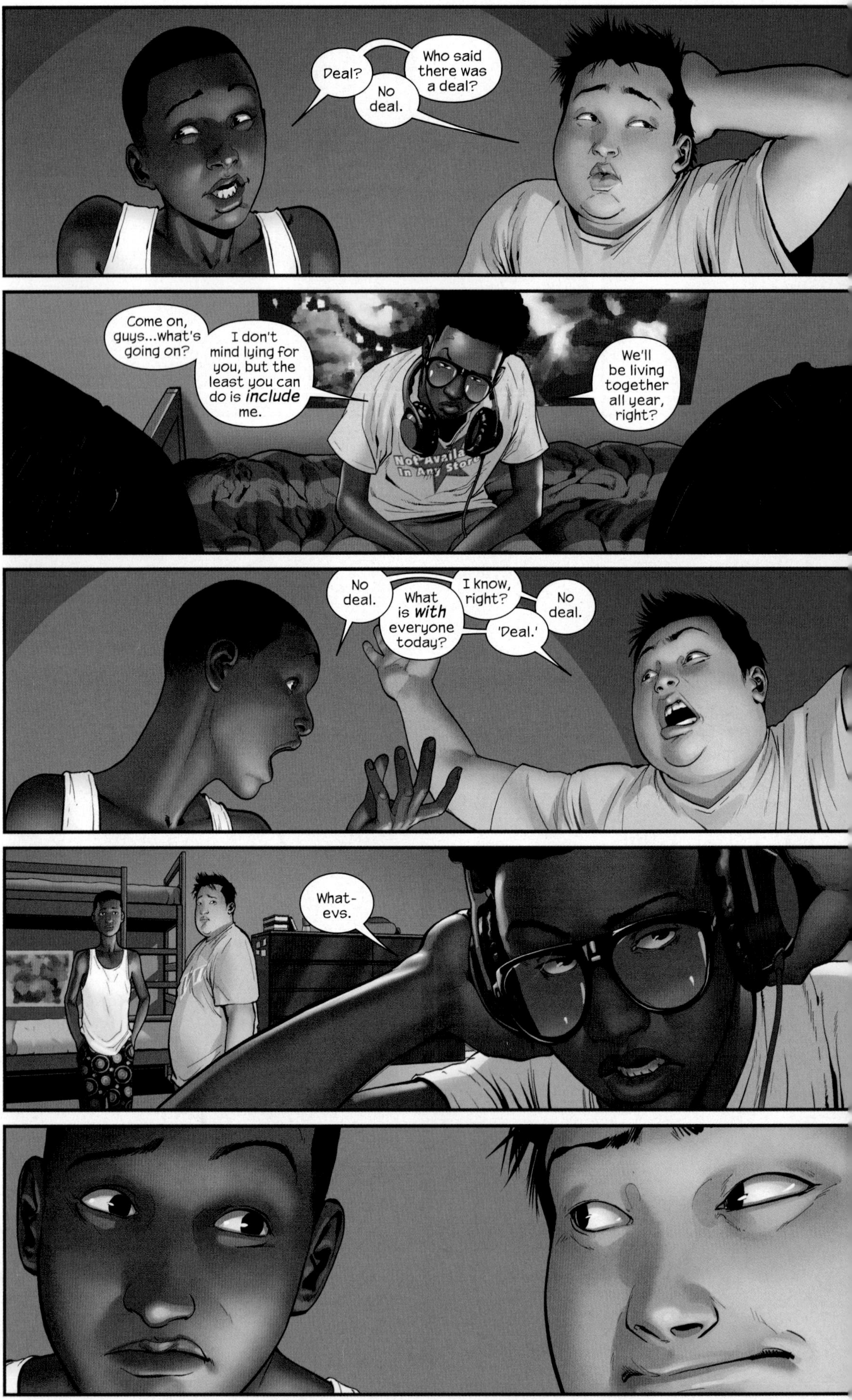
Deal?
Who said there was a deal?
No deal.
Come on, guys...what's going on?
I don't mind lying for you, but the least you can do is *include* me.
We'll be living together all year, right?
Not Available In Any Store
No deal.
I know, right?
What is *with* everyone today?
No deal.
'Deal.'
What-evs.

STARPICS

Z100

Ganke THE AWESOME:
today, 12:21 am

saw what you did tonight. Car-razy.

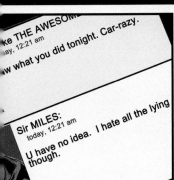

ke THE AWESOM
ay, 12:21 am

w what you did tonight. Car-razy.

Sir MILES:
today, 12:21 am

U have no idea. I hate all the lying
though.

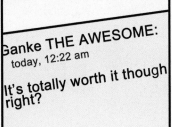

ough.

Ganke THE AWESOME:
today, 12:22 am

It's totally worth it though
right?

Sir MILES:
today, 12:23 am

We'll c

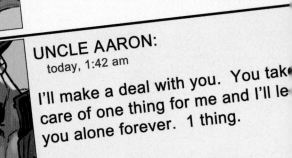

UNCLE AARON:
today, 1:40 am

hey, little man.

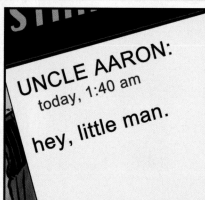

Sir MILES:
today, 1:41 am

No.

UNCLE AARON:
today, 1:42 am

I'll make a deal with you. You take
care of one thing for me and I'll le
you alone forever. 1 thing.

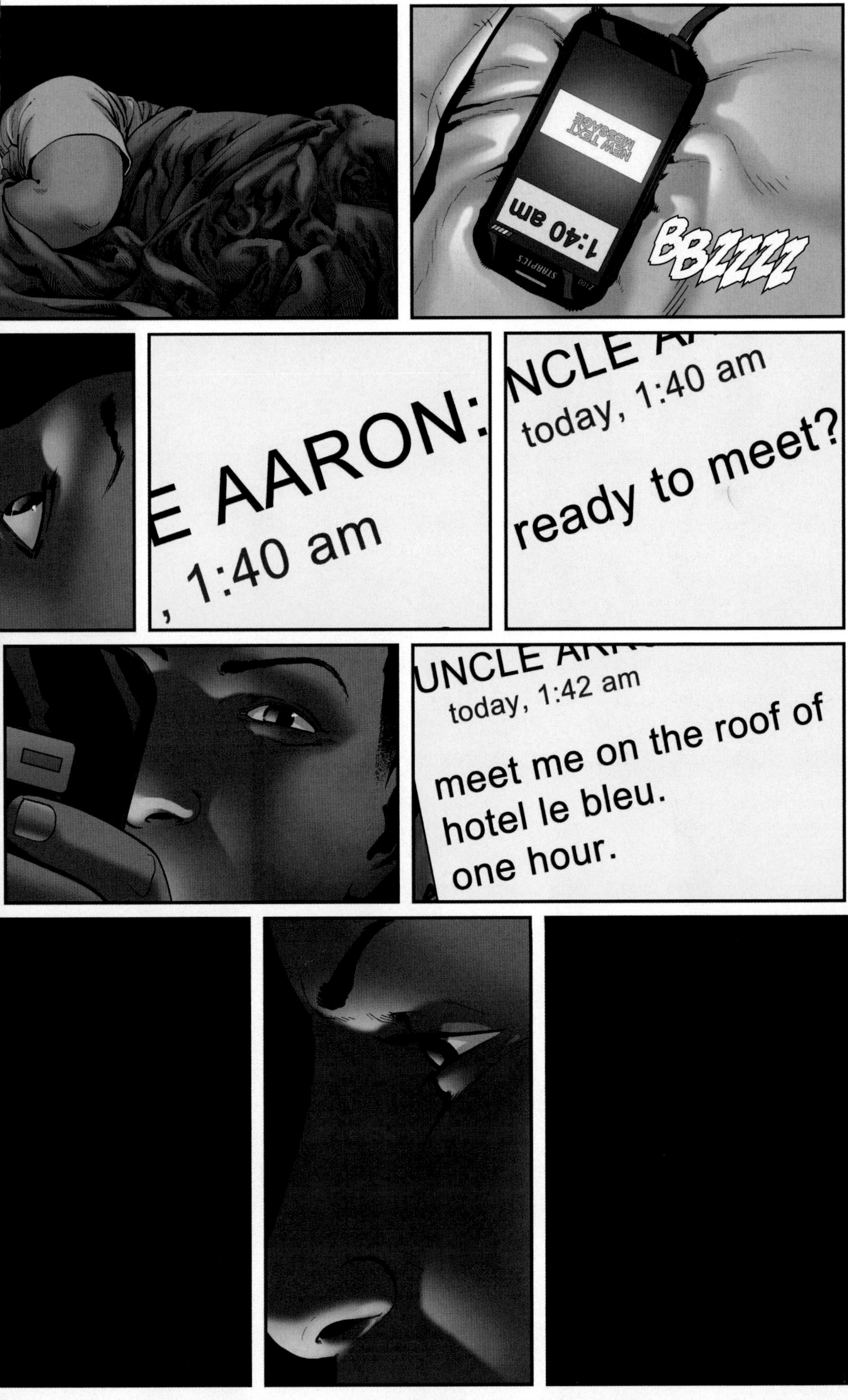
1:40 am
NEW TEXT MESSAGE
BBZZZZ
AARON:
1:40 am
today, 1:40 am
ready to meet?
today, 1:42 am
meet me on the roof of
hotel le bleu.
one hour.

#6 VARIANT
BY MARK BAGLEY

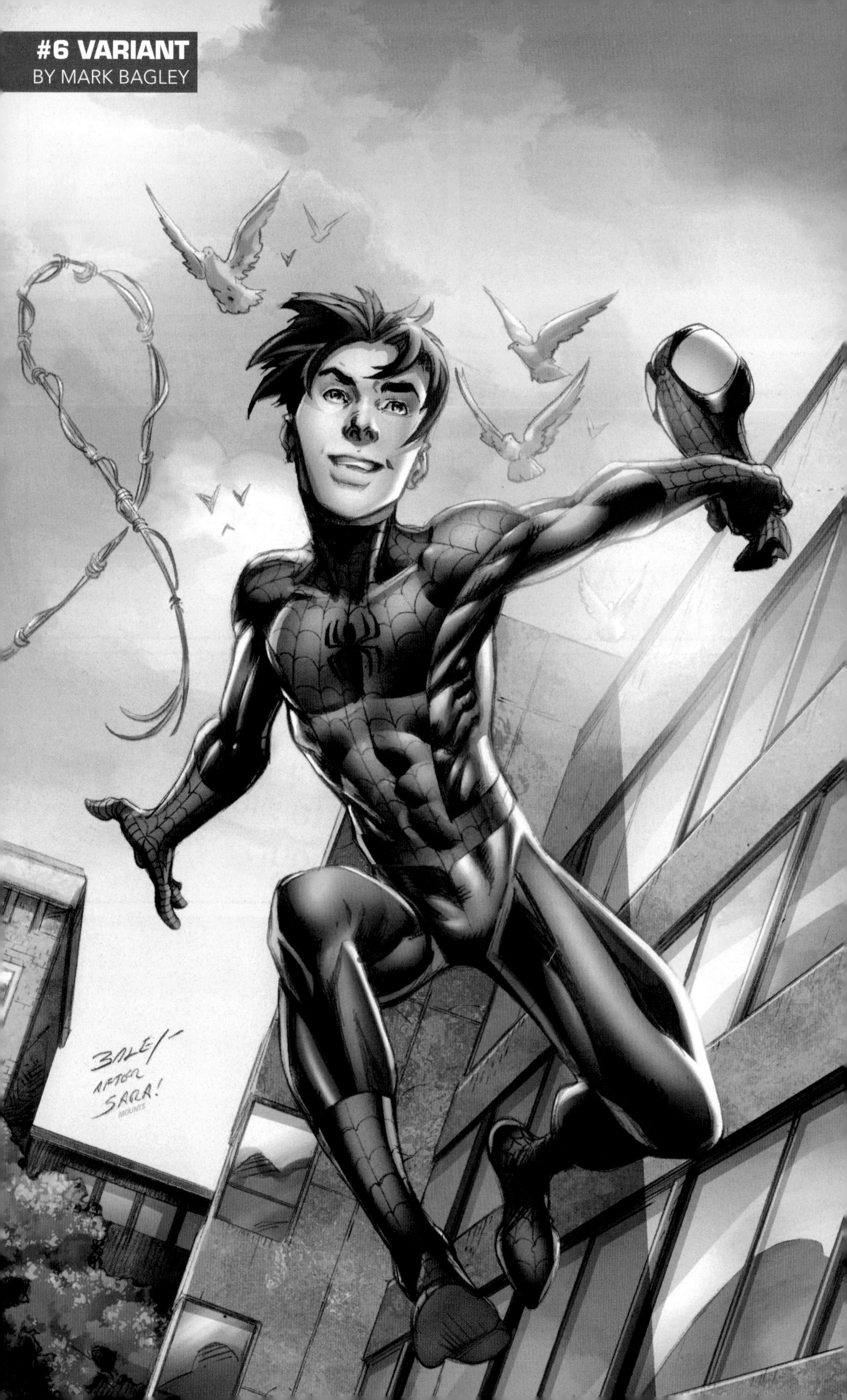

10

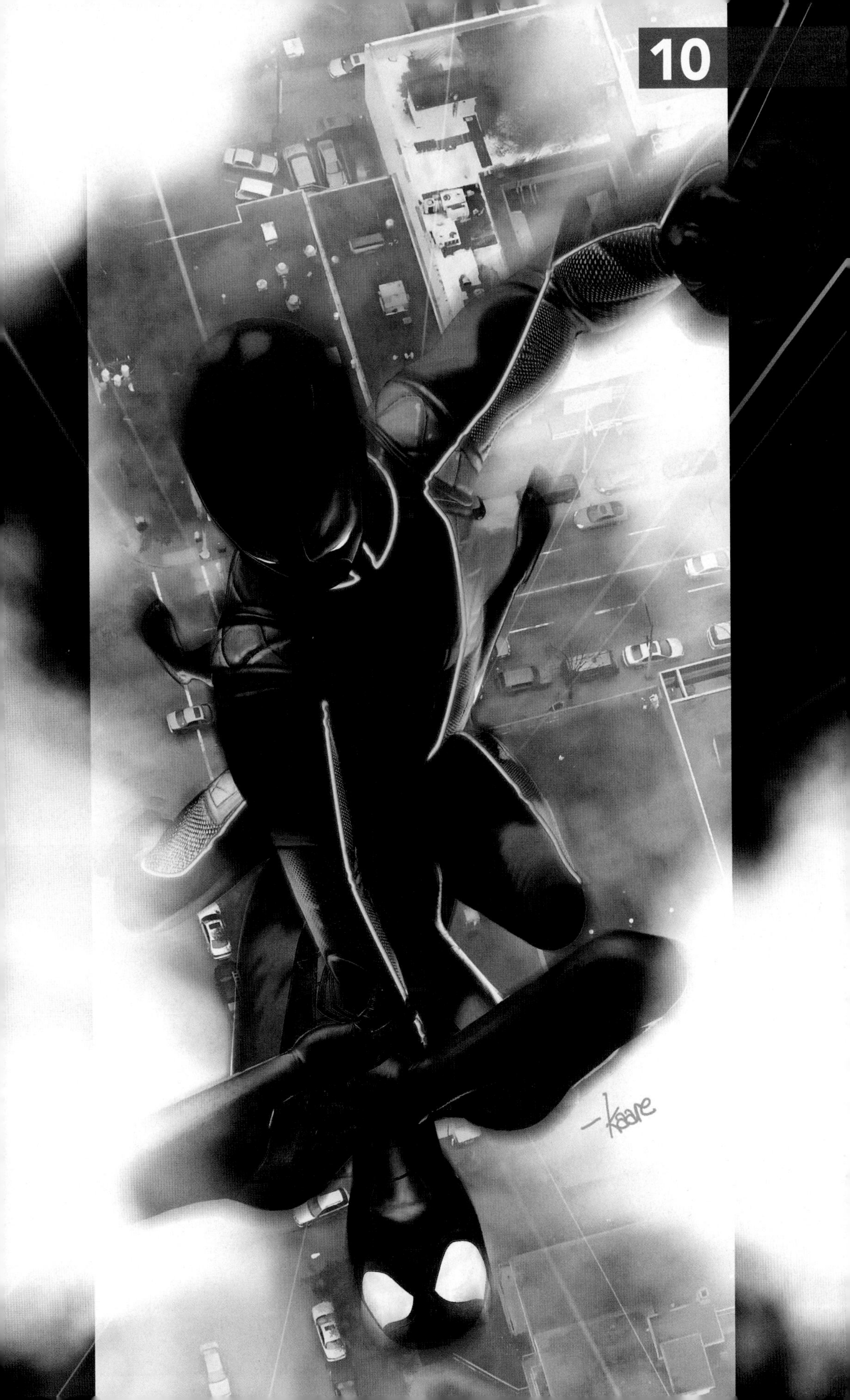
-Kaare

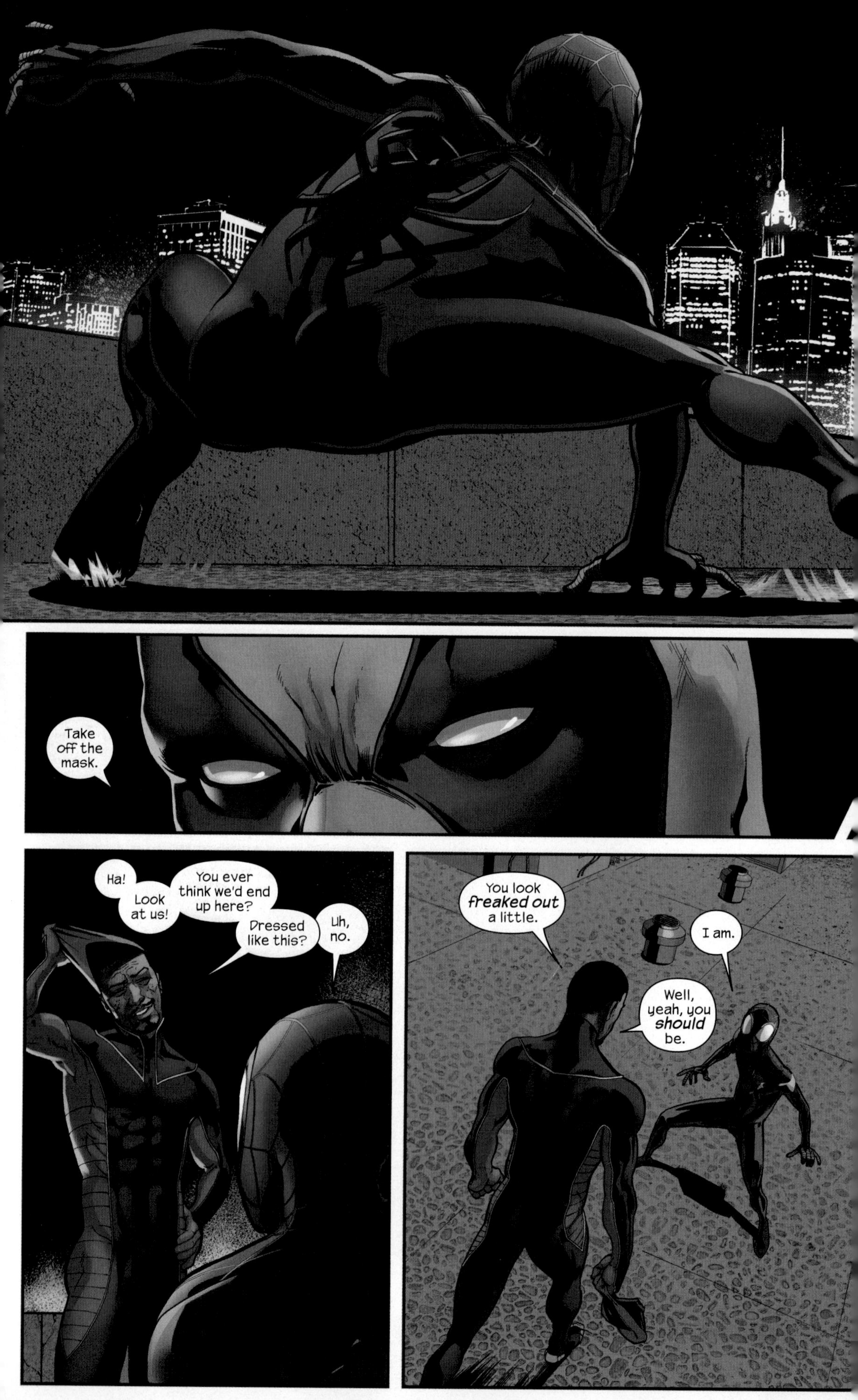
Take off the mask.
Ha!
Look at us!
You ever think we'd end up here?
Dressed like this?
Uh, no.
You look *freaked out* a little.
I am.
Well, yeah, you *should* be.

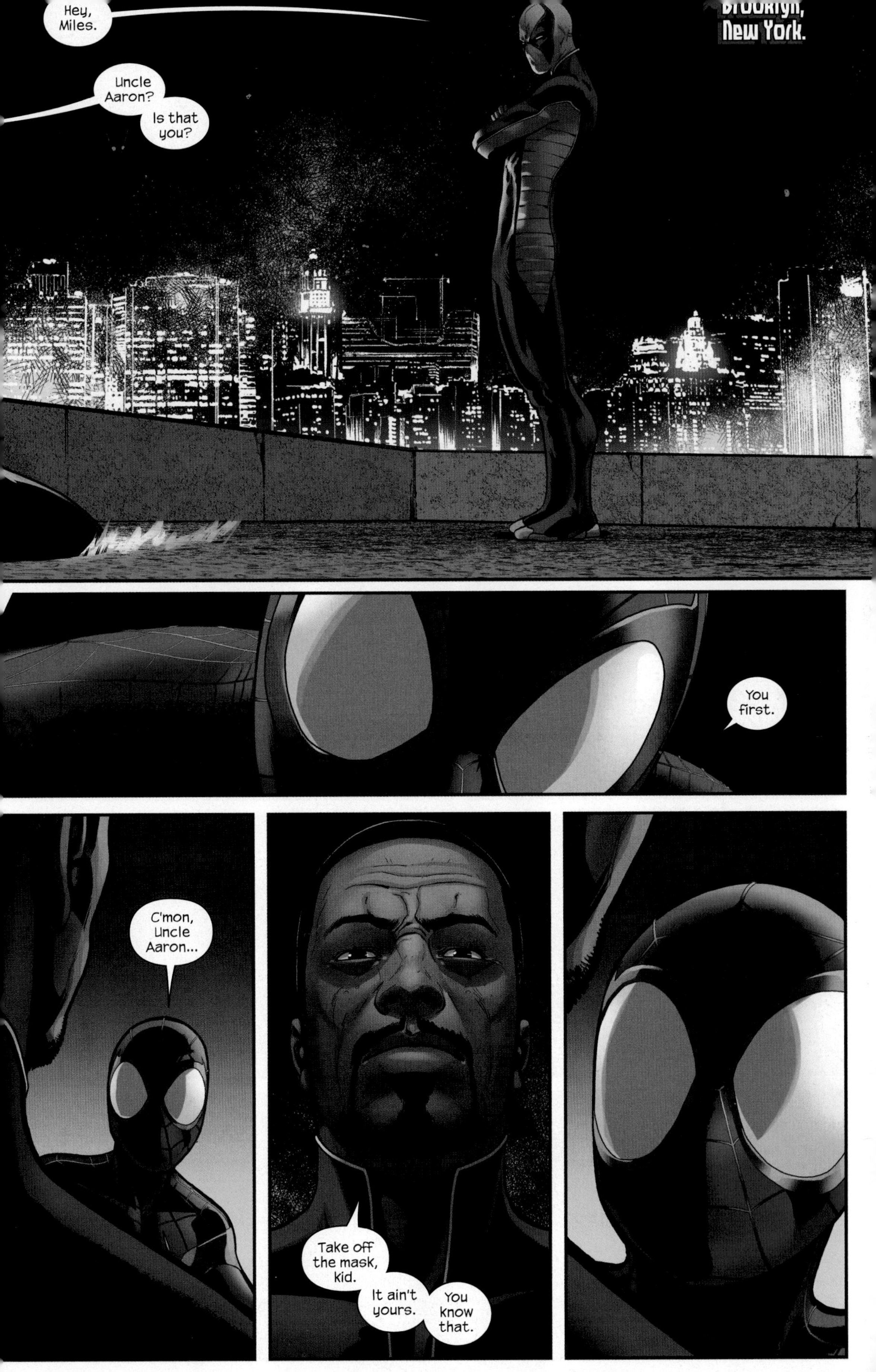

Brooklyn, New York.
Hey, Miles.
Uncle Aaron?
Is that you?
You first.
C'mon, Uncle Aaron...
Take off the mask, kid.
It ain't yours.
You know that.

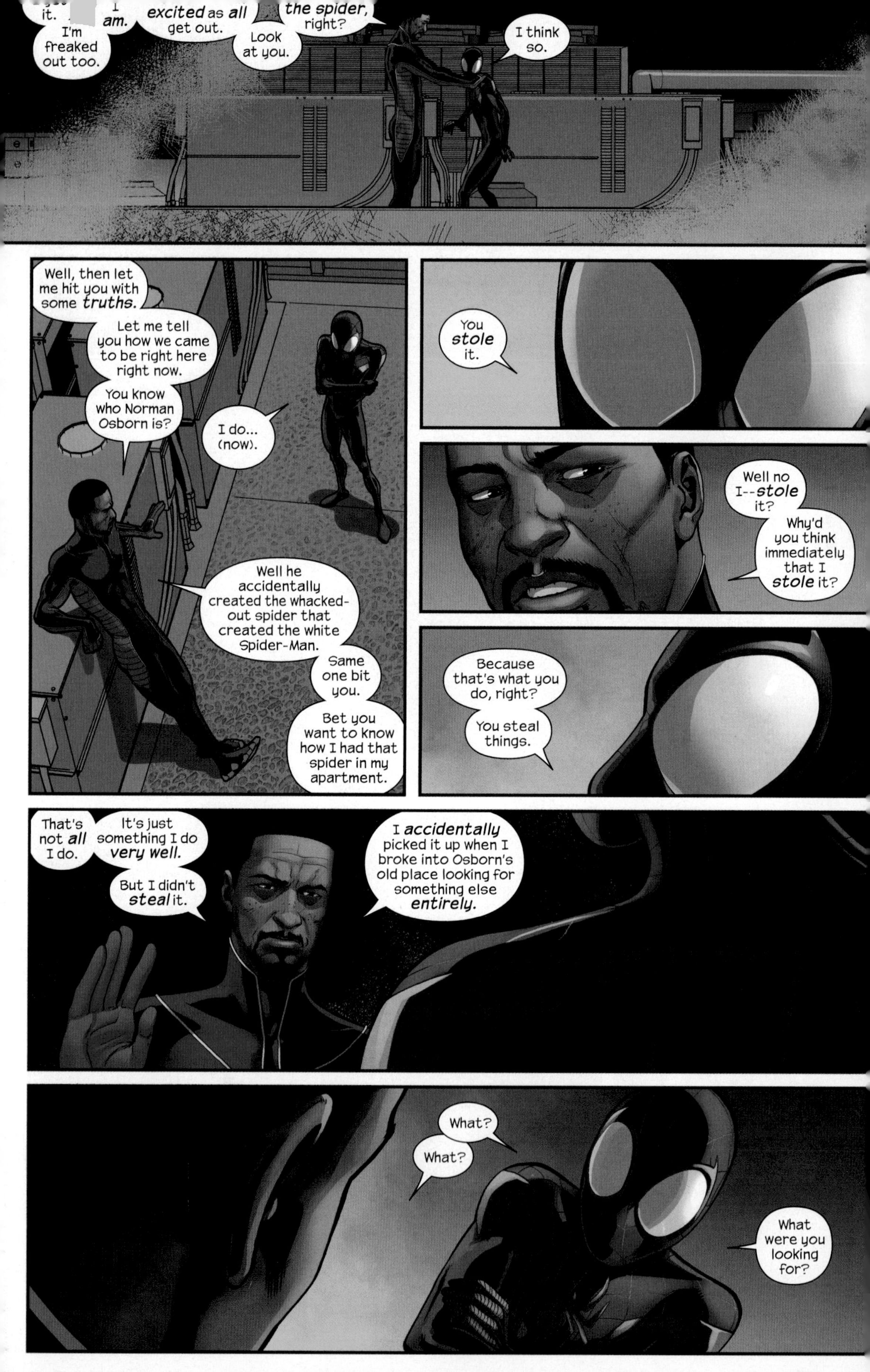

it.
I'm freaked out too.
I am.
excited as all get out.
Look at you.
the spider, right?
I think so.
Well, then let me hit you with some truths.
Let me tell you how we came to be right here right now.
You know who Norman Osborn is?
I do... (now).
Well he accidentally created the whacked-out spider that created the white Spider-Man.
Same one bit you.
Bet you want to know how I had that spider in my apartment.
You stole it.
Well no I--stole it?
Why'd you think immediately that I stole it?
Because that's what you do, right?
You steal things.
That's not all I do.
It's just something I do very well.
But I didn't steal it.
I accidentally picked it up when I broke into Osborn's old place looking for something else entirely.
What?
What?
What were you looking for?

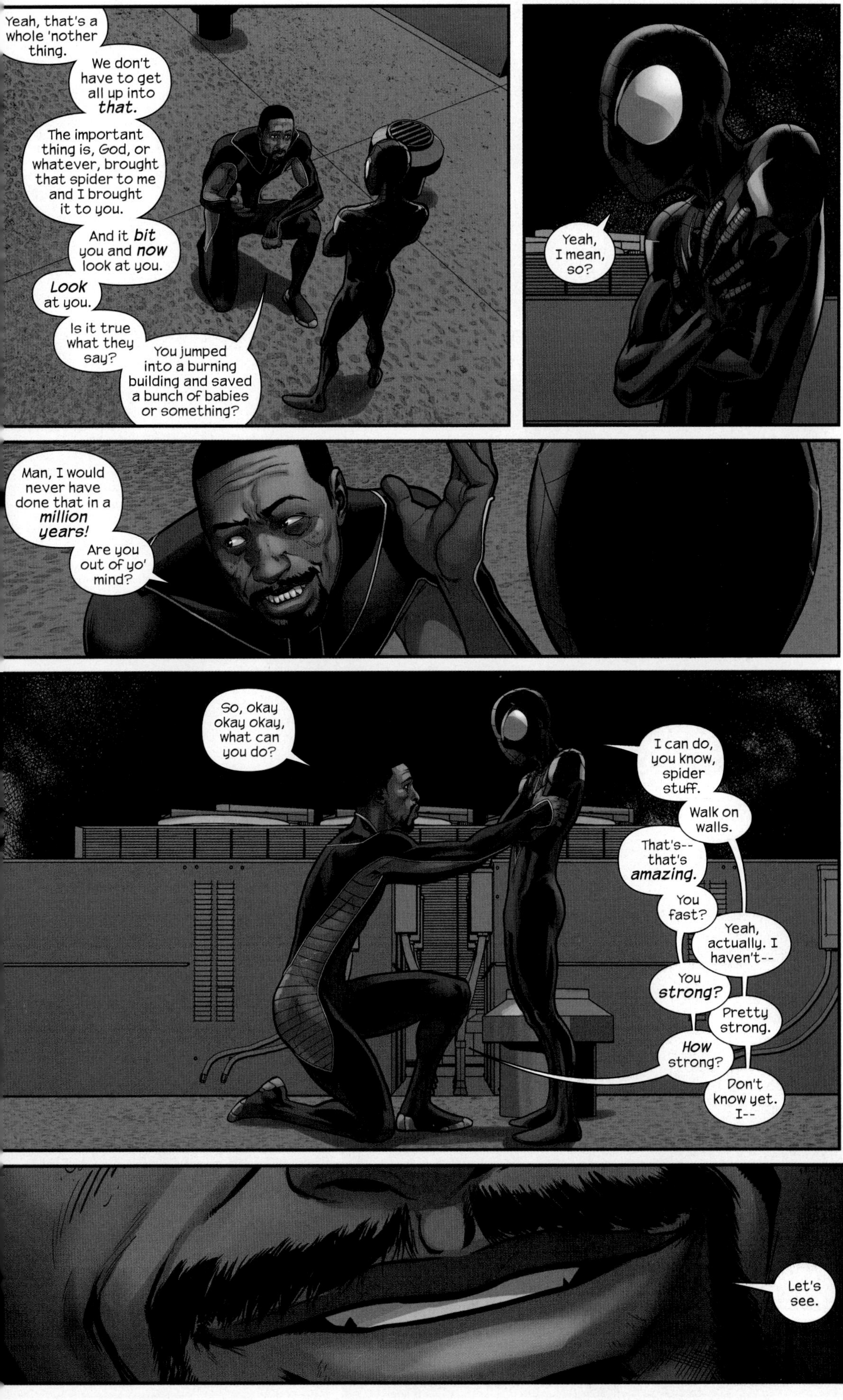
Yeah, that's a whole 'nother thing.
We don't have to get all up into *that.*
The important thing is, God, or whatever, brought that spider to me and I brought it to you.
And it *bit* you and *now* look at you.
Look at you.
Is it true what they say?
You jumped into a burning building and saved a bunch of babies or something?
Yeah, I mean, so?
Man, I would never have done that in a *million years!*
Are you out of yo' mind?
So, okay okay okay, what can you do?
I can do, you know, spider stuff.
Walk on walls.
That's-- that's *amazing.*
You fast?
Yeah, actually. I haven't--
You *strong?*
Pretty strong.
How strong?
Don't know yet. I--
Let's see.

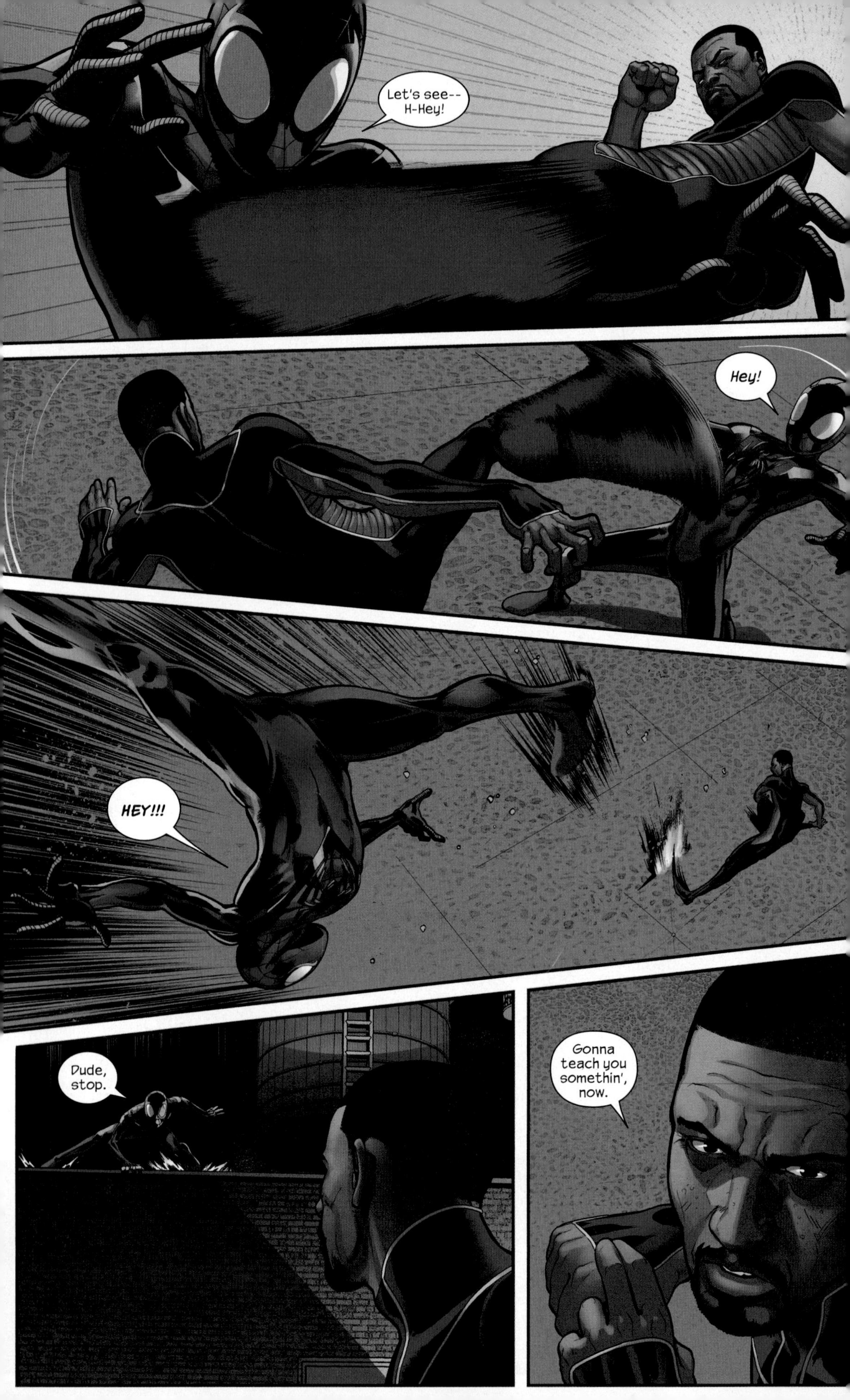
Let's see--
H-Hey!
Hey!
HEY!!!
Dude, stop.
Gonna teach you somethin', now.

AAGH!!

ZATTT

SMACK

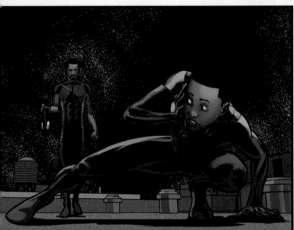

Come on, Miles!!

You can do better than this!!

You're **stronger** than me, you're faster than me...

Why are you letting me whup you??!!

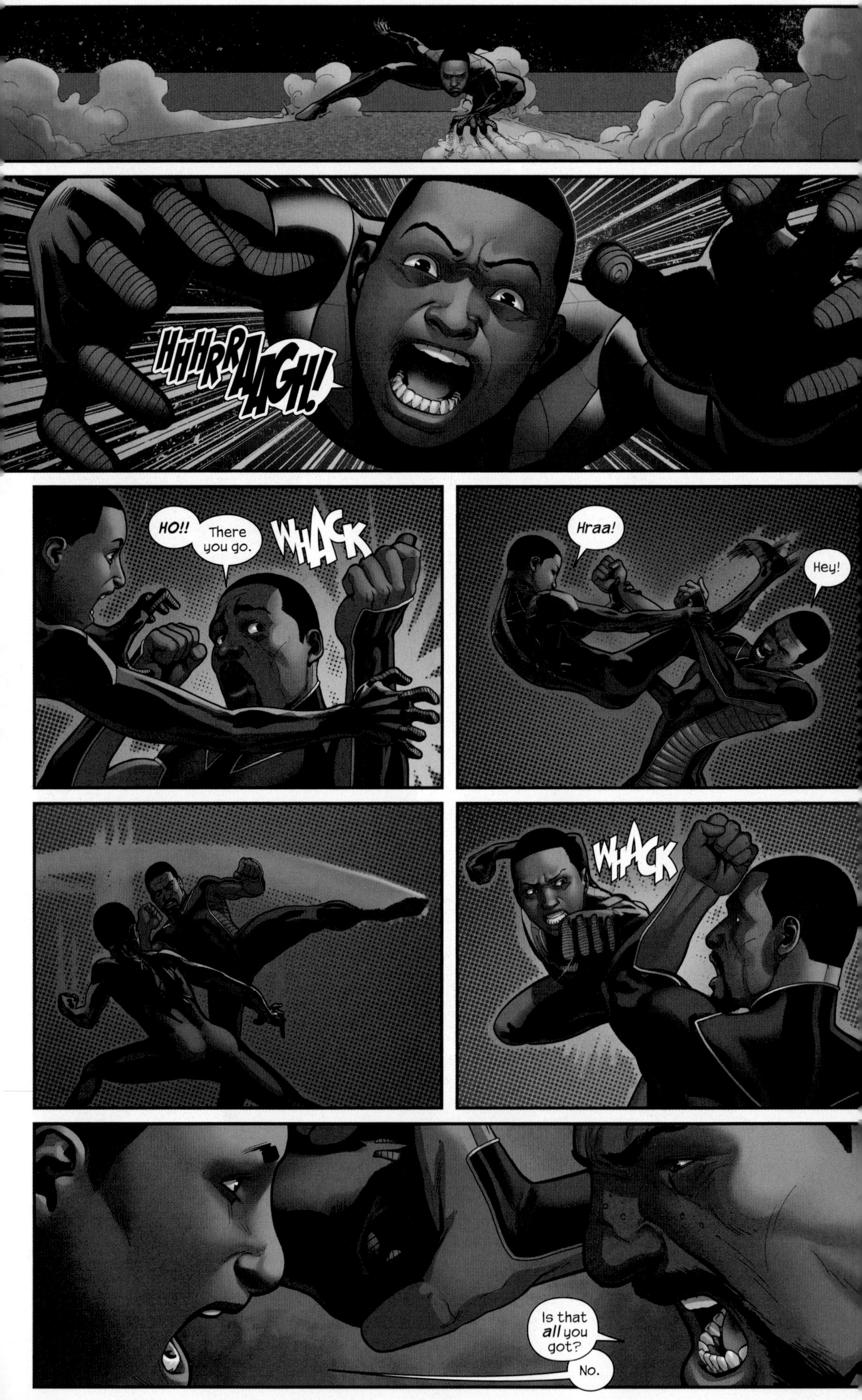

HHHRRAAGH!
HO!!
There you go.
WHACK
Hraa!
Hey!
WHACK
Is that *all* you got?
No.

ZTT

Agh!

What did you just--

GAAARRGHH!!

SMACK

Agh!!

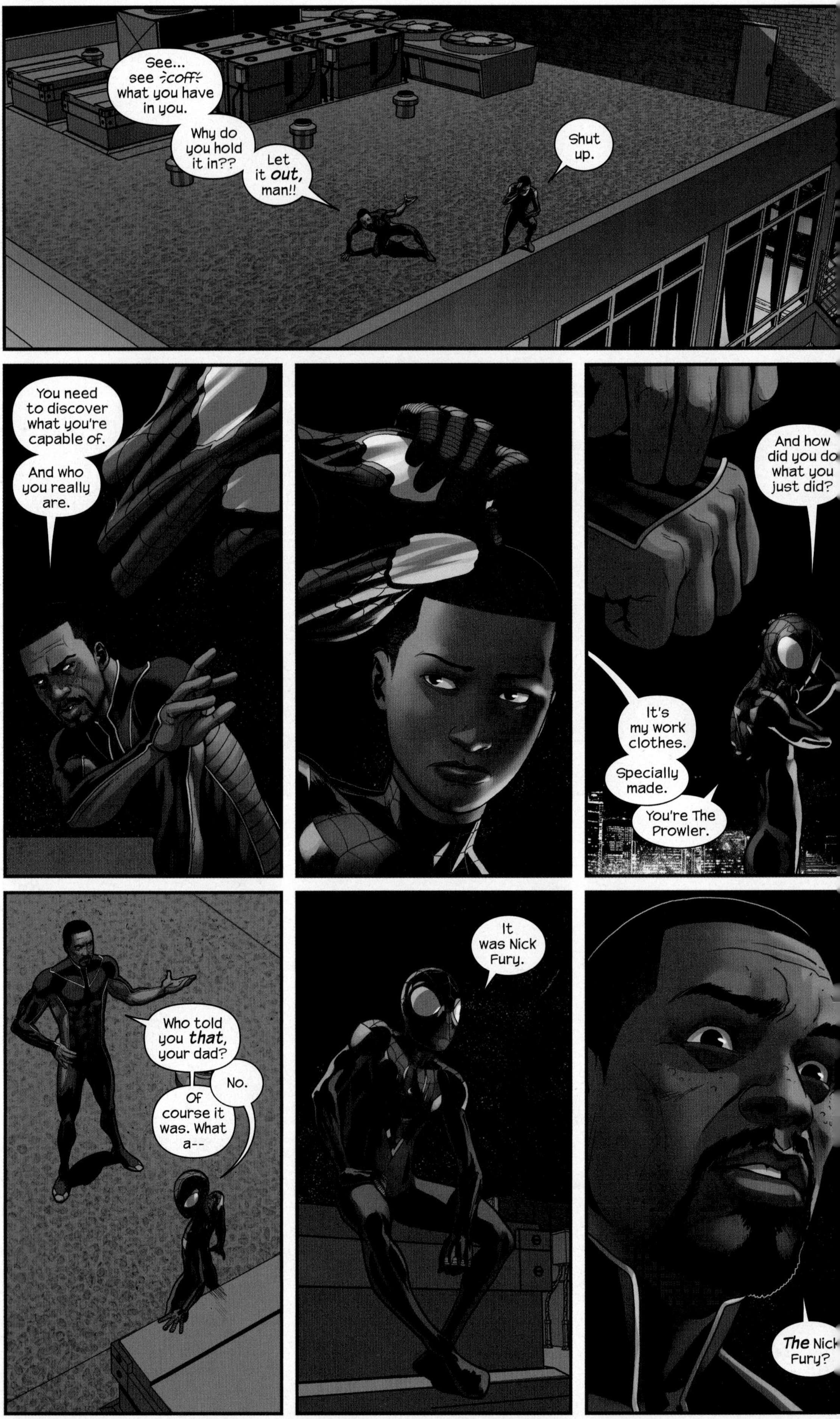
See... see ≈coff≈ what you have in you.
Why do you hold it in??
Let it *out,* man!!
Shut up.
You need to discover what you're capable of.
And who you really are.
And how did you do what you just did?
It's my work clothes.
Specially made.
You're The Prowler.
Who told you *that,* your dad?
No.
Of course it was. What a--
It was Nick Fury.
The Nick Fury?

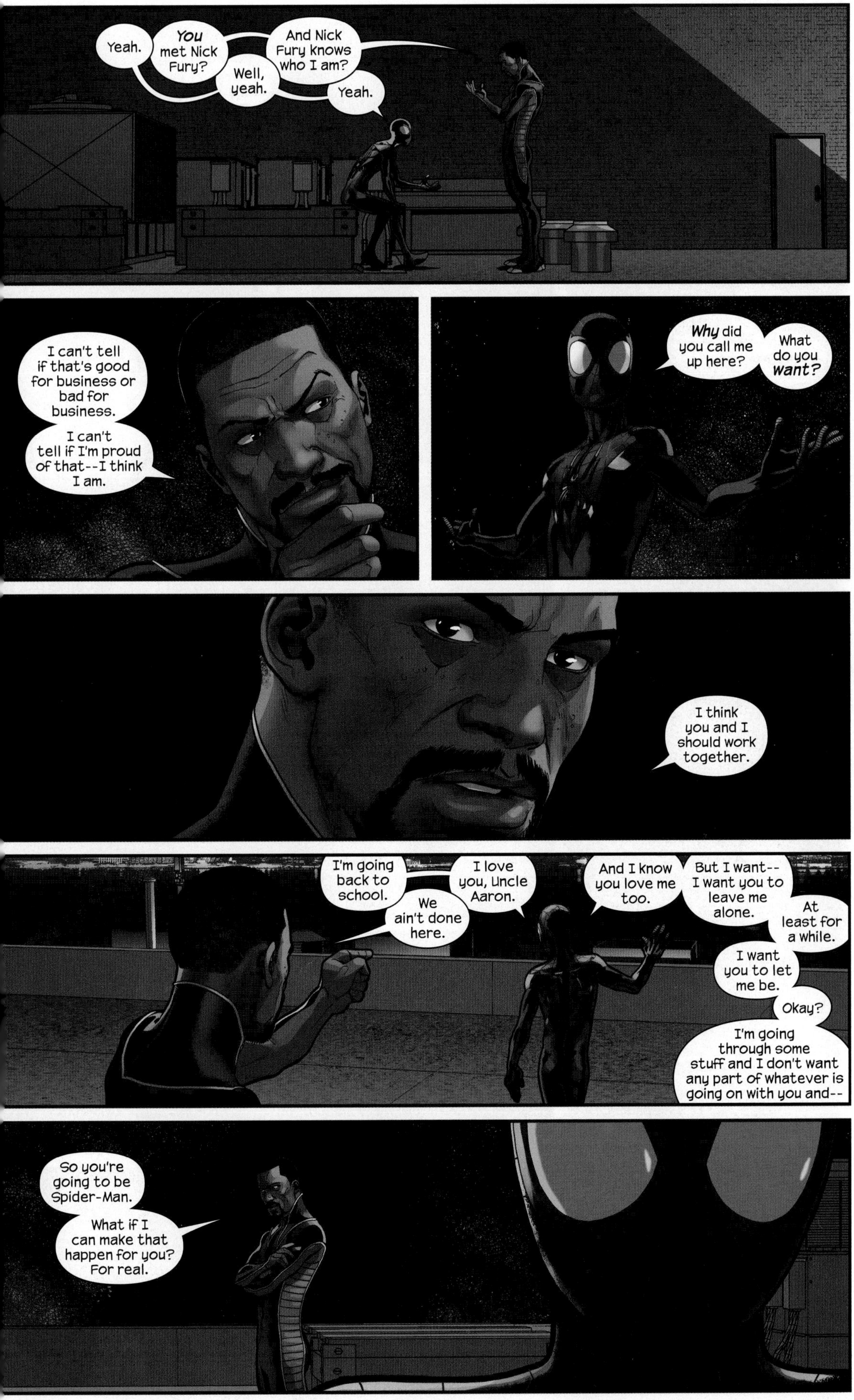
Yeah.
You met Nick Fury?
Well, yeah.
And Nick Fury knows who I am?
Yeah.
I can't tell if that's good for business or bad for business.
I can't tell if I'm proud of that--I think I am.
Why did you call me up here?
What do you want?
I think you and I should work together.
I'm going back to school.
I love you, Uncle Aaron.
We ain't done here.
And I know you love me too.
But I want-- I want you to leave me alone.
At least for a while.
I want you to let me be.
Okay?
I'm going through some stuff and I don't want any part of whatever is going on with you and--
So you're going to be Spider-Man.
What if I can make that happen for you? For real.

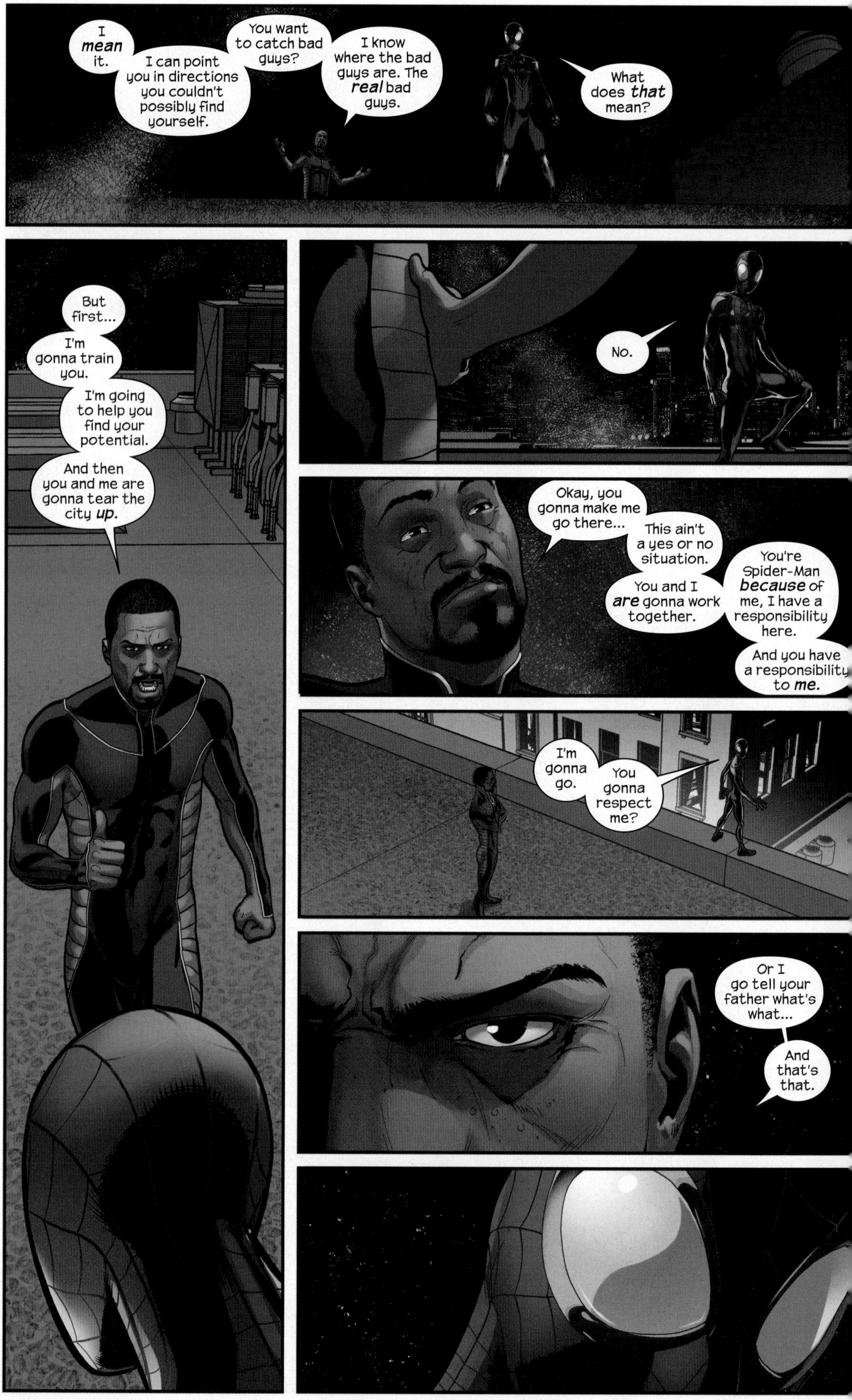

I mean it.
I can point you in directions you couldn't possibly find yourself.
You want to catch bad guys?
I know where the bad guys are. The real bad guys.
What does that mean?
But first...
I'm gonna train you.
I'm going to help you find your potential.
And then you and me are gonna tear the city up.
No.
Okay, you gonna make me go there...
This ain't a yes or no situation.
You and I are gonna work together.
You're Spider-Man because of me, I have a responsibility here.
And you have a responsibility to me.
I'm gonna go.
You gonna respect me?
Or I go tell your father what's what...
And that's that.

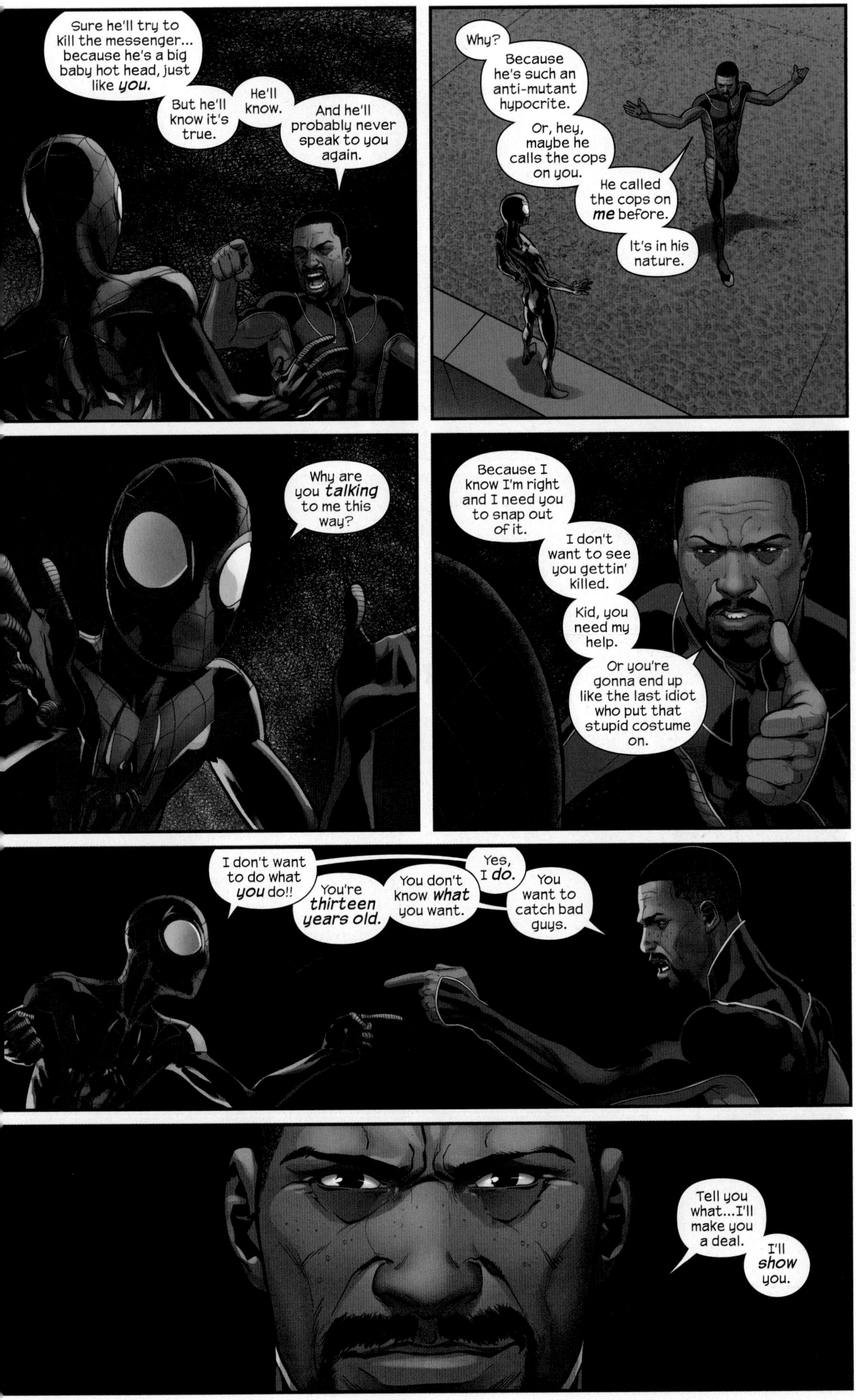
Sure he'll try to kill the messenger... because he's a big baby hot head, just like *you.*
But he'll know it's true.
He'll know.
And he'll probably never speak to you again.
Why?
Because he's such an anti-mutant hypocrite.
Or, hey, maybe he calls the cops on you.
He called the cops on *me* before.
It's in his nature.
Why are you *talking* to me this way?
Because I know I'm right and I need you to snap out of it.
I don't want to see you gettin' killed.
Kid, you need my help.
Or you're gonna end up like the last idiot who put that stupid costume on.
I don't want to do what *you* do!!
You're *thirteen years old.*
You don't know *what* you want.
Yes, I *do.*
You want to catch bad guys.
Tell you what...I'll make you a deal.
I'll *show* you.

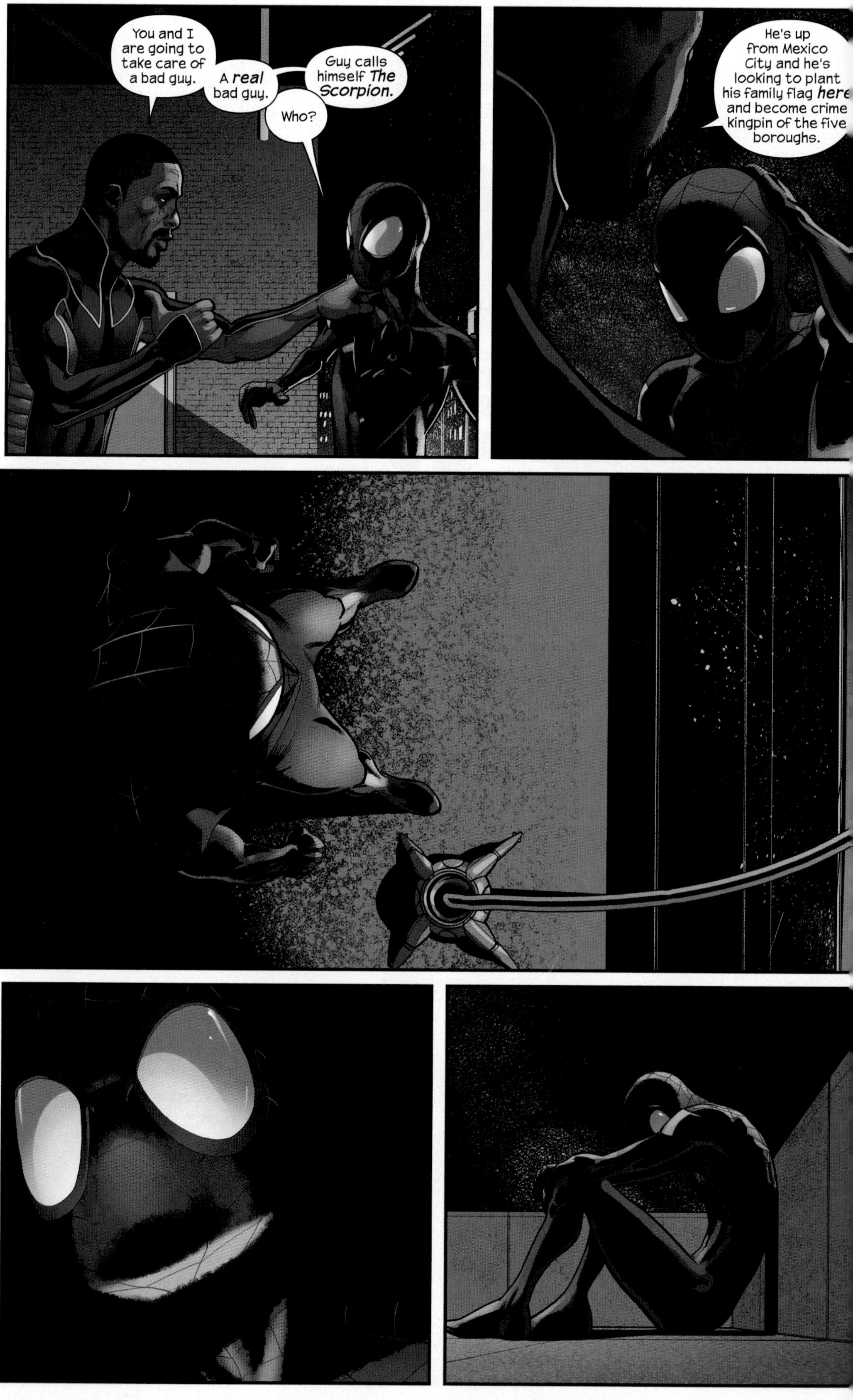
You and I are going to take care of a bad guy.
A *real* bad guy.
Who?
Guy calls himself *The Scorpion.*
He's up from Mexico City and he's looking to plant his family flag *here* and become crime kingpin of the five boroughs.

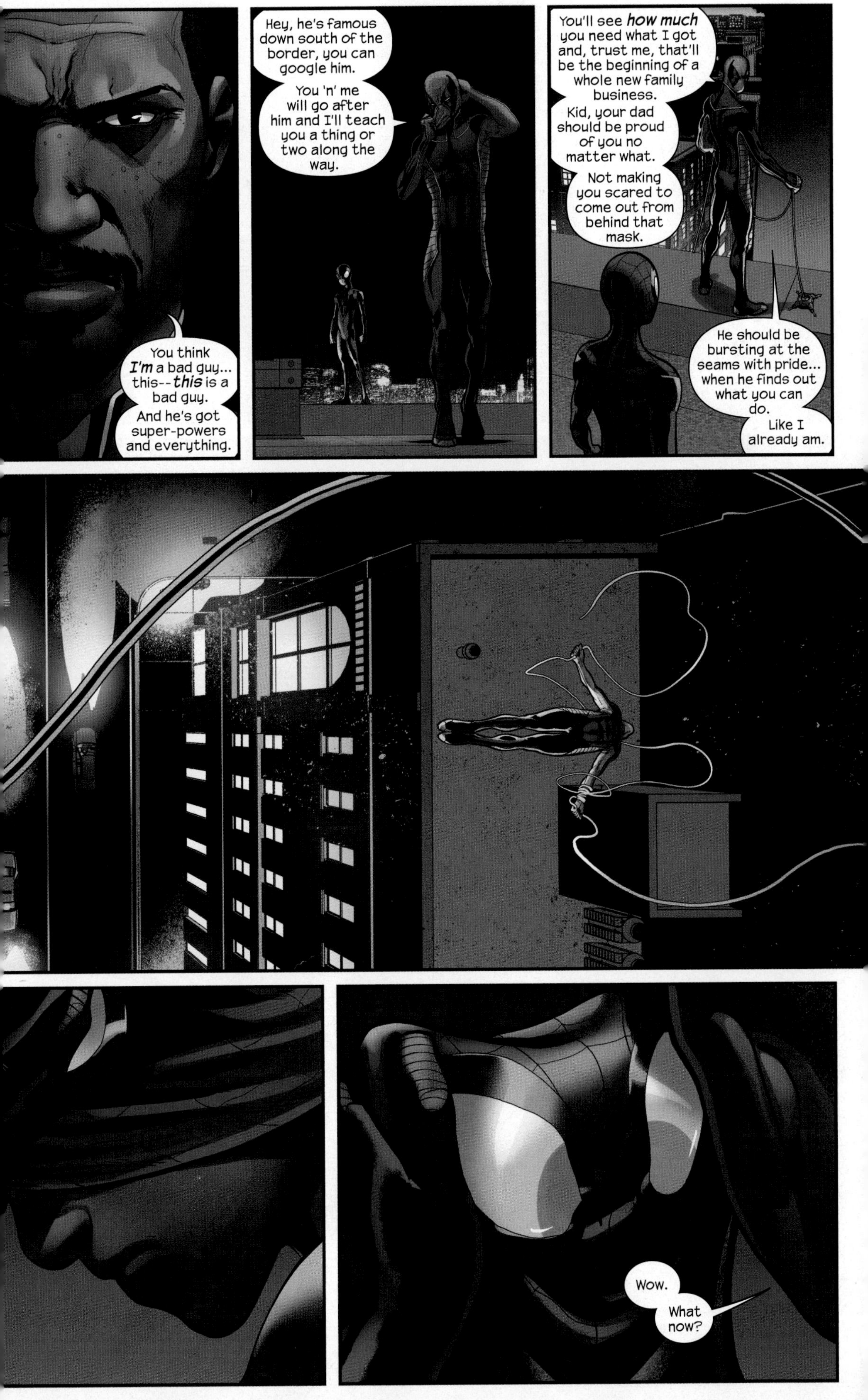
You think *I'm* a bad guy... this--*this* is a bad guy.
And he's got super-powers and everything.
Hey, he's famous down south of the border, you can google him.
You 'n' me will go after him and I'll teach you a thing or two along the way.
You'll see *how much* you need what I got and, trust me, that'll be the beginning of a whole new family business.
Kid, your dad should be proud of you no matter what.
Not making you scared to come out from behind that mask.
He should be bursting at the seams with pride... when he finds out what you can do.
Like I already am.
Wow.
What now?

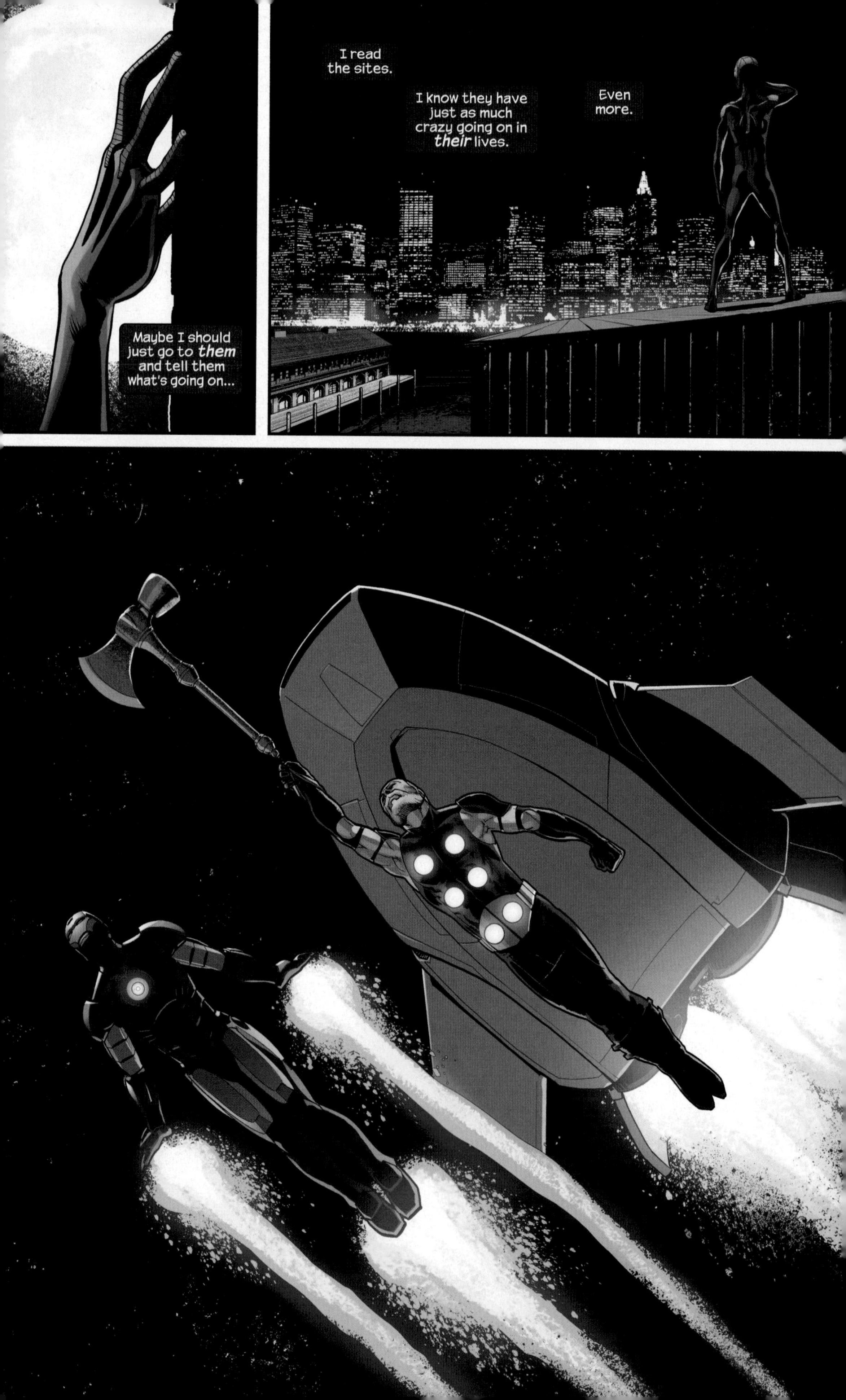
Maybe I should just go to *them* and tell them what's going on...
I read the sites.
I know they have just as much crazy going on in *their* lives.
Even more.

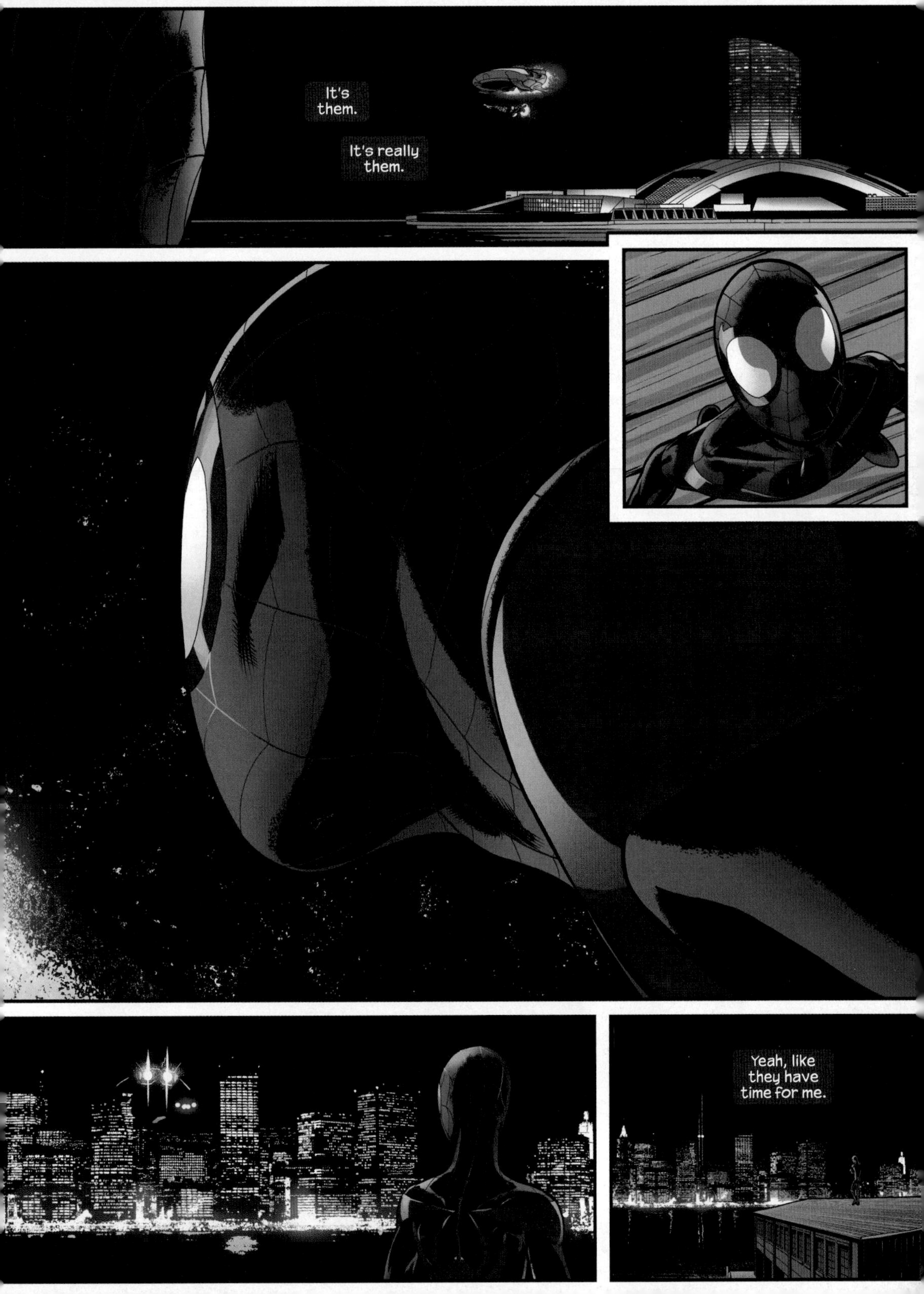
It's them.
It's really them.
Yeah, like they have time for me.

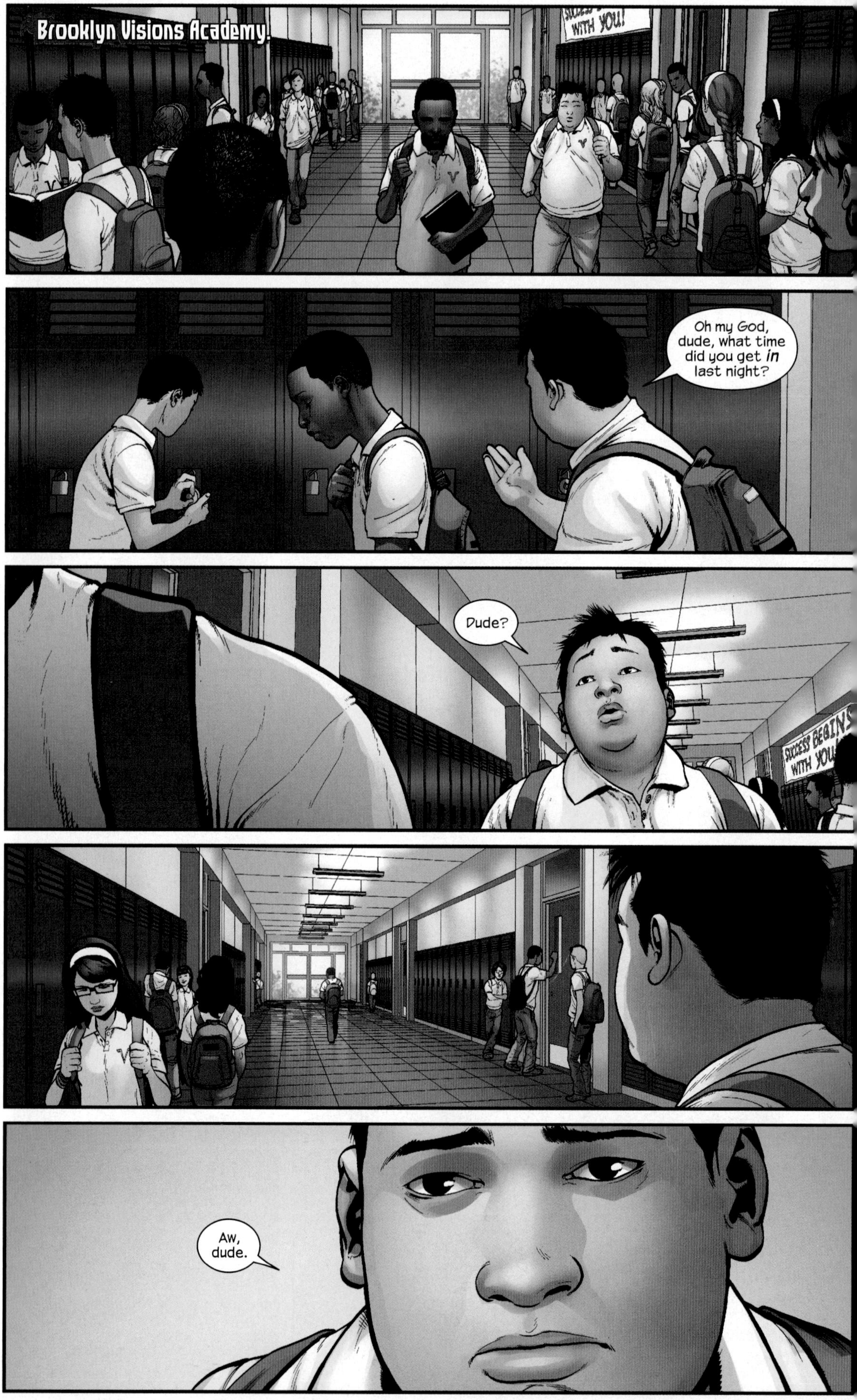
Brooklyn Visions Academy.
SUCCESS BEGINS WITH YOU!
Oh my God, dude, what time did you get *in* last night?
Dude?
SUCCESS BEGINS WITH YOU
Aw, dude.

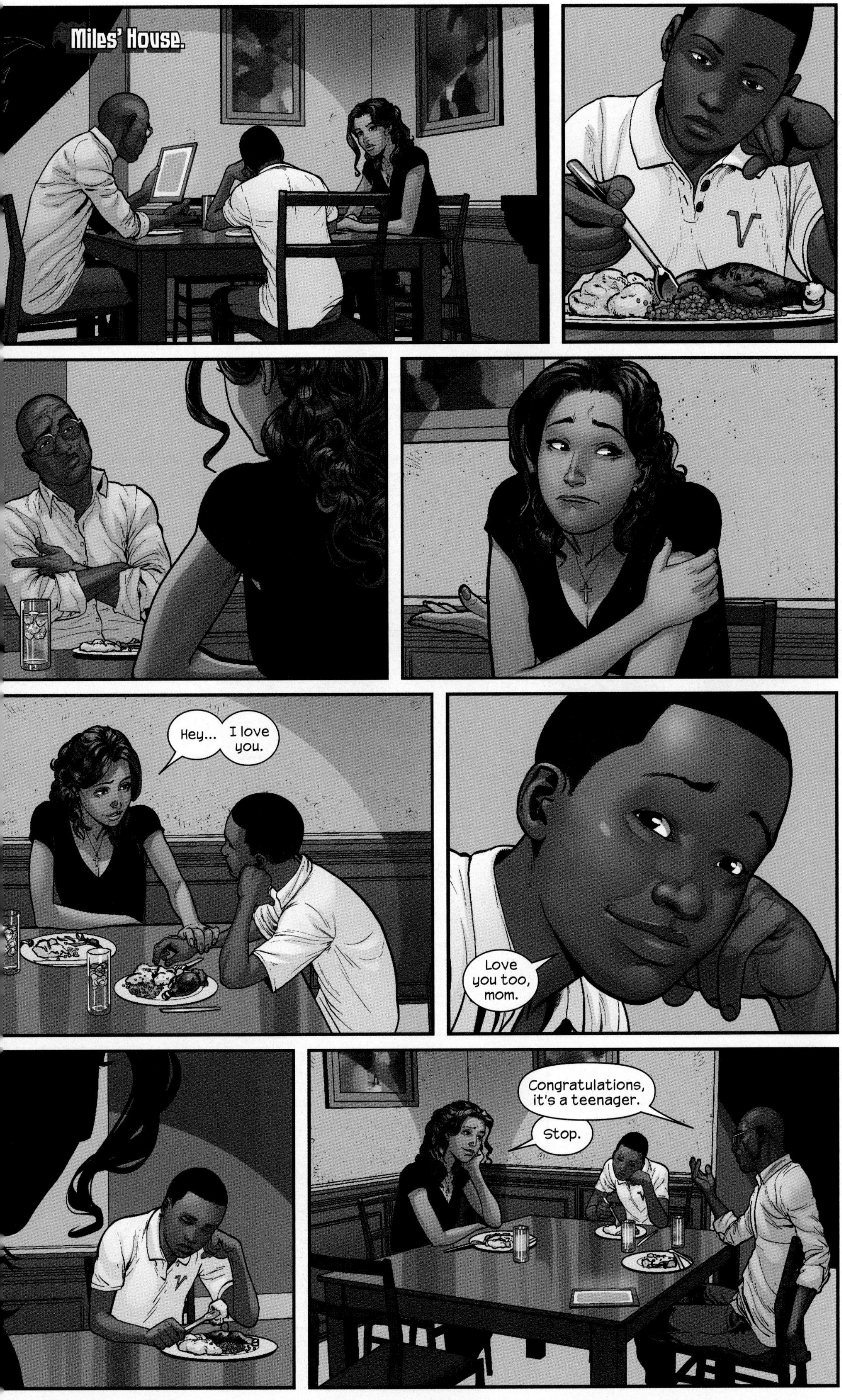

Miles' House.
Hey... I love you.
Love you too, mom.
Congratulations, it's a teenager.
Stop.

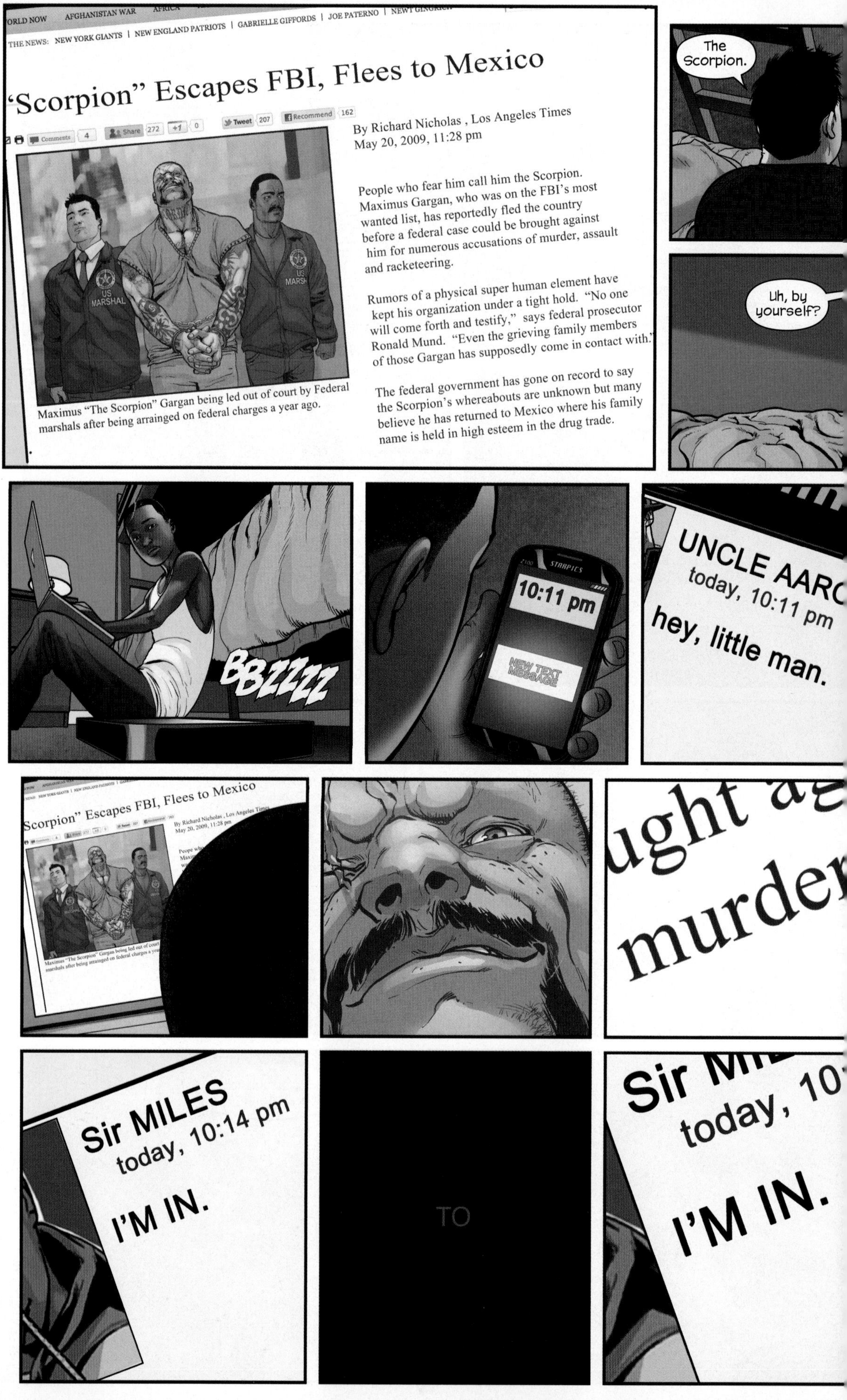
ORLD NOW AFGHANISTAN WAR AFRICA
THE NEWS: NEW YORK GIANTS | NEW ENGLAND PATRIOTS | GABRIELLE GIFFORDS | JOE PATERNO | NEWT
'Scorpion" Escapes FBI, Flees to Mexico
Comments 4 Share 272 +1 0 Tweet 207 Recommend 162
By Richard Nicholas , Los Angeles Times
May 20, 2009, 11:28 pm
US MARSHAL
US MARSH
People who fear him call him the Scorpion. Maximus Gargan, who was on the FBI's most wanted list, has reportedly fled the country before a federal case could be brought against him for numerous accusations of murder, assault and racketeering.
Rumors of a physical super human element have kept his organization under a tight hold. "No one will come forth and testify," says federal prosecutor Ronald Mund. "Even the grieving family members of those Gargan has supposedly come in contact with."
The federal government has gone on record to say the Scorpion's whereabouts are unknown but many believe he has returned to Mexico where his family name is held in high esteem in the drug trade.
Maximus "The Scorpion" Gargan being led out of court by Federal marshals after being arraigned on federal charges a year ago.
The Scorpion.
Uh, by yourself?
BBZZZZ
STARPICS
10:11 pm
NEW TEXT MESSAGE
UNCLE AARO
today, 10:11 pm
hey, little man.
Scorpion" Escapes FBI, Flees to Mexico
By Richard Nicholas , Los Angeles Times
May 20, 2009, 11:28 pm
ught ag
murder
Sir MILES
today, 10:14 pm
I'M IN.
TO
Sir MI
today, 10
I'M IN.

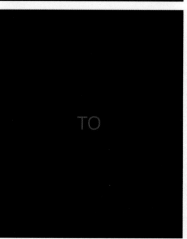

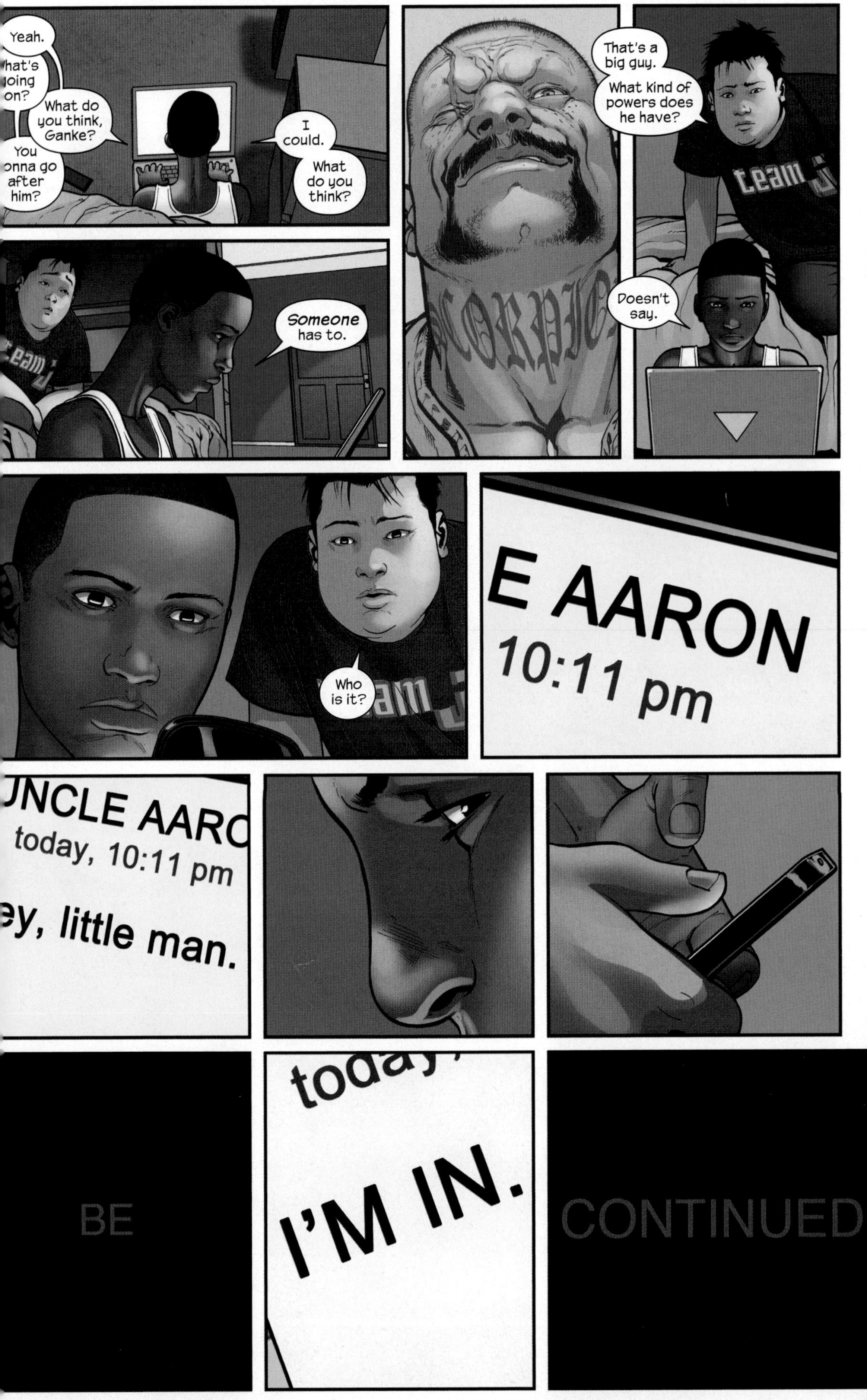

Yeah.
hat's oing on?
You onna go after him?
What do you think, Ganke?
I could.
What do you think?
Someone has to.
That's a big guy.
What kind of powers does he have?
Doesn't say.
team
Who is it?
E AARON
10:11 pm
UNCLE AARO
today, 10:11 pm
ey, little man.
today,
I'M IN.
BE
CONTINUED

#8 VARIANT
BY SARA PICHELLI

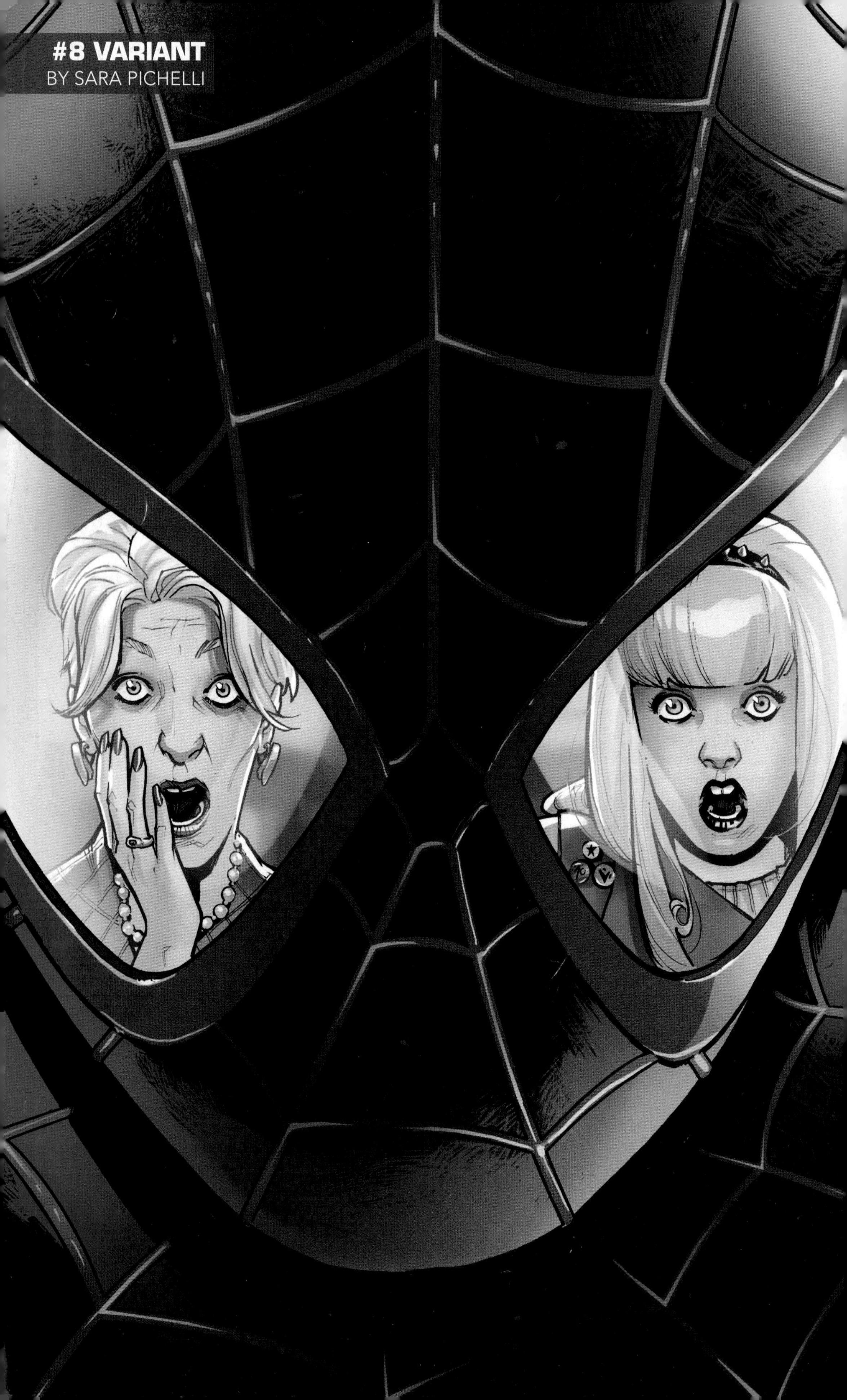

BEST NEW CHARACTER OF 2011

- USA TODAY

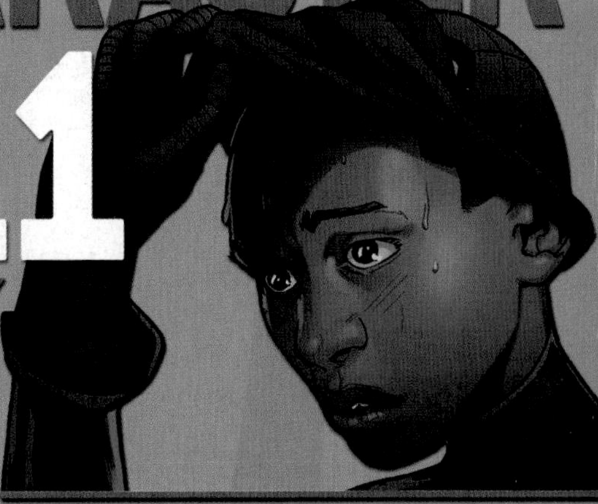

"Miles Morales is the absolute BEST Spider-Man for 2011."
- ComicBookResources.com

"Meet Miles Morales. You'll be glad you did."
- iFanboy.com

"I'm definitely with Miles Morales for the long haul."
- Newsarama.com

"Here's to another ten years of great comics."
- MTV

"Say hello to a new era of Spidey."
- BET

"This is good comics, and the start of something cool."
- ComicsAlliance.com

"A Spider-Man for a new generation"
- AV Club

"2011 was Miles Morales' year — we just lived in it."
- ComicBooked

"Forget about Peter Parker, the new Spider-Man is swinging through the pages of Marvel Comics, and his name is Miles Morales."
- The Colbert Report

"Best of luck, Miles Morales. You've got a world to change."
- Washington Post

"Long live Spider-Man!"

- Entertainment Weekly

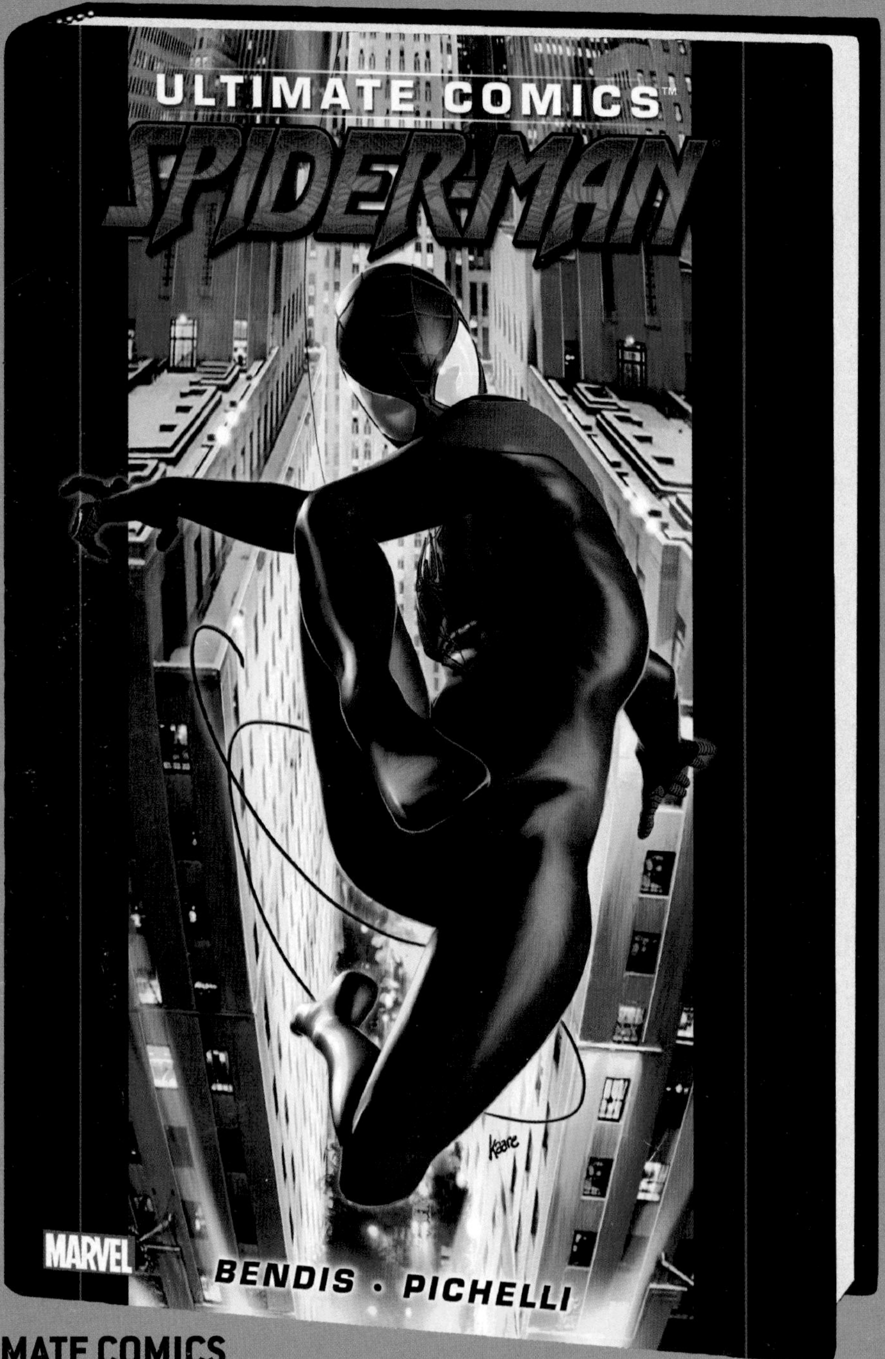

ULTIMATE COMICS
SPIDER-MAN
MARVEL
BENDIS · PICHELLI

ULTIMATE COMICS
SPIDER-MAN BY BRIAN MICHAEL BENDIS
VOL. 1 PREMIERE HC
ISBN: 978-0-7851-5712-0

ON SALE NOW!

MARVEL

ULTIMATE COMICS DEATH OF SPIDER-MAN: FALLOUT PREMIERE HC
ISBN: 978-0-7851-5912-4

Also available February 2012

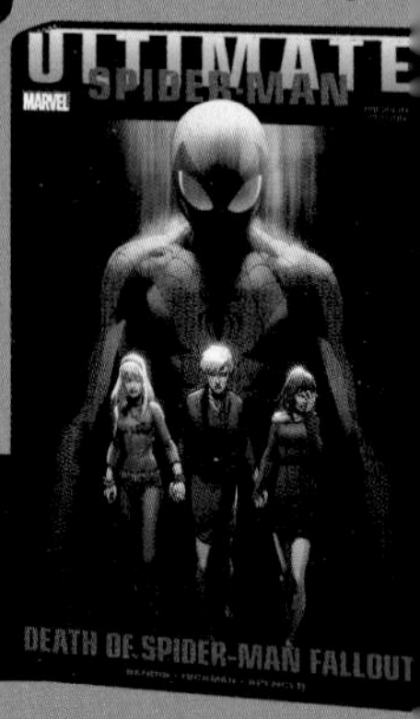

ULTIMATE
SPIDER-MAN
MARVEL
DEATH OF SPIDER-MAN FALLOUT

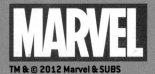

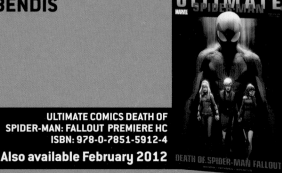